D1629866

E P Nunn

THE HOUSE IN THE PARK

THE HOUSE IN
THE PARK

by

F. D. OMMANNEY

Author of
"SOUTH LATITUDE" and "NORTH CAPE"

WITH FRONTISPIECE

LONGMANS, GREEN AND CO.
LONDON ✧ **NEW YORK** ✧ **TORONTO**

LONGMANS, GREEN AND CO. LTD.
OF PATERNOSTER ROW
43 ALBERT DRIVE, LONDON, S.W.19
NICOL ROAD, BOMBAY
17 CHITTARANJAN AVENUE, CALCUTTA
36A MOUNT ROAD, MADRAS

LONGMANS, GREEN AND CO.
55 FIFTH AVENUE, NEW YORK

LONGMANS, GREEN AND CO.
215 VICTORIA STREET, TORONTO

First published 1944
Reprinted November 1944

CODE NUMBER: 12465

PRINTED IN GREAT BRITAIN
BY WESTERN PRINTING SERVICES LTD., BRISTOL

To

ERIC GILLETT

ACKNOWLEDGMENT

The first two chapters appeared originally in the *Fortnightly* and are included in the present volume by courtesy of the Editor.

I

THERE was a time when the old Duke of Cambridge used to shoot rabbits in Richmond Park. I am not quite sure which Duke of Cambridge this was, or whether indeed there was ever more than one, but I have a vague idea he was a cousin of Queen Victoria. Anyhow he shot rabbits in Richmond Park and might have been seen early on any fine summer's morning potting at them in the bracken around White Lodge. There were primroses in those days growing wild as you please in the coarse grass and there was no one to pick them. In those days my great-grandfather used to look through his french windows that overlooked the park, across his soft green lawn bounded only by an open iron fence, and be pleased if he saw a solitary human figure walking in the wide near distance. It gave life to the scene, he said. He should see it now!

By degrees life became more and more difficult for harmless and rather ineffectual old noblemen with their fowling-pieces. Rude democratic voices were raised inquiring why the likes of him were allowed to go potting Crown rabbits on Crown lands. In due course the privileged sportsman died and went potting celestial rabbits around a residence even more Palladian than that very incommodious one in Richmond Park. They said they could never keep servants there because of the lonely walk through the park on dark winter's nights. Then the primroses retired to the depths of the Hickman plantation where two small boys one day, trespassing, of course, attracted by a strange odour, suddenly stumbled upon the disintegrating remains of Mrs. Hickman, a doctor's wife from Richmond. Dr. Hickman did it. No doubt the small boys went home and had nightmares for weeks afterwards, as I did after seeing my first performance of *Peter Pan*. But as for human figures, the level turf beyond the smooth green lawn of my great-grandfather has been asphalted over to make a car park and the rest of it has been cut up to make football pitches. On the round pond, where you used to be able to fish for pike by special permit, you may now ride in a paddle-boat at "tuppence" a ride. The rushy margin of the pond, once the home of tadpoles and sticklebacks and other muddy joys, is bounded now by a concrete rim. The tall proud elms have been judged a danger to the public and have lost their sorrowful heads.

It is progress, I suppose, and it hurts. But the little old house where my great-grandfather lived has remained, gazing out upon progress

9

from under its thatched eaves, deep embowered in trees, an island of holy quiet surrounded by a rising tide of ugly and unsympathetic clamour. The far distances, ridged with trees, that you can still see from its windows, rising gently to Wimbledon Common crowned by a wind-mill, are broken and toothed now by rows and rows of villas. Out of the gimcrack windows of w.c.'s and back bedrooms the twentieth century looks down into the eighteenth-century pleasances of that dear garden where the ghosts walk.

I am one of those ghosts myself, I think, for if I close my eyes at night and turn my face to the pillow, or even if I lay down my pen now and think back a little, I am again upon those mossy pathways, under the resinous firs, and running over the smooth soft lawns covered with dew and the droppings of hedgehogs, illicitly dropped at night when all things slept. I can smell again the hot scent of box and privet and see the insects weaving in the patchy sunlight. It is all so long ago and yet so near to me.

The memories of one's childhood become hallowed at this distance of time. I do not know that my youth was a very happy one. I was a lonely, nervous, timid little boy. But the remembrance of early days seems to have burned itself into my mind in a way that the memory of later days has not done. Perhaps you live and feel more intensely in youth, more like an animal, when the world is new to you. Old Words-worth was right. The child has a very special magic power which makes life shine with a lustre that leaves it in later years. He has a consciousness of beauty and the sense of a presence in the world which slowly dims. The knowledge dies, the entity fades and becomes diffuse and presently fades away. It is doubtful if you recognize the vision splendid for what it is until after it has faded.

Because I am nearly forty and because the vision has almost left me, I am trying to recapture it, "to recover only for a moment the wistfulness that is the past." I remember lying in my little bed in the downstairs bedroom in that old house, always called the "dressing-room" because it adjoined another downstairs room where my parents slept, praying in the darkness to be made grown-up. "Oh, please God, make me grown-up soon." The only answer to my prayer was a long sigh from the tall elms and firs that waved their branches against the sky outside the window. Now God has answered my prayer and ah! how soon. Half the journey lies behind me already. Half the show is over. Let's go out and have a drink and see what we think of it.

At nearly forty I am that I am. Whatever I was going to be when I lay in that little bed and heard the dark trees sighing, that I have become.

It is too late to turn back. It is too late to say "I'll know next time" or "I'll do better next time." There will be no next time. There is no sillier remark ever made than "It's never too late to learn." Of course it is and at middle life, at this half-way house, you have either learnt or failed to learn. You have either seen or not seen, felt or remained insensitive. If you are blind or deaf or insensitive now you always will be. It is possible that I may fall in love in the years between this moment and the end of my life but it is doubtful. The passionate friend or the heart's desire may be waiting round the corner but I think it rather unlikely. There may be new experiences, emotions, feelings still to be aroused, but it seems improbable. There may be some new chords to be struck but I have an idea these strings have played all the tunes they know. Some of them were pretty discordant. They jangled a bit. But some linger sweetly in the memory and I shall try the strings again even if for their sake alone.

The little house in Richmond Park was the centre of my life for many years. At times we lived in it, at others we lived near it. But always my family seemed to revolve round it like attendant satellites round a sun. The exact relationship which we, the satellites, bore to our sun depended, it seemed, upon the rather tyrannical capricious old lady who ruled at the centre of our solar system. She was my grandmother. She had what was perhaps an unwarrantably large share in the control of my destinies throughout many formative years. When she died a whole structure collapsed in my little world. She had seemed to be an old lady when I could scarcely walk, and had lived for more than thirty years in this same house. Her masterful personality had stamped itself upon the house and upon all of us so that her tricks of speech and mannerisms were already family legends in the earliest days I can remember. They still remain so, twenty years after her death, old jokes and old sayings, stored in a kind of metaphorical lavender, brought out and smiled over still in private moments. Can this, I wonder, be her immortality?

So that when she died it seemed like the end of a chapter. We seemed rather like a boat suddenly adrift, its anchor cable parted. When we had to leave the house at her death we felt we had left harbour and set sail upon a wide and desperately lonely ocean.

This extraordinary, dominating little old lady had inherited the house from her father-in-law, the great naturalist, Richard Owen. Besides conferring such benefits upon the community as the Natural History Museum (he was not, I think, responsible for its architecture) he held the post of Lecturer in Natural History to the Royal Family and who knows how he may not unconsciously have guided the course of history as he held forth in his resonant voice to rows of little princes and princesses, and even to the old Queen herself sometimes? He expounded the manners and habits of beasts, carefully skimming, perhaps, over the less delicate aspects of his subject. Not that the old gentleman had any qualms himself, for his wife, in one of those interminable diaries which people found time to write in those days, recorded rather wearily how he brought back the remains of a hippopotamus from the Zoo to dissect at home, filling the house with too-African odours. A faint note of protest was perceptible in the patient diary. When Thomas Henry Huxley was championing Charles Darwin and setting orthodox opinion by the ears, Owen came down heavily on the side of the angels. He said that there could not possibly be any affinity between man and the apes because of certain important points of difference in the brain. Perhaps as much for this as for his services as lecturer he had a charming little house in Richmond Park bestowed on him for life.

The old man lived in this house until he died at a great age—over ninety. He too was a dominating and masterful spirit with great personal charm, which he could turn on and off like a tap, and a biting sarcastic humour which he apparently reserved for his large family circle. He had stamped his personality upon the little house to such an extent that when we came to live in it many years afterwards, long after his death, his spirit still possessed it. It seemed redolent of him. To my mother who knew him in life it was almost as if he were still there, or had gone away only for a short time and might be seen again at any moment, tapping along the garden walks with his stick. Or shuffling down from the library in his carpet slippers to interrupt the most subdued conversation by remarking in a terrifying voice that there seemed to be a lot of noise going on. The house was full of heavy Victorian furniture which had been his and there were huge dark oil paintings which were supposed to be immensely valuable but, of course, were not. "My nice things," my grandmother affectionately called them. In spite of her affection for them she used to get experts to come down from London periodically to pronounce upon them with a view, perhaps, to selling them. The experts always made the same pronouncements and went away leaving her indignant and incredulous. There was a library upstairs lined from floor to ceiling with dusty volumes. It adjoined the old man's bedroom and at the last he used to sit here all day reading and making marginal notes in a quivering hand in all the books in the great collection, underlining, scoring through passages, marking them with angry exclamation marks, or indignant comments such as "Rubbish!" or "This is nonsense!" I still have a little leather-bound Keats. Where

Hyperion is chasing a golden butterfly through the happy vales there stands, for all posterity to see how science regards the Muses, a long list of generic and specific names—the butterflies which science thought perhaps Hyperion was chasing! But at the end it was always the same book he read, upside down for he could no longer see and scorned the use of glasses. It was called *Imaginary Conversations with the Duke of Wellington*. Reading it in the gathering gloom of his little room he would periodically tug the bell-rope and, when the summons was answered, acidly remark that it must be nearly dinner-time. When told that he had dined only ten minutes ago he grew angry and inferred that his family were all in a conspiracy together to starve him to death. Poor soul, that dies at last before the temple that holds it has quite fallen!

In this quiet and cloistered room there lingered for years after his death a faint indefinable odour which I called "the library smell" but which my mother called "the grandfather smell." At certain times, particularly when his grandchildren and their families were in the house, at Christmas for instance, this faint aroma in the library became a live presence. It wandered like a spirit disembodied down the stairs and into the hall. Into the downstairs bedroom where I lay and prayed to be grown-up, into the drawing-room with its satinwood furniture and marble figures where all his medals and decorations were displayed on purple velvet in a glass-topped cabinet. Possibly it comes there now when we have all gone and the house has central heating and electric light. Is this, too, his immortality? . . .

II

MY people were gentlefolk. Upon this earth-shaking assertion no false interpretation need be placed. I am not trying to explain to the reader how blue my blood is underneath this somewhat plebeian exterior for I am only a moderate snob and quite honestly do not care what colour it is. Such questions, of absorbing interest to so many, do not concern me.

At one time, however, I think I might have been called a snob with some truth. I seem to remember getting a kick out of knowing the right people in the suburb where we lived and by that, of course, I meant the rich people, those who lived aloofly in the big houses behind high walls overtopped by cedar-trees as opposed to those who lived in small houses surrounded by low railings overtopped by privet hedges or by nothing at all, unashamedly open to the street. I also had intellectual pretensions, I think—especially at college where, failing to shine in the athletic sphere, I cast about for some less exhausting, more easily attainable sphere to shine in. But nowadays I realize that I am an average moderately, but certainly not exceptionally, well-educated middle-brow. I think I must be that elusive individual "the man in the street." My tastes and opinions—I hardly know them. As with most people, I suspect, they are mainly a collection of attractions and repulsions. At any rate at nearly forty I have no pretensions. The balloon of my youthful self-conceit has long ago lost all its gas, as indeed it should have done by now, and floated gently down to earth. I have no particular social position, no wish to fill my address-book with high-sounding names or to frequent fine houses that do not belong to me. No mantelpiece of mine has ever been a gallery of invitation cards. I have a fair number of friends with all sorts of tastes and inclinations who earn their living—or did before the war—in all sorts of ways. I have a little money, but only a little, and have earned it all.

So there I am. I can say with truth that I do not pretend to be anything that I am not. On the other hand I do not affect to despise all these things that I do not possess, like the fox gazing at the grapes, for inverted snobbishness is the silliest variety of this harmless laughable vice. I should like to be better read and better educated than I am but from now on I expect I shall gain experience but not culture. And it must be fun to be rich, to move about in expensive and gilded circles, to be surrounded by beautiful things and decorative gay people. I enjoy lunching at the Ritz. I love the delights and graces of this world and sometimes sigh, as we all do, for a fuller, richer life than has been granted to me. But I know that, having got thus far with much but without a good deal, I am not now likely to add very much to myself. I might find a nugget lying in the street or someone might suddenly leave me a million pounds, but I am afraid I should find these benefits less useful now than I should have, say, twenty years ago. So I must make do with what I have been given, as we all must in the long run, and not pretend to have gone further or climbed higher than in fact I have lest I be one day compelled, publicly and with shame, to take a lower place.

And if, when I say that my people were gentlefolk, you object that I am using a long-dead language, heard only faintly now in Kensington and Bayswater boarding-houses, reviving words that no longer have any meaning, or returning to a forgotten set of values now grown pathetic in decay, I can only agree. Yet, they belonged to the upper middle class.

My father's family were at one time tolerably well landed and tolerably well off. During the nineteenth century the male members distributed themselves liberally and fairly evenly among the honourable professions of the Navy, the Army, the Civil Service, the Law and the Church. Many of them achieved moderate distinction in these professions and rose to be naval officers and soldiers of fairly high rank, senior civil servants, prosperous lawyers and eminent, very C. of E., parsons. Knight-hoods and honours descended upon them in a gentle shower. They were proud, class conscious, typical and looked upon the world as their oyster, which indeed in those days it was. They had large houses behind garden walls overtopped by cedar-trees, enormous numbers of children and believed that not voting conservative was a sign of mental derange-ment. In their eyes commerce and trade were dishonourable and anyone remotely connected with them was beyond the pale. To obtain money by any means other than by receiving it as a fee, stipend, salary or legacy was looked upon as receiving it by false pretences. They were C. of E.; they killed things for fun; they read *The Times* and *Punch*. They were honest, upright, God-fearing, intensely patriotic in an inarticulate way, and not terribly intelligent. Intellect made them feel slightly uncomfort-able. They held the reins of England in inflexible hands—or so they thought.

The female members of the family learnt deportment and fancy needlework when young, the pianoforte and a little French but no house-keeping or domestic science. They were mostly finished abroad and then returned to engage in a carefully veiled but none the less anxious, at times even delicately acrimonious, competition with each other and with the other young women of the neighbourhood for the prizes of the local marriage market. These were all young men destined for the honourable professions of the Navy, the Army, the Civil Service, the Law and the Church. When a girl secured one of these prizes she became the object of universal congratulation. She was held to have made a "good marriage." Whatever might have been the promptings of her own heart her future happiness and well-being were taken for granted and it was assumed that she would settle down in an enormous house, bear quantities of legitimate children and bring them up to be soldiers, sailors, civil servants, lawyers and parsons, to be C. of E., to vote conservative and to continue to hold the reins of England. And even if she had secretly preferred the young man who came daily to her carriage door to take orders for groceries such little seeds of desire were by all her training and upbringing quickly and easily suppressed. Indeed they never really sprouted at all or attained any life but lingered only as a certain coldness, a lack of real enthusiasm, for the oft repeated undignified performance inseparable from the production of so many red foetal-looking future admirals, generals, permanent under-secretaries, Queen's Counsels and archdeacons.

These people and all those like them in their stately houses lived rigidly encompassed lives. For them society was divided by a definite but intangible line into two distinct and opposing sections—gentle people and common people, the high and the low, the rulers and the ruled. The former were their own kind who lived by means of salaries, fees, stipends or, even more Olympian, by inheriting fortunes they had not earned at all. The latter class were those who existed by means of wages, paid weekly in vulgar cash rather than monthly or quarterly by means of aristocratic cheques in sealed envelopes. Among these also were those who stooped to gain their livelihood by selling things, which, as everyone knew, was really a form of swindling. It was next door to living by one's wits. To have wits to live by was slightly discreditable in any case.

The recipients of cheques drawn monthly and quarterly, the drawers of dividends on preference shares, the inheritors of unearned wealth lived in an exclusive Olympus where narrow lanes ran between high walls and where wrought-iron gates gave glimpses of Georgian and Queen Anne houses amid smooth lawns. But down towards the river was another region of shops and trams and row upon row of villas where dwelt the recipients of weekly wages in cash, the people who sold things and even that mercifully submerged tenth who had no means of livelihood at all. Down to this Avernus in their carriages the Olympians swept daily to give their orders at the pavement edge without alighting. The fact that they were then really buying things that the less exalted were selling was as carefully disguised as possible and commerce was tacitly given the aspect of command and performance. Then the carriages swept them back again into Olympus, back to the groves of cedar-trees and the striped level lawns where no sound but a distant murmur reached them from the underworld in which men bought and sold and worked and went ill-clothed and starved. But yet who knows what strange stirrings, what germs of ideas the young brought back from that world where the pace of life was higher and where blood ran thicker and more red? There it was, perhaps, that the girl, leaning back in her carriage beneath her parasol, learnt to drop her eyes before those of the young man who took her orders for groceries and felt her heart give a sudden and strictly interdicted thump.

In order to preserve themselves from vulgar contacts and to guard their way of life from disagreeable intrusions the inhabitants of this sanctuary hedged themselves about with a barrier of conventions more formidable than a brick wall armed with spikes. This was carefully designed to keep the two classes apart and to ensure that those who inhabited the region of shops and villas down by the river remained there. For any dweller in that dim twilight to attain the rarefied air that was breathed higher up the hill was more difficult than for a camel to pass through the eye of a needle. A system of scrutiny, inquiry, formal visiting and card-dropping made certain that no undesirable elements, no taint of common trade, no stranger from without the gates could gain admittance to the charmed circle. "One had to be so careful, don't you know." Relics of this system linger in country districts to this day I believe, but, looking back on it, it seems incredible that it could ever have so universally existed or the standards upon which it was based have been those of educated Christians, who went solemnly to church on Sunday to chant "Oh Lord, have mercy upon us, miserable sinners," and then emerged into the Sabbath sunshine bowing right and left to some, but pointedly ignoring others in the same congregation.

But with my father's generation a melancholy decline began. Slowly there came creeping insidiously up from the river companies and platoons of little houses. They formed up in rows and stood complacently where there had been green lawns. They were the advance guard of what would, in the not very distant future, become an invading host. One by one, but only very slowly at first, the great old houses began to fall on evil days. They became shabby and weeds sprouted in their drives.

Patches of dampness appeared and spread on drawing-room walls. At last they fell empty and at long last they were broken up, their fair gardens given over to the spoilers. Boards appeared above the old walls, looking impertinently over them upon the leafy lanes of that select suburb. They told a sad story to anyone who could read it, the story of a *Götterdammerung*, the twilight of a caste.

This decline was greatly helped and accelerated by the last war but it was not entirely due to it. For even before its outbreak those promising careers on which some of my male relatives found themselves launched, somewhat to their own surprise occasionally, through the influence of powerful fathers, began to falter and show signs of sinking beneath the waves of rude ungentlemanly competition. My relatives mostly failed to make the grade. The pace was becoming too hot. Or else they just never got started at all, never got launched on that smooth sea which it was intended that life should be for them. The influence of those powerful fathers was on the wane. Only the fathers themselves retained any faith in strings and their ability to pull them adroitly, and in those suave letters —"I assure you that anything you may do on his behalf will be very greatly appreciated as a token of the long and harmonious, etc. . . ." Early in the twentieth century these well-chosen phrases were beginning to fail to ring bells in the right quarters. After the war, I suspect, the bells were no longer there to ring.

So it began to be discovered that professions less exalted than the Navy, Army, Civil Service, Law and Church offered hitherto undreamt of attractions. Other ways of gaining a living were gradually promoted in status and it began to be less despicable to buy and sell. Before many years had passed it became highly enviable. Perhaps it was the girls who made that surprising discovery first. They found that you might be just as happy if you married a sanitary engineer, a butcher, a baker or a candlestick maker as if you married a Foreign Office official. Anyhow your life was not likely to be more uninteresting and you might be richer. So the marriage market changed its character slowly but definitely as the twentieth century grew and all sorts of people became my uncles by marriage—motor engineers, salesmen, stockbrokers and people vaguely and ambiguously "in the City."

And slowly, year by year, battalions and companies of little houses came marching up the hill from the direction of the river. The high walls fell before them. This invading host encamped on the smooth lawns, levelling the old homes and the stately trees or leaving them forlorn amid a sea of brick and slate. The place was changing so, my people said. There was hardly anyone left. And yet, in spite of the fact that there was hardly anyone left, more and more people from all the rows of little houses came pouring up the hill into the park, more every year. They came up on fine sunny days with their push-carts and their picnic baskets and their strings of children and sat down on the grass beneath the trees. They swarmed around the pond and kicked footballs on the level turf beyond it. Unfamiliar shouts and laughter grew louder in the summer air as the years went on and only in the evening when the park gates closed did a holy peace descend again with wreaths of mist that curled upwards from the water.

So we declined in wealth and power and position and the reins of England slipped from our hands. In the new, crude, vulgar world in which we found ourselves we were markedly less successful than we had been in the easier days. We were not good at this buying and selling business so that from being tolerably well off we presently became very badly off. And, as there seemed to be enormous numbers of us, owing to the philoprogenitive tendencies of the last generation or so, each of us inherited but little from the break-up of the old homes.

Thus it happened that I and my generation were born into a kind of twilight. We inherited rather expensive tastes and an upper middle-class tradition which made life difficult for us because we had not the means to carry on that tradition. We found ourselves in a world that had little respect for it unaccompanied by wealth. Not only did we inherit that fine old cumbersome, unpractical and somewhat threadbare tradition but also the picturesque idea of a world still divided into two distinct categories of human beings. We had that sense of still holding reins that had long ago escaped our grasp, that pride and that class consciousness but also that uprightness, that devotion to duty and to the state. All of this was injected into us in liberal doses by elders who either did not perceive how their world was changing or shut their eyes to change. Continual protests against what was said to be the deterioration of society assailed our impressionable ears. I for one, with the cocksureness of youth, felt convinced that, contrary to what my elders ceaselessly intoned, the world was really getting better and better. The up-and-up-and-on-and-on thesis is one of the innocent illusions of youth but, looking back now, I begin to see that my elders were not so wrong after all. Much has changed for the worse, there has been a lowering of standards and a decline of values everywhere since they were pushed off their pedestals.

Dethroned in their Wimbledon flats—taken "when my dear father died and the old place was sold"—in their Bayswater and Kensington boarding-houses they sit surrounded by fading photographs of people in wigs, robes, ecclesiastical regalia and elaborate old-fashioned uniforms.

All these bear witness to past renown. Dear Cousin John, who was in
the 17th at Quetta during the trouble with the natives, with his hand
on his sword and his helmet on his crooked arm, grows yellower every
year. Dear Arthur, who did so well in the Sudan, looks out from over
his high collar upon a world smaller and less generous than the world
he knew. A year or two ago, by elaborate research in Bayswater and
Kensington, by diligent inquiry in Cheltenham and Bath and after long
correspondence with Bournemouth, there was prepared an enormous
scroll, the swan song of a retired admiral in Somerset. When unrolled
it revealed itself as a family tree. There for the edification and enlighten-
ment of many old ladies, retired admirals or generals and country parsons,
were displayed, like the complicated diagrams that unfold at the end of
history books, the intricate series of respectable conjunctions, combina-
tions and copulations that finally culminated, among other surprising
results, in the production of me. This mountain, which had produced
this mouse, lay on the top of my wardrobe for a year or so collecting
dust. I do not know where it is now.

I was always rather scornful of this family business—as soon as I grew
old enough to have a mind of my own about anything. In the world I
found myself growing up in I saw that it was more blessed to be rich than
genteel, that however much you might wish to know the "right people"
they did not particularly want to know you unless you were one of them
yourself. This you could never be if you were impecunious and all the
grand conversation in the world, all the dark pictures in gilt frames, all
the old medals on velvet cushions, all the photographs of people in
regalia could not cancel out the fact that you had no money. High-flown
talk about grand relations now dead and portentously unrolling family
trees had a dead and hollow ring for me and I soon learnt that reflected
glory is a poor substitute at best. And I wished that the soldiers, sailors,
civil servants, lawyers and parsons had been butchers, bakers and candlestick makers. I wished that my aunts had married their grocers.

III

SHE was dead. At first it was almost impossible to believe this for the room in which she lay was exactly as it had always been. As though this were any sunny morning of her life her silver-backed brushes and mirror lay on the dressing-table. In the wardrobe all her small dresses were hanging like frail empty shells or cast-off skins. It was as though they were waiting as they always had for one of them to be chosen for that day. On the wash-stand a large soft sponge was scarcely dry from its last use. There was a cake of scented soap, a bottle of eau-de-Cologne, bottles of perfume, a bowl of powder. All the little intimate familiar things with which she was surrounded when she rose at morning and when she retired at night, and which had caught my eye so often when I had come in to say "Good morning" and "Good night," still seemed to hold in themselves some lingering embers of her life. Only the bed itself was already denying her. It had been stripped and the blankets and pillows had been heaped in the middle under the counter-pane as though their owner had gone on a very long journey. Now, so soon, the bed seemed ready to receive in its softness some other form than hers. On the little round table at the bedside were still her Bible and Prayer Book, full of silk bookmarkers and ornate cards bearing texts.

These were the betrayers. It was these, and I my own stupid self, who had brought her at last to the final certainty of death. She had been lying ill for over a month, bearing pain at first in the belief that she would soon recover, then that she would recover some time. And then that she would recover at long last. But presently, from the doctors who came daily and said nothing much and from the coldly efficient nurses with their mechanical bright cheerfulness, she began to get less and less reassurance. They said nothing. They brought her flowers, opened the windows to let in fresh air, smiled cheerfully and said what a lovely day it was, smiled and went away. "Try and get some sleep," they said. "There's a dear."

"Am I dying, Olive?" she would say to my mother.

"No, Mother dear, of course not."

And she was not reassured. She laid her plans and came by the truth by devious but certain means. One of the vessels that held this truth was a frail one, I myself. It was an old truth like an old wine, the ineluctable fact of death, and it was held in a new skin that could not contain it. It burst at the first trial.

21

Three days before her death my mother had said to me, "Your Grannie wants you to go and read to her."

"Oh, no. I can't."

I knew how badly I read for the old lady had often made acid remarks about it in the past.

"I can't read," I said. "I can't. Why can't somebody else read to her?"

My mother was suddenly very angry. "Because she particularly asks you to do it. Your Grannie's very ill and you'll please go along at once and do as you're told. And for Heaven's sake try not to be so selfish. Really, you ought to be ashamed of yourself."

I was not intentionally selfish but afraid, frightened of my own weakness. Nevertheless, sheepishly and considerably ashamed of myself, I went.

She was sitting in an arm-chair before her bedroom window which looked out over the park. One side of the window was filled with the dark August green of the chestnut-tree that stood in the front garden. Its big palmate leaves fingered the sunlight. In the other half of the window lay the glittering strip of the pond, the open stretches of the park and the soft blue of distant trees, the familiar and well-beloved prospect that was part of her life and of mine. The tiny figures of people moved against the green background and the morning was full of the sound of children's voices and of dogs barking shrilly. The sounds seemed to come from a long way off and all those figures weaving like insects out there in the sunlight seemed remote and detached as though they belonged to another world. Her long silver hair that I had always loved and admired so much was done in a thick plait that fell over her shoulders and reached down to her waist. Her eyes were still brown and keen and sharp as needles as she turned towards me where I stood awkwardly before her chair, a little sullen and half-rebellious and yet ashamed. Her face was waxen and the hand she placed on my arm seemed light as paper.

"Darling boy, I want you to do something for an old woman."

"Yes, Grannie."

"Kiss me."

I kissed her cheek which seemed cold and already death-like. It was a contract and I was bound by it.

"I want you to read to me. I felt sure you would, dear boy, because you've always been my favourite. Old women are strange things, you know. Rather horrid, I'm afraid, but strange. They have favourites. It's one of the privileges of being an old woman that one can have favourites. Dr. Roberts was only asking me the other day which of my grandchildren I loved best and I said you. Horrid man, I don't know what it had to do with him, but I said you were my favourite, my dear, and it's quite true. I want you to read a bit of the burial service to me."

"Oh, Grannie!"

I saw through the plot at once and felt trapped. I knew what it was she wanted to find out and felt certain that I should betray the dreadful secret that everyone in the house was keeping from her. A hot flush of rebellion mounted to my forehead and burst forth there as a dampness. It made a moisture in the palms of my hands. Yet I could not refuse. I had not the strength of will. I knew that I was her favourite and had felt it for years in spite of, and perhaps because of, the lash of her acid tongue with which she had often wounded me. She was an old lady who, like God, chastised those whom she loved. She had often slain me with hurtful stinging words and harsh judgments, goading me into those fits of uncontrolled rage and desperation, impotent, futile and spiritually exhausting such as only the young know. They were followed by the bitter tears of shame and remorse that only the young know too. I bore the scars of many such battles. Yet I did not need to be told of her love for me and wanted to die in the moment of telling. It was only that in this I knew I should fail.

"Oh, no, Grannie. Please. I can't."

"Now, now. Now, now," she said gently. "Take that chair, my dear, and sit down."

So I took a chair and sat down, trembling and fumbling through the thin pages of the little leather-bound book that fitted into the palm of my hand. She closed her eyes and there was silence. Presently I began in a halting, ill-controlled voice, thick with the tears that were already flowing and could not be kept back.

"I am the resurrection and the life, saith the Lord: he that believeth in me, though he were dead, yet shall he live. . . ."

"I held my tongue, and spake nothing: I kept silence, yea, even from good words; but it was pain and grief to me. . . ."

I could not continue but let the book fall to the floor between my knees, sobbing bitterly and without restraint. She laid her hand on mine.

"It's all right, darling. It's all right, quite all right. I'm not afraid."

I had failed and knew that she knew.

Three days later she lay in her coffin which was supported upon chairs in that same bedroom. The shutters were half-closed but when I entered the room the nurse folded them back and let in a shaft of sunlight. Then she stood with her back turned to me and to the dead, an impersonal figure. Only the small face was to be seen, aloof and austere with the waxen skin stretched tightly over the bones of the cheeks and temples. Her brow was smooth and the bridge of the nose seemed carved from ivory. I bent down and kissed her forehead. It was cold as stone, indifferent, utterly without life. In that moment, not through the eyes but through the lips, I knew that she was gone quite beyond recall.

My first meeting with death left me with a sense of loss which seems mercifully absent now from this periodic dread encounter. There was the shock of discovering that faces which were a part of life could thus suddenly vanish, that beloved voices might be abruptly stilled, that dear familiar things could come to an inexplicable end and all at once be no more. No one could say what had happened to the voice or the face. It was just death. The blankets were piled in the middle of the bed, the wardrobe and cupboards emptied of their contents, and presently the shutters were opened again and the sunlight streamed once more into the room. Yet where was its occupant? Later in life one begins, I suppose, without realizing it perhaps, to form some sort of belief in immortality. The seeds of a faith in the hereafter begin to sprout from the thin soil of hope or of fear of the negation of hope. The sense of loss which death brings grows less acute. The dead no longer seem wholly to depart until time itself brings its inevitable, though partial, forgetfulness and comfort. But in those days I knew only what I had been taught. It was that at death something called the soul left the body and went to God. This always seemed vaguely unsatisfying since I was very confused as to exactly what the soul was and no one had ever succeeded in describing it convincingly. Nor was it clear to me where and, indeed, what God was. For years I pictured Him as a testy old gentleman peering through a hole in the sky at the doings of small boys, a sort of omnipotent all-seeing and vengeful schoolmaster. He inspired dread and a superstitious dislike. But to His safe keeping, they said, went the souls of the Good. I did not envy them. On the other hand terrible things happened to the souls of the Wicked and for such small offences as refusing to eat sago pudding a dreadful vengeance was meted out in the hereafter when all these sins, recorded down the years, would be brought forth, judged and expiated. Yet nobody that I could think of was really Good. Almost everyone flew into tempers, said things that were obviously unkind and spiteful and often things that were deliberately untrue. And least of all, I secretly felt, had my grandmother been really what you would call Good. But now everybody said she was safe in the Old Gentleman's keeping. If she was not I revolted against the idea that this indomitable, beloved, irritating old lady was now enduring punishments, long and vindictively stored up against her, for all those occasional little transgressions against me which I myself had long ago forgotten and forgiven and had often richly deserved in any case. So it was all unexplained, baffling and mysterious, a reasonless curtailment of a precious part of my life. I felt a mocking emptiness and a sense of incompleteness which I carried around with me for many months. And sometimes in bed at night I used to try to think her back to me, thinking hard about her silver hair and hearing her voice in my imagination. I used to fancy I could feel her in the room with me. Sometimes the sense of her nearness was so great that I believed I had succeeded and thought I could feel her hand upon my wrist as it had been when I had tried to read to her and she had said, "It's all right. I'm not afraid." It is over twenty years now since she died and I think I can still do this, though it is not so easy as it was. And, such as it is, I have formed my belief. In the poor soil of hope a slender tree is growing. For the dead are one with us and all about us, part of us, dwelling in the stones and earth of our country.

We went to live with my grandmother when I was about six years old. But I have early memories of her from days which, as a child measures time, were long before that. I remember lying in a big bed in the downstairs bedroom, where later I lay and prayed to be grown-up, suffocating with bronchitis. People moved to and fro in the room softly by the light of a candle. A small figure in a dressing-gown with her grey hair in a plait, as I saw it at the very last, bent over me and said, "Give him a poultice—a good hot poultice, child. That's the thing." And presently they brought in a scalding thing between two plates which seemed to burn my heart out but which saved my life. Then I see myself driving in the park with the old lady, for she always seemed to be that, in a two-wheeled trap behind a white pony whose bobbing smooth white rump seemed to be pushed along by the trap it drew along the yellow roads until suddenly the pony stopped for no very evident reason and became suddenly deaf to all threats or entreaties. My last remaining unmarried aunt and my grandmother, dressed in grey with veils floating in the wind, seemed to quarrel a great deal and grew bitterly acrimonious together. Then they would suddenly remember my silent diminutive presence, all eyes and ears, and to my rage continued their dispute, whatever it was, in voluble and baffling French. "Pas devant l'enfant, ma chère," my grandmother would say. "I know French," I would lie. "I do know French. 'Au clair de la lune, mon ami Pierrot . . .!' I do know French." But the pony would suddenly stop and, taking advantage of the strife among his foes, would begin to nibble the grass at the side of the road. There had to be an armistice then while he was cajoled into resuming his busy trot homewards. Yet chiefly I remember her sitting in her bedroom in the morning sunshine or by lamplight at night combing her long silver hair. This, the first and the last thing that I remember about her, always held for me a magic fascination. I would pluck the grey tail from my faithful rocking-horse and, having woven it into a silver plait such as the old lady wore when she went to bed, would run up and down passages and in and out of rooms shouting "Here's Grannie with her hair down! Look! Look! I've made Grannie with her hair down!" And one day, seeing my mother sitting in front of her mirror combing her hair which was long and thick too but jet black, I said, "I do believe your hair's going to be like Grannie's soon. There's grey hairs in it. Oh, hooray! Hooray! Mummie's going to have hair like Grannie's! Hooray! Hooray!"

In those days we lived in a little house some distance out of London and I used to be taken over to visit my grandmother in her old house beside the park where she lived with my last remaining unmarried aunt.

"Why! He's grown!" the old lady would say each time I went to see her. She would take my hand and stand me in front of her chair. "What a great boy he's getting!"

"I wonder," she would say presently, looking at me speculatively with sharp brown eyes over her glasses, "if his brain grows with his body, my dear."

And this at a time when my mother was a little anxious with the impatience of a fond parent because I showed no signs of learning my alphabet or of wanting to do anything but play imaginative games. It would bring my mother sailing into action in my defence with all guns.

When I was five or six my last remaining aunt got married. She had lived somewhat uneasily at home since her sisters had gone, for it was my grandmother's idea, an idea which prevailed in her time, that it should be the aim of every young woman to find a suitable husband. It was the old business of the marriage market again. Any girl who did not do so was looked upon as unwanted, wasted and "on the shelf." My grandmother saw this shameful state approaching for her last daughter and goaded her with all the slings and arrows of which she could dispose. And they were many. Underlying the disputes and the tears and the recriminations, mostly in French—"pas devant l'enfant, ma chère"— had been this marriage question, this reproach, unspoken usually but often openly alluded to at the last, this veiled accusation of being unwanted. Life was a race and the penalty for losing it was a shameful, barren and bitter spinsterhood. But in due course my aunt did make what was held to be a good marriage. She married a tall soldier with

26

a black moustache. There was a grand wedding and the reception was held in the old garden on a lovely summer's day. It was the last time the garden was ever "en fête", its flower beds ablaze with colour, marquees on the lawn and a band playing largely unheeded under the trees. But it was for me the first of an apparently unending series of other people's wedding receptions which I have been attending ever since. One day the gay procession will end, no doubt, but only with my death and then I shall find myself toasting happy celestial couples in ambrosial nectar in the tents of heaven. I remember little about this one, however, except my mother in a large floppy hat which I thought the most beautiful hat I had ever seen. I still do, though I cannot remember in the least what it was like. I remember crowds of people moving about and deck-chairs and a mountainous lady in brown, sister of the tall gentleman with the moustache that everyone seemed to be making such a fuss about. She sat down heavily in a deck-chair which collapsed under her. While horrified solicitous guests were helping the humiliated lady to her feet I was led away with tears of uncontrollable laughter rolling down my face. I had behaved so badly, they said, that I should never attend another wedding. How wrong they were!

But when the guests had gone, leaving the path to the front gate strewn with rose leaves and scattered rice, and when the marquees had been taken away, the old lady was left alone with only the thought to comfort her that she had now successfully married off all three of her daughters. Life became suddenly empty and the house full of beds with the blankets folded in the middle of the mattresses. She sold the pony and trap. She spread dust sheets in the drawing-room and closed the shutters. But presently the silence and the emptiness of the house oppressed her and she wrote begging my parents to come and live with her with their children. And this they did, but before my grandmother died ten or eleven years later two more were born and there were five of us.

With what joy I greeted this change! There was that old enchanted garden full of mysterious ways and friendly trees, bright with flowers in summer. There was the old house with its comforting ancient smells, its little bedrooms with flowered wall-paper and windows overlooking wide stretches of park or striped lawn, its stairway that wound spirally in a tower and its ghostly library filled to the ceiling with books and books and books for a winter's evening. There were few of these I could understand but many I could pore over, lying on my stomach before the fire. There were secret and forbidden cupboards, lofts full of forgotten treasures and a dear companionable spirit that I have met in a few old houses since. It is as though something of those quiet lives that once were led within them still lingers in the rooms. Love leaves its ineradicable pattern in old homes. When they are pulled down loving-kindness, gentleness and peace go with them. The number of these benignly haunted houses is not increasing, alas! The world grows poorer, colder, emptier every year.

Yet did I but know it I was approaching, as the change of homes drew near, one of the crises of my life. Had my parents decided not to listen to the old lady's entreaties but to stay away in their own little house my life, and I myself, would have turned out very differently. This would have been another story, written by somebody else with my name.

My world now became richer than I think it has ever been since, warmer with a romantic glow of its own, more full of strange fancies. I, and my sister two years younger than I, lived in a kind of dream world. It was far more exciting and significant than the real world in which one got up and dressed and ate meals and went for walks in the park. To begin with we were the centres of it. I, of course, was rather more the centre than she was. We had the power, the importance, the wealth and the beauty which, as a small boy and a small girl, we sadly lacked in the real world in which we could be forced to sit all a long summer afternoon rebelliously over a plate of sago pudding. Or into which one could be suddenly whirled out of the midst of some scene of royal splendour to be sat on the lavatory or bustled into a bath.

There was an enormous beech-tree in the garden. From the stout striped green bole the branches spread outwards and swept the ground on all sides making a great translucent green tent with a mossy floor. This became for us the centre and focus of all those romantic imaginative games of childhood which I wish I could play now. Whatever we wanted to be we made ourselves as completely as if a magic wand had been waved over us, so completely that to be recalled to earth from our day-dreams was almost physically painful. We made ourselves Kings and Queens, holding court in our emerald palace, and walked proudly erect with crowns on our heads among our loyal but entirely imaginary subjects.

"What are you wearing, Your Majesty?"

"I'm wearing my ermine robe sewn with seed pearls and scattered with diamonds and rubies."

"Oh, but you wore that yesterday."

"Don't care. I'm going to wear it again to-day."

"Oh well. If you're going to be an ass I shan't play."

A dreadful threat this, often levelled at one by the other, involving the sudden destruction of a whole fabric of bright images.

28

"Oh, all right then. I'm wearing my cloth of gold with ostrich feathers."

And, our sartorial differences adjusted, we resumed our royal progress among our applauding subjects. But Grandmother, arranging flowers or sewing or polishing silver at an open window, would see the royal cortège go past and the King would hear her voice in loud and acid *lèse-majesté*:

"What a great boy he's getting, Olive. And so backward. Such a pity he's so aimless, my dear. So bad for a great boy of his age."

And then His Majesty would wander unhappily away across the lawn, his royal magnificence sadly depleted, the ermine and the cloth of gold having suddenly become a dirty blue jersey and short knickers. For my grandmother was beginning to make discoveries about her grandson. His size was one of them and whenever she referred to me it was as "that great boy."

There were other days when the beech-tree became a theatre and we the stars performing dramas of our own composition to vast but mercifully imaginary audiences. Only robins and blackbirds hopped about undismayed in the stalls. Pigeons cooed their appreciation from the gallery. When we gave a musical performance the garden was filled with the sound of our flat tuneless voices which stopped abruptly if we saw a figure approaching in the distance or heard the faint warning rumble of a wheelbarrow. Sometimes the curtain would be run down abruptly because of the sudden appearance unobserved across the lawn of Grandmother, walking busily with her head bent as she always did, carrying a bunch of roses or a basket of eggs or a cabbage or some other of the kindly fruits of the earth still wet from its moist bed.

"What lovely games!" she would say as she passed, like a chorus of fates across our stage. "What lucky children to have nothing to do all day but play lovely games!" But later she would remark to my mother:

"What a pity, Olive, that he can't have something done about his voice."

"About his voice, Mother dear?"

"So tuneless, I mean. I'm afraid he'll never be able to sing."

"I don't know that it matters if he can't sing."

"No. No, it doesn't matter, of course. But I couldn't help noticing when the great creature was playing some game in the garden this morning. Not a note, my dear. Just like his father."

On other days I rushed about the garden with my sister obediently in tow. As time went on she grew less obedient at this, for I had turned myself into an express train and she was compelled to undergo that painful metamorphosis also, though trains had no special charm or magic for her. But for me they had a majestic and enchanted beauty. I endowed them with a personality, as I did all inanimate things that I loved, and I assumed that personality myself as I raced noisily about the garden in the form and image of a giant locomotive. I still possess this passion for trains which I share with many distinguished people. But unfortunately my grandmother never shared it. She felt no thrill of satisfaction when the great express came clanking on to the veranda and drew up with a shriek outside the drawing-room window.

In an outbuilding there was a large room where, on wet days, we were confined with great difficulty and where we played for hours. Here was my rocking-horse whose tail was such a joy on account of its resemblance to Grandmother's hair. Here was a large collection of those instructive and manly playthings which all boys are supposed to love— the Meccano, neglected and rusted because it bored me to try and make anything with it; the expensive model trains which took up an immense amount of space on the floor and were constantly being trodden upon and broken; the air-gun which shot rubber darts and was held, rightly, to be dangerous; the Red Indian outfit which had no charm for me because I never wanted to feel like a Red Indian. All these were forgotten and neglected. Instead we acted our endless melodramas, which was particularly satisfying in this confined space as there was an echo which improved the voice as a bathroom does. Or we went to Church and chanted endlessly and monotonously with dust-sheets round our shoulders. Or we knelt down and prayed and said, "Oh God, please God send us wings and let us fly."

"Well, it says if you have enough faith you get anything."

"Well, I've got lots of faith. I have got faith and I will fly."

"So have I. Let's try jumping off the ladder now."

"There. I believe I did fly just a little bit."

"I know—let's pray again and then jump off a step higher after each time we pray."

"Yes. Only you must *really* believe when you pray. That's terribly important it says."

"Your-Grannie-says-to-stop-making-that-awful-noise-whatever-are-you-doing, she says. She's resting, she says."

I do not know at what age I began to feel that I was too big to be playing these games or when it first occurred to me that there was an age at which dignity forbade me to be a king or to be a train or to raise my voice in unmelodious song upon my imaginary stage. At any rate I know that as time went on a sense of guilt would overcome me more and more whenever I suspected that anyone might be looking on. My grand and terrifying elder brother made occasional descents from school or from Osborne and would jeer unmercifully, so that I would never dare to be a king when he was around and the theatre was closed down for the holidays until he went away.

"Great ass!" he would say. "Look at you. Great ass!"

But chiefly it was the old lady herself who made me feel that the romantic imagery of childhood was no longer becoming to me. I was outgrowing it as though it were a garment which had become too small for me without my noticing it.

"I wonder you don't take some advice about that great boy, Olive," I would hear her say.

"Why, Mother? He's very well."

"Oh yes, he's well enough I suppose. Oh, I'm not suggesting he's not well."

"But what are you suggesting?"

"Nothing, dear. But still one can't help wondering, you know. I'm not sure it wouldn't be just as well——"

Until at last everyone began to tell me I was no longer a child. I was getting a great boy, they said. I know perfectly well now that they lied for a part of oneself remains always a child. I still love trains and turn to see them pass with a catch of the breath. I still like royal pageants, though I feel slightly ashamed of doing so. I still like to imagine myself grander and richer and more glamorous than I am. I still have my fancies but keep them locked away within myself while the other half of me, the nearly forty half, makes occasional descents upon them and says "Great ass! Look at you, you great ass!"

But for the first year or two after we went to live with my grandmother no one thought it was wrong for me to be a child and all my days were spent weaving these romances around myself and around my sister who was my often rebellious satellite. But our sky was clouding over. Often, as a punishment for making too much noise, we would be separated and told to "amuse yourselves quietly" and to stay apart. Sometimes we were whisked away and sent to bed early or sent up to durance vile in our little bedrooms. I would spend the first hour of this penal solitude in a storm of tears and rage and then, calming down, would draw trains or look at pictures in a book. When I had forgotten that I was alone and enduring punishment my mother would come up to set me free. Then I would be astonished to see that she had been crying too.

IV

I COULD not prevent myself from growing up but my grandmother's constant reminders that I was becoming a great boy made
little impression upon me until it was suddenly decided to take me
out of short trousers and put me in long ones. I was immensely proud
of this promotion and went about with my new garments as self-consciously as a young officer with his second pip. But they lent a greater
force to my grandmother's remarks. "Fancy a great boy like you in
long trousers playing such silly games all day long." It was obviously
wrong that such a great boy in such grand long trousers should spend
all his days in happy but unprofitable idleness. It was decided that I
must begin my education.

I must say at the outset that I never learnt anything at school or was
ever any particular credit to any school that I attended, and I attended
several. Somewhere there are a couple of leather-bound volumes with
my name inscribed on the fly-leaf. "The Romance of Modern Railways,
1st Prize for Divinity." "The Poetical Works of Wordsworth, 1st
Prize for English Composition." But my name does not figure in gilt
letters on any board in any school dining-hall. No school magazine
has ever recorded my prowess in any field and I have no photographs
showing myself among rows of scowling little boys ranged behind a
cup or a football. And yet, wait! Yes, I did once win a silver cup as I
shall tell later. For years it stood on the mantelshelf in my bedroom,
sole evidence that I ever had any athletic prowess. It was worn on my
head as a helmet when, in rare illicit moments home from school, I
became the king reviewing his troops.

My chief memories of the several schools which I inconspicuously
attended are the pain of homesickness, the feeling of dreadful loneliness
in a hostile world, the recurring desolation of farewell.

Parting is half dying. I seem to have been continually saying farewell
throughout my life and the pain of leaving familiar scenes and faces
never grows less. One leaves a part of oneself behind on each occasion
and there must be little bits of me all over the world. Whenever I see a
train go out of a station or a ship leave a quay I can feel something of
this death of the spirit even if I am alone among strangers and no answer-
ing eye meets mine. The pain of leaving my own country to-day is
every bit as great as that of leaving my home for school at the first of all
those many leave-takings.

32

The first of my many schools was that of Miss Beatrice Grey, a tall soldierly Victorian lady who ran a school for little boys in a tall barrack-like Victorian house. I went to her as a weekly boarder. On the first Monday morning, and indeed all subsequent Monday mornings, I memorized tearfully every object in the room while I sat over my lonely early breakfast, every stick and leaf in the garden as I walked with my mother to the front gate and I kept my eyes fixed on the house until it was out of sight, stamping it upon my memory. I half believed that everything would vanish immediately my back was turned. I have never quite been able to stifle this suspicion that things cease to exist when I am no longer there to see and perceive them. When I return after a long absence and find everything apparently exactly as it was before I went away I am still slightly incredulous. I go about looking for change among scenes and people only too evidently unaware of my absence and quite unaffected by my return. I greet the least sign of change with triumph and say, "Ah! That's new!" as though I had established proof that when my back is turned things do indeed dissolve and fade away.

The five-day week I spent at Miss Grey's seemed to me like an eternity when I faced it on Monday morning. It passed quickly enough. When later I went to boarding school an eight-weeks' term seemed no less formidable in advance but seemed to have passed as quickly in retrospect. Later still, when I went away for two or three years at a time, they too seemed like all eternity ahead of me. But they fled and were in the memory no more than six days or six weeks had been. For as one grows older one's perception of time seems to change. When I played all day in the garden each one of those days was divided into its long morning, afternoon and evening. There were seven such days in the week. But now years seem to slip away as swiftly as days did then. Are the days so full when one is young because each brings some new discovery, some yet untasted joy? Perhaps each hour is marked by its peculiar flavour, its foretaste of what will later become the common experience of life.

I learnt very little at Miss Grey's. Monday and Tuesday of each week I spent in an agony of homesickness and tearful loneliness. It was the first time I had ever been away from the safe harbour of home and I felt like a rudderless ship on a wide stormy sea. The dozen or so other little boys, all two or three years older than I, seemed like giants and ogres. And Wednesday, Thursday and most of Friday I spent in a fever of excitement at my approaching departure for the week-end. My mother fetched me away on Friday afternoon and on that day the sun shone with an especial radiance. On Friday morning the whole world awoke transformed. Miss Grey found my unconcealed delight at leaving her house extremely distasteful. She looked upon me with disfavour. She was a deeply religious lady with strong views about Heaven, Hell and Original Sin, and her constant references to Hell, inspired me with a kind of superstitious dread of her. I shuddered at the mere thought of her erect soldier-like figure, her armour-like clothes and her fuzz of white hair. My dread of her was increased by the fact that there seemed to be some mystery about her sex. To begin with it was quite impossible to imagine her without her clothes. Harry, the red-haired boy with whom I shared a bedroom, and I, tried many times in secret to picture Miss Grey naked but we always failed. It seemed as though those starched white blouses that she always wore, those high collars and that skirt that swept the ground without falling into folds, so that she seemed to move on wheels, must be as much a part of Miss Grey as her fuzz of stiff white hair. Spanners and screwdrivers would be necessary to remove them, we thought. In addition to being made all in one piece, like Mrs. Noah in a Noah's ark, there were the extraordinary noises she made at night. Harry and I slept in a shabby bedroom high up under the slates. Our hard little iron beds stood in opposite corners of the room. Miss Grey slept on the floor below. Waking in the night Harry and I would hear trumpetings such as we had heard elsewhere only in the elephant house at the Zoo.

"Harry, are you awake?"

"Yes."

"Do you hear anything?"

"It's old Bee snoring."

"Snoring? But my father snores like that."

"So does mine."

"I thought only men snored—do you think Miss Grey is really a man dressed up?"

Then we would get out of bed and creep down to her door to listen. It seemed impossible that anyone could make such a noise in the small hours and still be female.

One night, while we were listening outside her door, Miss Grey's inseparable and boon companion, her horrible little dog Betsy, who occupied her bedroom, suddenly gave a shrill muffled bark. The reverberating noise stopped suddenly and presently we heard a movement and Miss Grey's voice—"Who's that? Who's there?" There were sounds indicating that she was getting out of bed and two small pyjama-clad figures fled up the stairs and lay quaking under the sheets. Soon through half shut eyes I saw the bedroom door open a little way to admit the dull glow of a night-light. In its feeble glimmer I saw a head appear round the door for a moment and then withdraw. Horror of horrors! It had no hair. "Harry—did you see?"

"Yes."

"She has no hair!"

But next morning there she was the same as ever with her stiff white blouse and high collar and her fuzz of white hair as correct and soldier-like as ever. But now we knew she was a man.

All the virtues of faithfulness, loyalty, integrity and gratitude, which Miss Grey found so sadly lacking in her pupils, she found abundantly in Betsy who was old and blind, who was so obese she could scarcely move. She had two rows of black udders which almost touched the ground beneath her and she snorted and dribbled continually. She was the apple of her guardian's eye and the most repulsive creature I had ever seen. She feared and hated me with reason. In addition to the sly tweaks and kicks with which we tormented the unfortunate Betsy Harry and I concocted elaborate plots for her discomfiture. This was fairly easy since Betsy had only a single emotion. It was greed. The devotion and lavish attentions of her mistress meant nothing to her. They provoked no response if no simultaneous appeal was made to her stomach. So we were continually offering her titbits at which she snapped ravenously only to drop instantly with a yelp of pain and surprise because they were scalding hot, or which set her coughing and sneezing because they were covered with pepper. Needless to say this could only be safely accomplished when Betsy's guardian was out of the way. Sometimes we lured Betsy, in the absence of her mistress, up to our bedroom and chased her round and round it until she was panting and goggling with exhaustion and terror. Harry and I laid ceaseless plots in our bedroom after dark or lying on our stomachs in Miss Grey's cat-ridden strip of back garden, chewing young stems of Japanese cane or nasturtium leaves. One day Miss Grey went shopping leaving Betsy behind, as she often did because she was too blind and too slow-moving for the dangerous bustle of the High Street. When she returned she found Betsy cowering and slobbering with terror. We had spent an enjoyable hour chasing her round the garden with a can tied to her tail. Betsy, of course, was unable to explain this but she laboured heavily into her mistress's lap and lay there snorting and slobbering. Her reluctance to come anywhere near Harry or myself aroused dark suspicions in the mind of her jealous guardian.

"What have you been doing to my darling little Betsy, you wicked, wicked boys?"

"Nothing, Miss Grey," lied Harry, making his rather fishy eyes round and innocent. But I had much less guile than he and was, and still am, a very inexpert liar. I blushed scarlet.

"But why is she so frightened? Look! She is quite quivering with fright, the poor darling doggie. Have you been unkind to her, Dick?"

"No, Miss Grey." But she knew it was a lie for I could not meet her direct penetrating glance.

Unfortunately, while we had been engaged in our furious sport in the back garden, we had forgotten the old lady next door who was a crony of Miss Grey's and shared her confidences, and her religious convictions. Her watchful hostile eyes had seen us at our game. That same evening she felt it her duty, as she said, to come round and apprise Miss Grey of what she had seen going on in her garden during her absence. She had no doubt that we were very good boys really but she hated to see poor dumb things tormented. She couldn't bear to think of boys growing up to be horrid spiteful men. Wickedness and wrong-doing always found their deserts in this world—or the next, she added with frightful emphasis. She felt she was only doing her duty.

So next day a terrifying ceremony took place in the front school-room before all the other boys. Miss Grey rapped the table with her ruler.

"Now, boys," she said. "I want you all to pay attention. Harry Martin and Dick Ommanney, get up and stand by the blackboard. You see these two boys? I want you all to take a good look at them and feel thoroughly ashamed of them. I want you to pray to God that you may never become what they are in danger of becoming. Cowards. For I am sorry to tell you, very, very sorry to tell you, that they have been discovered behaving in a cowardly, deceitful, cruel and ab-so-lutely disgusting manner. Ab-so-lutely dis-gusting!"

Here a wave of excitement, a tremor of delighted expectancy ran through the two rows of little boys who stared at us as we stood sheepishly facing them in front of the blackboard. What ever could it be that Ommanney and Martin had been doing?

"They have been caught doing something that no decent man, no Christian would dream of doing, something every Gentleman considers beneath contempt, something I would rather see a son of mine die than do——" The rows of eyes regarding us became round with amazement and fascinated horror. "They have been caught in the very act of tormenting a poor dumb, defenceless animal," continued Miss Grey with the majesty of a judge pronouncing the death sentence.

The air of expectancy and quick interest collapsed like a pricked balloon. Oh was that all!

"So now"—Miss Grey went on, fixing us with a terrible stare—"I am going to make an example of these two boys. Harry Martin, step forward."

The excitement increased again. They were no longer two rows of little boys. They were a Spanish crowd at a bullfight, a Roman crowd watching the Christians thrown to the lions. Silently, with wide eyes, they watched Miss Grey take a cane from a drawer beneath her starched bosom. I watched fascinated too, but on this afternoon nothing that Miss Grey could do had any terrors for me for it was Friday and nearly three o'clock. At five my mother's familiar and comforting figure would appear outside the window signifying my release. Nothing that Miss Grey could do had any terrors for me as long as she did not tell Mother. There were tears rolling down my cheeks and on to my jacket, not because of the thought of the cane but because of the thought of my mother learning that I had done something that any Gentleman would consider beneath contempt. For, to tell the truth, I was already considerably ashamed of myself. For the first time in my life I had been led into evil by somebody else. Now, suddenly, I wished I had not been. I wished I had had more strength, as I have often wished since. But not because I had displeased Miss Grey nor because I had ill-treated Betsy, whom I hated as much as ever, but because I felt guilty and was afraid my guilt would hurt Mother. So when the cane appeared out of the drawer I thought of Mother and of her distress when she knew and the tears flowed faster than ever. Miss Grey saw them and relented a little, misconstruing them. But Harry's mouth was set. His colourless eyes seemed to have retreated into the back of his head. There was no repentance there and he certainly was not in tears.

"Harry Martin," said Miss Grey, "you are several years older than your fellow sinner—I might almost say, your partner in crime. I think you were the ringleader. You have led a boy younger than yourself into evil. So I am going to punish you the more severely of the two. Bend over."

Unrepentant and stiffly Harry bent over. "Lower. Touch your toes," directed Miss Grey, and she struck with her cane four times sharply on the shiny posterior that was presented to her. "Now go back to your place." And unrepentant, unforgiving, defiant, dry-eyed, Harry went back to his place at the table while Miss Grey turned her attention to me.

"Dick Ommanney, stand forward! You are a younger boy. I expect you were misled. Nevertheless I have had my eye on you for some time and I have noticed, I am sorry to say, that you are very easily led into

37

the wrong path by others. When you are tempted by the Devil
disguised as a bigger boy than yourself you must say, like Our Lord,
'Get thee behind me, Satan,' and you must pray to the Lord for
strength."

"Yes, Miss Grey."

But I was praying to my particular Lord for something quite different
and as Miss Grey spoke I was silently addressing him. "Oh Lord,
don't let her tell Mummie. Oh don't let her and I'll never tease Betsy
again."

"I shall give you a lighter punishment than I intended because I
can see you are repenting and I shall pray to Our Lord for you to-
night myself to give you strength to resist temptation. Hold out your
hand."

I held my hand out and she delivered two stinging cuts on it with
the cane.

"Now go back to your place."

I went back to the table with tears running down my face. As I sat
down I caught Harry's resentful tearless eye. "Oh Lord, don't let her
tell. Please, God, don't let her." But there were no prayers in Harry's
heart and, as Miss Grey glanced down to put her cane back in the drawer
under her bosom, he stuck his tongue out at her.

"Did it hurt?" whispered the boy next to me.

"Y-yes," I murmured in reply.

"Did it hurt?" I heard another whisper to Harry.

Harry smiled and shook his head. But he sat a little carefully on his
seat.

I don't know if Miss Grey prayed for me that night. If she did the
Lord turned a deaf ear to her for He never gave me the strength she said
she would ask for me. But it seemed that He heard my prayer, for when
the magic hour of five o'clock came and I beheld with joy my mother's
familiar figure at the gate, Miss Grey led me to the front door, all
smiles.

"Here we are, Mrs. Ommanney. We've had a *very* successful week
and we know our five-times table right off by heart. Don't we now?
Say the five-times and let's see how clever we really are."

"Five times one are five. Five twos are ten. Hooray, she didn't tell.
Five threes are fifteen, five fours are twenty. Five fives are twenty-five.
Oh, God, I thank Thee she didn't tell. Five sixes are thirty. I've a good
mind to tell myself now to pay her out."

But I did not tell. I kept quiet about it for I was not really very
pleased with myself for having tormented Betsy and never did it again,

though Harry plotted his revenge incessantly and was contemptuously angry with me for holding back.

"You're frightened," he said under the Japanese canes. "You're afraid, that's what you are. Well, of course, if you're a coward—— Cowardy, cowardy, custard!"

I dreaded his disapproval but would not be drawn. But Betsy never forgave me and would never come near me again.

But in spite of the fact that I was unhappy at Miss Grey's and found myself for the first time in conflict with another human being, I also made friends for the first time. I remember two of them particularly. One was a Welsh boy named, inevitably, Jones. He was a handsome pale-faced little boy who always wore a blue serge suit. At the age of about nine he played the piano most beautifully and I used to go to his home to tea sometimes and sit in a drawing-room filled with flowers watching his slim hands fluttering over the keyboard. I wonder where he is now. Dead, I dare say, for this was in 1910. But why is it that of two influences, good and bad, one so often deliberately chooses the bad? Little Jones hardly influenced me at all apart from the fact that I loved to hear and see him play, but my other friend, the red-haired Harry Martin, had a strong influence over me. He was a good deal older than I and I thought him wonderful. We shared, as I have said, a bedroom on the top floor, for Harry was a weekly boarder like myself. What intrigued me more than anything else was the mysterious knowledge that he used to impart to me in the bedroom after Miss Grey had seen us safely beneath the sheets and had blown out the candle. It appeared that there were words and facts about which I knew nothing. I was amazed at the ignorance in which I had lived hitherto. "But didn't you know *that*? Well, I must say——" A great flood of light burst in upon me. I was enormously proud of this new fund of knowledge and felt that I had attained a new sophistication. Looking back I can see that this was no worse talk than all small boys engage in but to me at that time it was something entirely new. It made me feel worldly, sinful. I had no idea that this sort of talk was ever indulged in at all.

One week-end I returned home bursting with a new worldliness. I longed to show off the extent of my new-found sophistication but was uncertain how I could do so. Certainly as yet no one seemed to have noticed it. On Sunday several people came to luncheon, as they often did after the morning service, relations, friends of my grandmother and my parents from neighbouring houses. Between courses, between the roast beef and the rhubarb tart, during a pause in the listless overfed conversation, I suddenly let fall, like a bomb into the heavy food-laden air, a Word.

There was a long horrified silence.

It was decided that I was coming under a bad influence and so I left Miss Grey's. I do not think there were any regrets on either side.

V

WHEN old Mrs. Shuttleworth died it was a disaster for about fifty little boys, myself among them. She was a kindly and gentle old lady who wore black silk dresses, covered with enormous cameo brooches in front, a lace cap on her head and a shawl around her shoulders. Her mildness and gentleness, however, were combined with an unexpected firmness of character which had a beneficent and curbing effect on her son and daughter who helped her to run her school in a popular south-coast watering-place. She ruled with firm motherly authority over her kingdom of fifty little boys who were noisily and boisterously happy all about the huge, red brick, hideous house and on the level expanse of playing field that lay behind it. Mr. Edward Shuttleworth, the son, was a little man with very short legs, pince-nez and an extremely red face which might have been the result either of a weak heart or whisky or both. No whisky was ever seen about the house, however, so one fell back on the weak heart theory. Mr. Edward had a violent temper, but he kept it under control during his mother's lifetime. He seemed to be curiously afraid of the old lady and would collapse like a pricked balloon when she turned towards him in her chair with a faint silken rustle and said, "Nonsense, Edward dear!" Miss Shuttleworth (I never knew her Christian name and never heard her referred to otherwise than as Miss Shuttleworth) was a small waspish woman, also with pince-nez, invariably dressed in sombre colours and with her mouth perpetually screwed up into a tight round disapproving O. She made a great deal of intimidating play with her pince-nez and would tower over you (even she could tower in those days) with her arms folded over her thin bosom or seated bolt upright on the extreme edge of her chair, looking with her fierce little eyes over her pince-nez, then through and then under them, all the time with her mouth screwed up into a tight dot. She was always surprised. "I never expected such a thing of you. I must say I'm surprised—very." But she, too, stood in awe of her mother and, in her mother's presence, screwed up her mouth and remained silent. "My daughter thinks so too—don't you, dear?" Mrs. Shuttleworth would say, looking keenly over the top of her glasses. "Of course, Mother," her daughter would reply sitting a little more stiffly in her chair.

Since I had left Miss Grey's, somewhat under a cloud, the problem which I presented in the home had become even more acute. As my grandmother constantly observed I was greater than ever. I had evidently learned nothing much at Miss Grey's, could not yet read and only knew the multiplication tables as far as the five times—Miss Grey's crowning achievement so far as I was concerned. I showed no very evident desire to press my search for knowledge any further. Moreover, the knowledge that I had acquired at Miss Grey's was not altogether of the kind that was considered suitable for young gentlemen at the early age of seven.

"Off to boarding school, my dear!" cried my grandmother continually and with triumph. "High time, I'm sure! High time! So bad for a great boy, idling about at home!"

My elder brother, the grand one who in due course went to Osborne, was deliriously happy at Mrs. Shuttleworth's school in the popular resort by the sea. All his letters home and his talk when he returned for the holidays were full of the fun he had there. "Last Wensday we went to the Warren and found lots of fossles. Poulton Major fell down and spraned his ancle but not badly. I made forty-two in a match against the Grange." Since my only experience of school had been Miss Grey's I was filled with astonishment and envy by these letters and by this talk. I began to feel some eagerness to share in these delightful adventures. I regarded my brother with admiration and awe and the thought of perhaps sharing this exalted life with him began to be exceedingly enticing. I too might find fossils and, who knows? perhaps I might make even more than forty-two against the Grange. Forty-two what? And what was the Grange? I was not very clear but that was unimportant.

It all began because my brother was good at cricket, a phenomenon unheard of in my family either before or since. With the idea in their minds that it might perhaps be a solution of the pressing problem to send me to Mrs. Shuttleworth's school, but without telling me of the idea, my parents took me down one summer's day in 1909 to see my brother play.

It was a lovely day. Huge white clouds like balloons drifted across the blue sky. White and gaily-coloured figures wove continually to and fro over the green expanse of the playing field. We sat in a long double line of deck-chairs facing the field where some of the boys, dressed in white, were engaged in what appeared to be a complicated dance which involved throwing a ball to a man with a bat. A ripple of hand-clapping, like rain on a roof, kept running along the line of chairs and a little red-faced man in a striped blazer, white trousers and a panama hat, who I afterwards learnt was Mr. Edward Shuttleworth, kept shouting out

42

things like, "Well hit, sir! Oh, pretty shot, sir!" and "Hard luck, sir! Well held, sir!"

These curious evolutions had no importance for me, however, because immediately above and behind me ran the main line of what was then the South Eastern and Chatham Railway. The engines had brass lips to their funnels and brass domes, so for most of the afternoon my back was turned resolutely on the cricket game except when a nudge or a touch from my mother compelled me to devote some attention to it. But the presence of that enchanting railway line predisposed me as much as anything else in favour of Mrs. Shuttleworth, as much as fossils or the thought of making forty-two, as much as the kind eyes of the old lady herself and the motherly touch of her hand upon my head. When she came and sat in the deck-chair, which I politely vacated for her, she took me by the arm and drew me towards her, beaming sweetly from under her sunshade.

"Are you coming to stay with me, tuppenny?" she said.

"Yes, please," I replied gazing up at the railway line.

"Look now, Dick," said the old lady. "Your big brother's going in."

My brother, with pads on his legs and a bat in his gloved hand, was striding confidently into the middle of the field. A ripple of applause ran along the line of deck-chairs. He stood his bat upright and a man, who for some reason was wearing four hats, made a sign with his hand. My brother moved his bat a little and then nodded. He began to pat the ground with it and stood ready. I watched round-eyed.

"Will he make forty-two?" I asked.

"I dare say. More if he's lucky or clever," said the old lady.

The boy with the ball walked away from my brother who stood defiant and alert, his body sideways and his eyes forward. Then, clasping the ball in his two hands, the boy walked back towards my brother for a few paces, broke into a run and, with a circular motion of his right arm, flung the ball straight at him. My brother raised his bat and stepped out. The ball struck the three sticks behind him with a brittle crack, knocking them sideways.

"Oh, well bowled, sir! Hard luck, sir!" said the man in the panama hat.

My brother was walking off the field looking curiously dejected.

"How many has he made?" I said in a loud bird-like voice.

"None, I'm afraid, dear."

"Why not?"

"Because he's been bowled, you see. He's out now."

43

"But you said he was going to make forty-two. I wanted to see him make forty-two."

"S-sh!"

I turned my back towards the cricket game and by tea-time, at which there were strawberries and cream, I had forgotten those senseless and boring evolutions that went on unheeded by me in the middle of the field until the shadows lay long and tenuous across the green.

On the way home in the train I was tired but happy. Everybody had been very kind and Mrs. Shuttleworth had patted me on the head and kissed me (not that I cared for that much) and said how much she was looking forward to my coming to stay with her next term. I was a dear little chap, she said, and exactly like my brother of whom they were all so fond. Mr. Edward Shuttleworth had said he would make an athlete of me, he had no doubt at all. He could see I had the makings of one. My mother had said how well I had behaved considering and I felt that I had, for I had been constantly leaping up, when nudged, to offer my chair to all sorts of people who wanted to talk to my parents. I had handed things at tea without spilling anything. I had seen lots of trains and my brother, even though he had not made forty-two, had given me a fossil he had found the previous Sunday. I clutched it in my fist all the way home. Most wonderful of all I had been introduced to my brother's friend Poulton Major ("I say, Poulton Ma., this is my young brother. He's coming as a new bug next term.") I went to bed that night with my fossil and dreamed of that magic world into which I was soon to be launched and which glowed, in my imagination, like mountains touched by the morning sun. In my dream I made forty-two and sprained my ankle very badly.

But before I ever started on that new exciting life Mrs. Shuttleworth was dead.

Alas! I was to learn for the first time something of the vanity of human hopes and wishes. To look forward, to live in the future and paint the days to come in colours more bright and glowing than the present or the past is the incurable disease of the human spirit. Disappointment and disillusion seem to be a treatment that only aggravates this obstinate complaint, the disease of chronic hopefulness, especially in the young subject. Later the treatment becomes more effective.

For, quite contrary to what I had so faithfully expected and dreamed, it was a lonesome unfriendly world into which I found myself launched, like a tiny paper boat on a wide river, when I arrived at the beginning of the next term. I seemed to be surrounded by enemies. All the friendly figures of my imagination turned themselves into a set of gargoyles. There were Mr. Edward and Miss Shuttleworth. There was Miss Watson, the matron, and there was Mr. Simpson, the assistant master. There was my brother and there was Poulton Major, perhaps the cruellest disappointment of all. It was a bitter disillusionment. I have had others since but this was the first so perhaps it was the most unkind and bitter of them all.

Mr. Edward Shuttleworth, now that the restraining influence of his mother had been removed by death, continually gave rein to the violent temper he possessed. Indeed, it seemed that there were moments when his temper possessed him and became quite beyond his control. He grew redder in the face than before. Often he disappeared from the scene for days together. When he flew into his sudden uncontrollable rages he cuffed and struck out at the small boys without any apparent reason. Or he would pull viciously at the short hair above their ears or twist the ears themselves until tears started into the eyes of even the strongest. I frequently became the object of Mr. Shuttleworth's vindictive attentions. Owing to the unfortunate presence of that beguiling railway line, which ran along the farther side of the playing field, my attention was constantly straying out of the window during lessons, and on the football or cricket field I was always watching passing trains instead of attending to the game. Mr. Shuttleworth would pounce on me in the middle of some trance or dream, buffeting and shaking me to the accompaniment of explosive and wrathful noises. But presently he began to find that mere cuffing, hair-pulling and buffeting was too easy a sport where I was concerned for I dissolved into tears almost at once. Before long, in fact, I got so that he could hardly speak to me or come near me without my preparing myself for the very worst and beginning to blubber with fright in advance. He became more refined in his methods.

"You, Ommanney Minor! Come up here. You were looking out of the window."

"Oh, sir. No, sir."

"Don't lie to me, sir. I saw you. Have I ever told you before not to look out of the window during class? Have I? Yes, I think I have. I seem to recollect something of the sort. Now, I wonder, can it be that you deliberately disobey me? Can it be? Can it possibly? And who do you suppose is the stronger of the two, Ommanney Minor, you or I?"

By this time I was in tears, of course, and stood with my chin just overtopping the edge of his desk, making incoherent gurgling noises by way of reply. Then he would take hold of the hair above my ears and pull my face towards him. I knew that he would do this sooner or later so that when at last he did it I usually felt a certain sense of relief. As time went on the intervals for ponderous playfulness grew longer and longer.

"Now answer!" he would say, holding my head near his face. There would still be no reply from me except for a gurgling sound indicative of pain, fright and impotent rage all mixed together. Then, suddenly abandoning his cat-and-mouse tactics, he would release my hair, catch me a resounding clip across the side of the face and send me back to my seat with my cheek feeling swollen to the size of a football.

In his study, which smelt faintly of leather, faintly of books and faintly of whisky, Mr. Shuttleworth made even better sport with me.

"You forgot did you? Perhaps, then, you would like your memory refreshed a little. Don't you think it would do you good if your memory were stimulated just a little bit? No? You surprise me, Ommanney Minor. I should have thought that with a memory apparently so poor as yours you would welcome the chance of a little refreshment. Just go to that sofa, will you? That's right. Now put your hand down behind the cushions. Do you feel anything there? I thought so. What is it? Quite right. Bring one of them out, will you? One will do, I think. Do you know what that's for? A very useful little instrument for refreshing the memory, Ommanney Minor. Most stimulating, I assure you. Give it to me. Yes, give it to me. . . ."

But there were times when Mr. Shuttleworth was quite different, usually after his periodical absences for a few days. Then he would suddenly reappear in the schoolroom with a large tin of bulls'-eyes which he would distribute, patting the boys on the head, lifting them up by the armpits and making jokes. All the boys would say that old Shuttlecock was jolly decent really and that his tempers didn't mean anything at all—all except me who thought, on the contrary, that these moments of sudden geniality didn't mean anything, had not forgiven or forgotten recent interviews in the study and could not be lulled into forgiveness and forgetfulness with bulls'-eyes. I hated these bursts of geniality almost as much as the bursts of fury, for while I understood the latter I was deeply suspicious of the former. I loathed being picked up by the armpits and held close to him. Something in my manner of receiving these advances must have been evident to him, for by degrees he began to leave me alone when he distributed these favours and I usually managed to lurk in the background and sneak unobserved out of the room. After these visits the outbursts of passion and rage grew slowly more and more frequent until finally there was some tremendous

46

scene about some trivial matter, after which he would be absent again for several days. The assistant master, Mr. Simpson, a seedy, sandy-haired young man with a ragged moustache and a perpetual sarcasm reserved for little boys, deputized for his senior in class. "Mr. Shuttleworth is slightly—er—indisposed. Ahem!" he would say gazing down his nose and fingering the ends of his moustache.

Mr. Shuttleworth's principal quarrel with me, I think, was that in spite of his prognostications the previous summer I showed no promise whatever of developing into an athlete. At first I was enthusiastic about football and wore enormous football boots and shorts much too big for me with great pride on the first day. "You look like a sparrow with cork legs," said Mr. Simpson. But I soon got bored, found that football involved an unnecessary amount of quite useless effort and running about which I could not manage, or of disagreeable standing about in all sorts of weather often wet and shivering with cold. After about twenty minutes play I had had enough and was ready to leave the field. On the first day I started to walk off the field saying I was tired. To my indignation I was called back. Unable to understand why I was not allowed to stop playing a game when I was tired of it I took no further interest in it and watched the trains instead. As the weeks went on I watched them more and more. But perhaps the real reason for my disinclination for violent exercise was that I was not strong physically and suffered severely from bronchial asthma until I was about fourteen. If I ran about too much the attacks began and soon had me choking and wheezing like an overworked steam-engine. As a result of standing about in cold winds and rain I caught frequent colds which, with unfailing regularity, descended to my chest and sent me to bed suffocating with asthma for several days. I do not deny that I worked this as hard as I could and with considerable success throughout most of my schooldays, incurring the dislike of a succession of schoolmasters, who saw no particular advantage, apart from a slight pecuniary one, in having me as a pupil. I began this subterfuge at the Shuttleworths' and continued in the same for many years. It did not endear me to Mr. Shuttleworth, nor did my constant presence in the sick-room and the extra work it entailed particularly endear me to Miss Shuttleworth and her elderly matron, Miss Watson. In the summer, however, I was usually in better health and had no convenient excuse for dodging cricket. I disliked cricket rather less because it taxed me less and called for less attention. But standing for long hours in the grilling sun or chill wind bored me to death and all my schooldays I resented being compelled to play a game I loathed. It was rather fun, however, to lie behind the pavilion when my side was batting, sucking the stems of long grasses, drowsily reading a book and watching the trains roar past above me. I particularly enjoyed school matches when whole afternoons could be devoted to this occupation. But it infuriated Mr. Shuttleworth who, between his enthusiastic shouts of "Well held, sir!" and "Well hit, sir!", would suddenly discover me drowsing in my retreat and, shaking me as a dog shakes a slipper, would order me to take some interest in my side. I had no idea what he was talking about.

Miss Shuttleworth ruled over the upper part of the house and seemed only to descend at meal-times or when the necessity of reaching the front door compelled her to go through the hall. Her headquarters were the small square drawing-room on the first floor which had once been her mother's room and still seemed to house the old lady's ghost. It was full of palms and pampas grass, cupboards and cabinets containing bric-à-brac and photographs, photographs and photographs. It had a stuffy drawing-room smell. There was a grand piano on which I made a pretence of practising for half an hour a day. My attention often wandered at this too, and whenever the unmelodious and broken rhythm of my scales ceased Miss Shuttleworth would come noiselessly in and sit on the edge of a chair, upright and silent, knitting. On Sunday evenings the whole school, over forty little boys, trooped into the drawing-room and perched themselves about it on chairs or on the arms of chairs, on the sofa or on the arms of the sofa, on stools or on the floor in order to sing hymns while Miss Shuttleworth thumped them out on the piano. Everybody chose a hymn in turn, so many each Sunday, and the game was to try to choose one that Miss Shuttleworth did not know. The winner was the boy who did this most often in a term. However, her repertoire, from constant practice over many years, was remarkable and she was familiar with the most abstruse ones suitable for the oddest occasions. When you chose one to be sung "At the Dedication of a Church" or "At the Solemnization of Matrimony" she would turn round from the piano and say, "But are you sure you mean that one?"

"Yes please, Miss Shuttleworth."

And she would launch forth into its unfamiliar melody with her elbows working so that the bracelets jangled, the thin boys' voices trailing after her in a shrill stream and Mr. Edward's mouth making extraordinary shapes as he sang.

Long and tedious hymns were strictly taboo among the boys themselves and the choice of an unpopular hymn was visited upon one's head in the boot-hole after the session was over. I frequently used my considerable knowledge of the "English Hymnal" and "Hymns Ancient

and Modern" (acquired during sermons at home) as a weapon with which
to chastise the school in general or to get my own back on the other
boys for real or imagined wrongs. "All right! All right! You wait till
Sunday evening!" I would pipe shrilly from under two or three larger
boys sitting on my head. "You wait that's all!" And next Sunday
evening, when my turn came, I would say, gazing maliciously at my
enemies and using a holy voice that I kept for such occasions, "Number
351—'Day of wrath and doom impending'." And for the next quarter
of an hour or twenty minutes, while Miss Shuttleworth pounded away
at the piano and the boys struggled manfully on, I kept my eyes, gleaming
with triumph, steadfastly on my book.

In the upper part of the house Miss Shuttleworth ruled with an iron
hand over the dormitories, the bathrooms, the linen cupboard and over
the oppressed and oppressive Miss Watson. Her tours of inspection,
which she conducted round the dormitories nightly, were like parades.
We lay silent in our beds while she regarded us from the door, her arms
folded and her mouth screwed up, Miss Watson a shadow in the background. She was much more to be feared, with her constant pained
surprise, than her brother with his sudden fits of fury. Her mouth was
always shaped into that forbidding disapproving dot and her arms were
always folded under her mother's cameo brooches which she now wore.
Miss Watson followed Miss Shuttleworth about creaking in a starched
blue uniform. She was for ever gathering up wisps of hair and patting
them into place behind her ear.

"Very well," she would say. "I shall report you to Miss Shuttleworth."

That meant an interview with Miss Shuttleworth in the drawing-room.
She sat very upright on the edge of her chair.

"I can only say," she would remark, gazing through, over and under
her pince-nez, "I can only say that I am most painfully surprised at
what Miss Watson has felt it her duty to tell me. I quite certainly
did *not* think it possible that even you could be so deliberately dis-
obedient."

Then would follow some tedious heart-breaking punishment such as a
thousand lines (her favourite) and no blots allowed, an extra hour's
practice in the drawing-room every evening for a week, while she sat
there like a spectre knitting, or, perhaps the most cruel for a small boy,
bread and water only for supper every evening for a week.

But after I had been at the Shuttleworths' for a month or two I became
more or less accustomed to Mr. Edward and his sister. From Mr. Edward
I learnt to expect cuffs and hair-pulling and learnt to avoid them by

D   49

keeping out of his way and by denying myself the pleasure of looking at trains during class. I learnt to stand still and endure in silence his ponderous fun during those interviews in the study. Silence and failure to dissolve into tears, I discovered, irritated him. He became exasperated and exploded into "So you refuse to answer me, do you?" and produced the cane more quickly, which shortened the interview. And from his sister I grew to expect disapproval, pained surprise and long lectures. I learnt to endure her punishments and to dodge them in various ways. When, for instance, Miss Watson said "Very well, I shall report you," I could forestall her by taking my courage in both my hands and reporting myself, making a tearful confession to Miss Shuttleworth in the drawing-room. Several times I got beneath her angular bosom and touched her heart in this way. On each occasion she gave me a long lecture, to which I listened with a great show of penitence, was painfully surprised and let me off without any sentence. So when Miss Watson said with lugubrious pleasure, "I feel it my duty to report Ommanney Minor," she was astonished to be cut short with "I know, thank you, Miss Watson. I know all about it." If, on the other hand I was unfortunate enough to incur one of Miss Shuttleworth's sentences I usually managed to produce an attack of asthma and went to bed for three or four days. This had a double effect for it not only enabled me to dodge punishment but it paid Miss Shuttleworth and Miss Watson back by giving them extra work. It also irritated them because, while they suspected me of malingering, they could do nothing about it because the asthma was visibly and audibly present. It was largely a nervous complaint and I could more or less produce it by taking thought. I could worry myself into an asthmatic state. The enemy countered with Gregory powder, with castor oil floating on milk, with powders on spoonfuls of marmalade, with liquorice powder, with meals consisting solely of sago pudding of the large type like frogs' spawn. But I was undeterred.

Thus, expecting the harshness of authority, I learnt to endure it or to avoid it just as one expects rain and learns to keep dry or to shelter from it. But what I found hard to bear was the unaccountable cold aloofness, changing occasionally to active hostility, of my brother and his magnificent friend Poulton Major. Instead of being the friend and protector, the bestower of fossils and the maker of forty-two that I thought he was going to be my brother floated in the upper air miles above me. He lived an aloof and remote existence as a prefect and a member of the first eleven in the first form, endowed with all sorts of special and mysterious privileges. He sat at the masters' table in the dining-room. At mealtimes and at prayers he came into the room ten minutes after the rest of the school and no one was allowed to sit down until these god-like creatures, of whom he was one, had taken their places. At bed-time he came up to the dormitory half an hour later than the others, was excused hymn-singing on Sunday evenings and lived in a special first-form room away from the rest of the school. I found to my astonishment that I was not allowed to sit at the same table with my own brother or live in the same room with him. It was not even proper to speak to him without being first spoken to. He seldom took any notice of me at all, but, when he did, it was to chase me across the junior football field and kick my bottom for not attending to the game or to punch my head for leaving my gymn shoes lying about the boot-hole. And frequently I incurred his displeasure by my shocking breaches of etiquette. One morning soon after the beginning of the term he saw me reading a letter in the school-room.

"Is that a letter from the mater you've got there?" he asked grandly in front of the other junior boys.

"No," I replied guilelessly, "it's from Mummie."

As for his friend Poulton Major he never spoke to me or looked at me save once. That once was on the first day of term on the asphalt square outside the schoolroom. I ran up to him eagerly and said, "Hullo, Poulton Major!"

He turned and looked at me with the crushing disdain of a patrician Roman for a slave, the disdain in fact of one unpleasant small boy for another.

"Great Scott!" he said. "What sauce!"

Both my brother and his friend left at the end of my first term. Poulton Major disappeared out of my life but the sense of disappointment which he created in me still lingered, the first wave washing at the foundations of my faith in human nature. My brother's ghost remained at the Shuttleworths' with me in the form of an unattainable standard up to which I was expected to live and in the form of an everlasting, always unfavourable comparison. It stood behind me and followed me about in everything I did, an ever-recurring reminder of his excellencies and matchless qualities as against my own most unfortunate shortcomings. "And what do you suppose your brother would say if he knew?" "How would you like your brother to see you now?"

But such is the resilience of the human spirit, especially the young one, that on the whole I was not unhappy at the Shuttleworths' in spite of the unpleasant skeletons in my cupboard, in spite of Mr. Shuttle-worth's rages, his sister's lectures, Miss Watson's tireless supervision and Mr. Simpson's sarcasm. I found happiness within myself, a blessed facility that children have and which I had perhaps more than most. I made no friends among the boys and was content to be mostly alone, playing strange games and weaving fancies within my own head. I was always mooning about as Mr. Simpson said.

On Sunday afternoons we were allowed to go for walks without a master until tea-time. Most of the boys went in twos or threes, but I, if I possibly could, preferred to go alone. I would go down one of the broad leafy avenues between tall houses and then come out suddenly on to a great green expanse which was like the edge of the world. And there ahead, shimmering, vague and infinite, was the sea. Tiny ships crawled upon its immensity trailing smudges of smoke. I would stand on the cliff edge and let my eye wander over those immeasurable distances wondering what could lie beyond that thin line where sky and sea met. And on clear days I saw, far off, drawn like a faint pencil line, remote, mysterious, the coast of France. One day an old man lent me a telescope and I made the pencil line resolve itself into white cliffs topped by green like the downs behind the town. On the green were white dots—houses. That was Abroad and there dwelt Foreigners, men and women like those I knew and yet not like, speaking a foreign language. Wandering along the shingle beach, watching the curl and suck back of the sea upon the stones, I entered another world than that of the Shuttleworths and forgot them altogether. I was away on voyages of my own. I was with the ships that I watched moving slowly up and down the Channel until they were each only a smudge far off and low down to the south-west by Dungeness or to the north-east by the South Foreland. Sometimes I went down to the harbour and looked at the fishing smacks and drifters, inhaling those ancient and fish-like smells that never lose their magic. Sometimes I would see a cross-channel boat go out, threshing with its paddles a white pathway over to France. No one ever spoke to me except the old man with his telescope. A dreamy round-faced little boy wandering about attracted no one's attention. Nor can I recall many of my thoughts on those moonstruck wanderings of mine but remember only the enchantment, the whisper of the tide on stones, the pale light, the cry of gulls. I remember that I was quite happy and quite alone.

In a tall red-brick house in one of the avenues that led towards the sea lived a comfortable old lady with five daughters. They were distant relations of my parents. When I had been at the Shuttleworths' for a term the old lady invited me to lunch one Sunday. I went unwillingly because I knew it would interfere with my afternoon wanderings. But Mrs. Miller gave me an enormous lunch and made me feel completely at ease.

She was gentle and kind and comfortable. I did not have to bother. The girls must have been in their early twenties or their late teens but they behaved towards me not as though I were a silly little boy of seven but as though I were their equal. This was new to me and for the first time in my life I found myself taking pleasure in grown-up society. I went again the following Sunday and soon their warm food-smelling house became a second home to me, one of the compensations of life at the Shuttleworths'. Every Sunday almost without fail after this I went there for lunch and stayed until it was time for the evening hymn-singing at six-thirty. Sunday became a day to look forward to throughout the long dreary lonely week. After lunch, at which there always seemed to be roast beef and Yorkshire pudding, the old lady rested from the fatigues of church in the morning and of consuming roast beef at lunch. Then some or all of the girls and I sat on the front and listened to the band or walked along the sea wall. To me the girls seemed exceedingly old and very grand. They wore large hats covered with flowers and carried large handbags. Chattering gravely beside them, and receiving their perfectly grave and serious answers to my silly questions, I was as proud as a pea-cock. No doubt they guessed that I was lonely and friendless at the Shuttleworths' though they never mentioned school at all but talked in a matter-of-fact way about ships and trains which must have bored them considerably, about the sea and about Abroad. Every winter, it seemed, their mother took one or more of them to that mysterious and exciting place which seemed to have such an attraction for grown-up people.

"Tell me about Abroad," I would say, sitting on the cliff-top and looking towards the far-off dim line of the French coast.

"Well, we went to Paris last spring with Mother. Paris is lovely in the spring. You'll go there one day when you're bigger."

"Will I? What for?"

"Oh, everyone goes to Paris some time in their lives. You're not educated, you see, till you have been."

"I've been to London."

"Ah, but Paris is quite different."

And they would tell me about Paris and about France. Sitting on the front at that English watering-place I did the round of most of the Continental resorts. After tea the tour was illustrated by picture postcards in an album. Deauville, Biarritz, Cannes, Baden-Baden—I got to know them all. In France you drank wine as you drank water in England. You went to the Casino which was a place so wicked that it was not allowed in England at all. You took your meals sitting in the street which, for some reason, was fun. In Germany there was wonderful music, though why the girls should enjoy that when none of them ever went to a concert at home was not very clear. And at Montreux in Switzerland there were huge mountains covered with snow. How high? As high as the Downs? Hundreds of times higher. Higher than the clouds, so high you could not see the tops. And that, I thought, would be rather fun. So from this kaleidoscopic picture, this jumble of images, I began to be aware of other countries, other peoples than my own. My horizon was widening and I began to look at the vague shimmerng edge of the sea with eyes newly awakened, full of hope. And from the girls themselves, to whom I am eternally grateful, came the first warmth of friendship like the sun in early spring.

At this time my own immediate world was a shell within which I lived and breathed, rejoiced and shed tears, unconscious of anything beyond it. Sunrise and sunset, the changing seasons and all the people that came and went about me were only the background of a picture of which I myself formed the centre. Only occasionally did something happen which might have told me, had I been old enough to understand, that I was a part of something greater than myself, that my tiny spirit was apiece with a larger spirit that strove even as mine did towards the undefined goal of human happiness. One of these was a special day, heralded by weeks of excitement and anticipation, called the Coronation. The school closed for a week and I went rejoicing home, not understanding what it signified. The family rose at the early hour of half-past five and trailed up to London in jostling crowds to watch the procession from my uncle's office overlooking the Abbey door. From this coign of vantage I looked down upon the ranks of red soldiers and upon the milling crowds, on the glittering people that stepped out of high-backed motor-cars into the cavernous darkness of the Abbey. I might also have looked down on King George the Fifth himself had it not been that at the moment when his magic coach appeared I was overcome by the one desire of all small boys that cannot be denied and was led away to the lavatory. But for the first time I had taken part in the pageant and drama which is the history of my country.

One summer's day during the desultory afternoon school hour an unbelievable noise like all the insect world let loose was heard above the roof-tops. Rushing with Mr. Simpson to the window we beheld a vast structure like an extremely complicated and clumsy box-kite charging with a sound of terror through the sky above us. We ran shouting into the street and saw the thing come down in a field some distance off.

It was soon surrounded by a swarm of people but we were in time to see a man seated in the midst of its mass of struts and ribbed planes. He was waving his cap, shaking hands among the crowd and posing for his photograph. He made a speech, standing up in his seat, but we could not hear what he said. But it was Grahame-White. He had just flown the Channel. Soon a huge space was cleared through the crowd. The thing began its crackling roar again. The little man, perched precariously in the middle of it, did something and it lurched forward. Soon, amid gasps of astonishment from the massed onlookers, it rose zooming into the air. Presently it was a tiny whirring dot far off towards the sunset. I had assisted at the birth of the greatest blessing ever conferred by God upon man, the greatest curse ever inflicted by mankind upon himself.

VI

THE summer term was the pleasantest. The sea was often azure to the far horizon and to the dim coast of France. On Sundays the people who thronged about the bandstand on the green facing the sea were gaily dressed, the women twirling their parasols, the men in straw hats and white flannels. Mrs. Miller abandoned roast beef and Yorkshire pudding for lunch in favour of cold beef with great bowls of salad and jugs of iced lemonade. During the week, especially on Saturdays, there were often first-eleven matches during which I could lie in the grass pretending to watch the match but surreptitiously reading *Swiss Family Robinson* or *King Solomon's Mines*. On some days we were taken by Mr. Simpson down to the sea to bathe—a crowd of white screaming little frogs—and on some Sunday afternoons there were long organized picnic walks to the Warren to collect fossils or on to the Downs to pick cowslips. One Sunday, I remember, we went by train to a place where there was a wood the whole floor of which was covered with lilies-of-the-valley, a sight I have never seen since in England and which held me transfixed with joy when I set eyes on it. I can recall the fragrance of them still and have often wondered if these lovely things grow there now or if that wood has long ago become what is called "ripe for development."

But the whole summer term was overshadowed by an event which seemed to dwarf in importance all others throughout the year. It was a day that stood above the level plain of days like Fujiyama gleaming above Japan. Indeed it had an almost religious significance for all the masters and boys as has that mystical mountain for those who live within its shadow. You could see it afar off, shining in the sun of an English summer—the school sports day, that day consecrated to the athletic clean-limbed god who rules the lives of English boys. I doubt if any religious festival was approached with more excitement and awe, or indeed if any Olympic games ever aroused more eagerness and high resolve, than that day in late July when Mr. Shuttleworth's young men showed their paces.

Very early in the term a huge white sheet appeared on the notice board outside the boot-hole. It was ruled into an elaborate arrangement of columns and squares and covered with Mr. Shuttleworth's neat tight handwriting. It was headed "DOWNFIELD SCHOOL SPORTS—SUMMER TERM, 1910." This was written in large and careful block letters. During school hours we had seen, with eyes that nothing escaped, that Mr. Shuttleworth had long been at work on this masterpiece with ruler and red ink. We had seen him carefully painting in the letters of the heading with the sheet spread upon his desk. When he came in carrying it, rather gingerly as one might carry a priceless and fragile painting done on thin glass, we heaved a sigh of relief and knew that we should be left in idleness and peace for an hour since he would not wish to be disturbed. Spreading out the sheet on his desk he would say, "Open your Golden Treasuries. Milton's 'L'Allegro,' line one—'Hence loathéd Melancholy' —to line thirty-two—'And Laughter holding both his sides.' I'll hear you at the quarter to the hour." For three-quarters of an hour we should be left alone to draw pictures in the backs of our books, to gaze dreamily out of the window, to flick blotting-paper pellets or pass notes as the spirit moved us while Mr. Shuttleworth, lost to all but his art, bent over his outspread sheet of paper wielding ruler and pen, breathing stertorously and pausing from time to time to adjust his glasses on his nose.

"Sir, please, sir! What does 'yclept' mean?"

"Eh? What's that? I'll answer all questions at the end of class."

Ten minutes, or sometimes less, before the hour he would call upon one or two to repeat what they had learnt. If you were unlucky enough to be called upon you stood up and began to stumble through what you could remember of that incomprehensible jumble of words. You could remember very little, of course, and as a penalty were ordered to learn it again out of school. But the chances were seven or eight to one you would not be chosen and could go down to Mr. Simpson's arithmetic class congratulating yourself on having filched another hour of idleness from the consuming demon of toil that was eating up all your time.

In due course the sheet appeared in final form pinned to the noticeboard outside the boot-hole. At the top of it, underneath the heading, was written, "Those who wish to enter for the undermentioned events should sign their names in the allotted squares." Each of the squares in the carefully ruled chequerboard below bore a title—"Mile," "Three-quarter Mile," "Half-mile," "500 Yards," "225 Yards," "High Jump," "Long Jump," and so on.

It took me a little while at first to discover what all this meant. But by degrees the virgin whiteness of the sheet became blurred and soiled and in each square, slowly at first but in increasing numbers as the days went by, uncertain and spidery signatures began to appear, some in ink with blots and smudges, some in smeared pencil, all immature and ill-formed, all embryos of that most characteristic and ineluctable of all that can be committed to paper, the signature of a man. The notice in time became dog-eared and torn at its edges, it came loose from its pins and was pinned up afresh. Blots and smudges marred its whiteness. But it was never without a knot of boys in front of it and often the masters came to stare at it, Mr. Shuttleworth snuffling and adjusting his glasses, Mr. Simpson morosely pulling at the ends of his moustache.

That this focus of so much interest and attention should have any particular reference to me did not occur to me until one day I happened to be looking at it in a detached sort of way when Mr. Simpson came and stood behind me. He wore soft slippers so that I was unaware of his presence. This was a habit of his which made him very unpopular for it was said that he wore the slippers in order to be able to move about silently and catch the boys out, stealing upon them unawares. This came under the category of "sneaking," the greatest of all crimes among boys, the synonym for slyness and deceit, and earned him the nickname of "Sneaker" Simpson. Now I was startled to hear his tired voice suddenly behind me saying, "Well, I don't see our celebrated Sparrow's name down here." Ignorant of the nickname he himself had earned he enjoyed bestowing nicknames on the boys and had always called me "the Sparrow" since the day when he had first seen me in football shorts and had made that excruciating witticism about my resemblance to a sparrow with cork legs. He was pleased with that blinding flash of wit and gave me the nickname as a sort of memorial to it, perhaps in the hope that the name would stick. It would have flattered his vanity had it done so but, probably because of his own unpopularity, it failed to do so. Nevertheless he persevered.

"No," he went on musingly, "I don't seem to see the Sparrow's distinguished signature anywhere. Strange—strange. But not altogether unexpected perhaps." And he walked silently and meditatively away.

After that I studied the notice guiltily and with a somewhat anxious care. I saw that indeed every boy in the school, even the smallest, apparently, had scrawled his name in at least one of the squares and observed with horror that I was the only laggard whose name appeared nowhere. The question began to haunt me. To which part or parts of this gladiatorial contest must I commit myself? The squares filled up with scrawled, almost indecipherable names, and still I stared at the board and wondered where I should add my own, like a hesitant swimmer staring at the water, not daring to take the plunge. The absence of my name did not, of course, escape the other boys and it presently became the subject of unflattering comment.

"Aren't you going in for anything? No, you wouldn't."

"If your brother was here he'd jolly soon make you go in for something. Awful little milker! Frightened, I suppose."

Then one day a slip of paper appeared, pinned across the notice. On it Mr. Shuttleworth had written, "Entries will close on Saturday, May 31st."

And in a panic, when no one was looking, I scrawled my name across the bottom of every square.

Almost every evening throughout the months of June and July we ran and jumped and stood about in the evening sunshine. From the schoolroom windows we looked as frail and purposeless as little white butterflies that gathered and separated and reformed into groups. I found that, surprisingly, I rather enjoyed this. I was taking part in something. I had a place in the general emotion that this protracted contest seemed to evoke and when I was eliminated from every event, as of course I was, long before the semi-finals were reached I had nothing to do on subsequent evenings but stand about in the sunshine watching the others, who still remained in the battle, exhausting themselves on the track. I had the feeling that I had at least tried even if I had failed. It was better to have run and lost than never to have run at all. When, in the hundred yards hurdles, I tripped over the first hurdle and fell flat on my face a magnificent individual of thirteen summers said "Jolly hard luck!" and my cup of happiness was full.

But for the 225 yards handicap race, the entries for which completely filled their allotted square and trailed into the Long Jump below, there were no preliminary heats. We ran a handicapping trial race one evening under the judicial eyes of Mr. Shuttleworth and Mr. Simpson. In all the long races I had run so far I had given up before I had flapped my way twice round the track so that on this evening, when I took my place in the long row of little butterflies poised on the starting line, I looked at the long curving green pathway that I was to follow and decided beforehand how far I should have to struggle before I could with decency fall out.

"Now remember," admonished Mr. Shuttleworth, "on the Day you will be started by pistol." He always referred to the coming festival in a sort of mystical way as "the Day," with a capital letter, as though to impart an extra religious significance to it. "I want every competitor to finish the course and no one to drop out. You can all run two-twenty-five yards easily enough."

And, put on their mettle like this, the lengthening procession of butterflies went languidly flapping round the green track. One after the other they fluttered on ahead of me and soon I found that I was wheezing and panting a long way in the rear of the procession. Its head was soon coming round to catch me up. At the head, bearing round the bend like an express train, came the hero who had condescended to say "Jolly hard luck" when I had fallen over the hurdles. As he passed me he said "Stick it!" and, in a trance of joy and admiration, I went doggedly on, flapping and panting far at the tail of the race, grimly determined not after all to give up. When I reached the finish most of the others, who had arrived there long ago, were lined up along the last few yards of the course and, as I came panting home exhausted but triumphant, I heard their shrill unkind laughter greeting my arrival—except one voice which, through the laughter, I heard say "That's right! Jolly well done!" And because of that voice, and not at all because of the laughter, I found myself in tears.

The Day was fine. Somehow I do not seem to remember any such Days that I subsequently attended ever being anything but fine. I suppose there were occasions when the white figures wove to and fro upon a field unlit by sunshine and beneath a sky that was not blue, when the gay frocks of mothers and sisters were hidden beneath coats and when sunshades gave place to umbrellas. But in my mind's eye the sunlit picture persists, the ranks of spectators with sunshades and white trousers lining the oval track, flags fluttering on the meticulously ruled white lines and the flocks of tame butterflies that performed along the lines between the flags. I hear still the thin cheering, the intermittent crack of the starter's pistol, the drumming of running feet and the rhythm of my own heart pounding.

My mother and father came down for this festive occasion. The arrival of one's parents was always a matter of some anxiety since their bearing and general appearance, their clothes and their manner of speaking were subjected to the sharpest criticism by the other boys. This criticism was always unspoken since the strange unwritten code that runs among boys of all ages forbade direct censure or outspoken opinions on subjects of this sort. Anyone who was sufficiently lacking in taste to give voice to the unexpressed thoughts of a majority was held to have committed an unpardonable breach of that code. And it was many years later, after some high festival of this kind, that a boy who was parent-conscious beyond the average, solicited favourable comment from me by saying, "Well, what do you think of the mater?"

"I think she's hell," I replied.

This was, I knew, the private opinion of nearly the whole community rbout that loud-voiced horsey woman, but I found that by voicing it I had earned general condemnation even more severe than had the boy himself by asking such a direct and indelicate and, in the nature of things, unanswerable question. Nevertheless one's parents could gain or lose one much prestige. One prayed that they would not exhibit those more noticeable, though in the shelter of the home doubtless lovable, peculiarities. One hoped that skeletons would remain securely locked in cupboards. Sometimes to one's nearest and closest friends, in moments of lover-like confidence, one might perhaps open the cupboard door a crack to let the skeleton within be glimpsed. It is so much easier to be haunted when you have described the ghost to someone else, someone you can trust, so that at least one person may understand why your eyes bulge and your hair stands on end.

"Swear on your oath you won't repeat it and I'll tell you something," whispered a boy to me one day when we were out walking. "Swear on the Bible! Cross your heart!"

"I swear," I said, flattered by so much confidence and avid for the secret.

"My mater wears a wig," he confessed in a hushed voice like a man confessing to a murder.

But above all perhaps one hoped that one's parents would not feel moved to kiss one in front of the other boys. This cardinal sin I myself once committed by kissing my sister in front of the school with never-to-be-forgotten consequences.

Luckily for me my parents always considerably increased my prestige and some years later, during the war of 1914–18, I distinctly remember being lifted out of a trough of unpopularity, one of those hidden troughs into which I always seemed to be falling, by the appearance of my brother in the uniform of a sub-lieutenant in the Royal Navy.

"Was that your brother I saw you with?"

"Yes."

"What is he?"

"He's a sub-lieutenant. He's in the *Imponderable*."

"Gosh! How jolly decent."

And at this, the first of these festivals which I ever attended, I was relieved of all anxiety immediately I saw my parents arriving at the gate, shaking hands with Mr. Shuttleworth at the entrance to the field. I ran forward and greeted them with joy and pride, walking proudly with them through the throng under all those furtive and appraising glances. My mother was charmingly dressed, very small and vivacious, and wore a pretty light scarf about her shoulders that floated in the breeze. Even Miss Shuttleworth unscrewed her mouth into a smile when my mother was talking to her. My father looked soldierly and distinguished in a grey silk suit. Even the biggest and most god-like boys in the first form called him "Sir."

On the Sunday before the Day I had lunched at the Millers', and told them shyly that I was running in the 225 yards handicap race.

"We must come and see you," said Mrs. Miller, sinking her chins into her bosom and beaming upon me. "Yes, we'll come and see you win."

That it was even remotely possible that I might win had never occurred to me. But the thought of the girls, my dear friends of whom I was so proud and whom I was so anxious to please, watching me sent me off immediately into the wildest and most extravagant dreams. Supposing——! There was a chance. My failure in the trial race had caused Mr. Shuttleworth to give me a start of nearly a hundred yards from scratch. But, in spite of my failure, I had finished the course without giving up which was in itself a triumph for me. Supposing, by an extra and supreme effort, I did manage to reach the finish first! I was rather silent that afternoon walking along the cliff top, nursing within myself the germ of this astonishing resolve. "Will you promise to come and see the race?" I asked when I took leave of the girls. And as I lay in my bed that night the germ of the resolve grew like a strong plant and became a great tree filling my mind and spirit with high determination.

Even I was infected with the general enthusiasm which the occasion seemed to impart, trailing my eight personable visitors about, parading them under the eyes of friends and enemies alike. For them Mr. Shuttleworth wore his mask of geniality and even laid his hand on my shoulder as he had done a year ago when I first met him but had certainly never done since. Miss Shuttleworth, making a special concession to the occasion by wearing light grey, unscrewed her mouth and looked almost pleasantly through her pince-nez. Even Mr. Simpson, in a startling blazer, said, "Well, and how's the Sparrow now?" And when the greatest moment of the day came, the crisis within a crisis, I saw my own public of eight persons lined up advantageously at the finish of the track. No star of the stage or screen could have had a public he was more anxious to please.

We stood spaced out along the green oval according to our various handicaps. I had to do about one and a half complete rounds of it before the prize was mine. The gods who started from scratch had to complete a little more than two and a half rounds of the track in the same time. I stood at the head of the long tail of boys trembling with excitement, waiting for the crack of Mr. Shuttleworth's pistol. "Don't look round. Remember now, whatever you do, don't look round," Miss Shuttleworth had enjoined before I went to take up my position. "Gently at first," Mr. Shuttleworth had said. "Go gently until you get your second wind. Save yourself for a final spurt." "Run on the balls of your feet," said Mr. Simpson. "Breathe gently and naturally."

The pistol cracked. But even as it cracked I was looking over my shoulder to see if my public was still where I had placed it. In recovering and getting on the move I lost a second of precious time. Now the whole extended train of panting figures was thundering behind me. I felt as a wild animal must feel as it flees before a bush fire with all the world stampeding at its heels. As I ran the whole of that familiar scene, the flagpoles, the green track, the rows of spectators, became a coloured moving scroll without features. It blended into a sense of desperate effort, an urgency blotting out individual sights and sounds. As I passed the bright barricade on either side of the track, dimly knowing it as the ranks of onlookers, I heard vaguely an indeterminate sound coming from it. I thought I could hear familiar voices within the wave of sound but could not be sure. The urgency of the moment was all I could be aware of and the only sounds that mattered were the pounding of my heart and the thundering of my rivals in hot pursuit behind me. They seemed to make a noise like cavalry in full charge. I was still ahead. Tight iron bands were about my chest. Something was labouring inside me like a steam hammer. I thought of the injunction "Take it easy until you get your second wind," but from the increasing thunder behind me I knew that I was being overtaken. I summoned up reserves of effort from hitherto unplumbed depths of determination and so still kept ahead. But the harder and more urgently I forced my feet to run the farther away the finishing post seemed to retreat like the goal of an unattainable ambition. My lungs seemed to draw in no air as though I were breathing in a vacuum and the bands around my chest grew tighter. Familiar asthmatic wheezing noises accompanied me as I strove forward, propelled as much as anything by rage on account of the steadily lengthening distance. And then I did an unpardonable thing. As I ran I glanced over my shoulder to see whose feet they were so inexorably pursuing me. In that moment my rival who had been following close on my heels for what had seemed hours, but was really a matter of seconds, overtook and passed me. It was the boy in the first form whose voice had struck so warmly on my ear at the finish of the try-out. He had overtaken me from scratch. So my rage that, after all my effort and after the immense start I had been given, I should still fail to finish first was tempered by a certain pleasure that it should be he who beat me. I thrust forward desperately in a new effort to overtake him and even drew up a little when suddenly people were all about me and I was face downwards on the grass panting like a landed fish.

At first I was conscious of nothing except that it was over. Then, as by degrees my heart began to thump less violently, I realized that although I had not won I had at least not been utterly defeated. I had come in second. That was something.

"That's something, isn't it?" said Mrs. Miller, enveloping me in folds of lavender-coloured silk.

"Better than nothing, my boy," said my father.

"Never mind, perhaps you'll be first another time," said my mother.

"We'll make an athlete of him yet," lied Mr. Shuttleworth.

But Miss Shuttleworth stifled any germ of self-praise that might have begun to sprout within me. She took me by the arm and drew me aside. Her mouth was formed into its familiar and customary shape and she shook me impatiently

"You don't deserve it," she said furiously and doubtless with perfect truth though I was not very sure what it was that I had failed to deserve. "You don't deserve it. You're a very stupid little boy and I'm surprised, after what I told you—very. If you hadn't looked round you'd have won." Almost, it seemed, she felt my failure more keenly than I did myself.

The sun went down upon that great day crimson above the Kentish chimney-pots. As the shadows of those same pots began to draw across the field, grotesquely elongated like fangs in a slowly closing jaw, all our high hopes and heroic resolves died down again for another year into the breasts from which they sprang. The dark jaw advanced to engulf them like the maw of age and time into which all our hopes vanish in due course.

The crowd scattered all over the field drew now towards the still sunlit end of it. Could Mr. Grahame-White have flown over the assembly in his flying machine he would have seen what looked like a host of tiny organisms obeying a tropism on a half-illuminated green slide. For there, on the eastern and still sunlit quarter of the field, stood a table bearing the gleaming glittering array of trophies which were to be the rewards of valour. Round this the microbes gathered as though it had some chemical attraction.

During the course of the afternoon I had often stolen sly glances at these tall vase-shaped cups of silver-gilt and these squat bowls standing on ebonite stands, at these embossed shields framed in wood and these medals in velvet cases wondering secretly what I should really do with one of them if I should win it. I wondered why they were so much coveted for I did not think, on close inspection, that they were really very beautiful and they were certainly not useful. And the largest and most expensive, I noticed, were not even intended as gifts but only to be loaned or even only to be kept at the school in a prominent place with the name of the latest winner engraved on the bulbous silver surface. The ecstasy and triumph of winning a race I could understand—had I not in part experienced it?—but if a prize was to be given I faintly and privately wished it could have been something useful like a bicycle bell or a postcard album or something beautiful like a model engine. To commemorate one's endeavour and one's triumph with a silver-gilt trophy was needless since one would never forget them. They would live in the memory and never die there. But from the memory of indifferent strangers one's triumph would fade if the silver cup that commemorated it were as large as a house.

So that when I knew that one of these prizes was to be mine I was surprised at the thrill of pride that I felt. I looked at the table furtively and with quickened interest, wondering which one of all those gleaming shapes I should carry off in my arms. That large one with the two handles, I hoped, which shone so proudly in the centre like a captain in the middle of his team.

Mr. Shuttleworth took his stand behind the table and, amid bursts of applause, made a speech thanking his guests for their support and "the Clerk of the Weather for smiling on us once again," and saying what a successful day it had been. He then introduced a stout, amiable, rather vague lady in deep purple who, he said, would now give away the prizes. I wondered why he should say "give away" when most of the prizes were not given at all but only on loan or only for exhibition in the school itself. Before the ceremony each boy, myself among them, who had to make an appearance before the purple lady was shepherded indoors by Miss Shuttleworth and made to wash, put on a blazer and a tie and brush unruly hair. When his name was called he then advanced, scrubbed and shining, with blushes and coy smiles, up to the table to receive from the hands of the purple lady the tribute due to his prowess on the field. To each the purple lady had something queenly and gracious and not very illuminating to say. "Mind you don't drop it—it's rather heavy. The harder the race the bigger the prize, you know." "That'll look well on your mantelpiece, won't it? I beg your pardon? A challenge cup? Oh, so it is. Well, on the schoolroom mantelpiece then." "With your shield or on it as the Greeks used to say. I still remember some of my Greek history, you see." And for each proud recipient a burst of applause, for each friendly quip from the purple lady a little ripple of appreciative laughter, as much a reward for her ingenuity as for her graciousness.

When my turn came I advanced towards the table grinning from ear to ear in the manner I thought appropriate for so public an occasion. To my joy and astonishment the purple lady lifted from its central position the bulging King of All the Cups and, with something of an effort for it was very heavy, handed it over the table into my outstretched arms. "Well," she said, "what a big prize for a little boy! And thoroughly deserved for a gallant fight, I'm sure." Mr. Shuttleworth was busy talking to some people behind the table and did not see me bearing my trophy away. Hugging it to my breast, blushing with pride and triumph, I bore it off into the crowd. I understood well now the elation which results from the winning of such trophies and if I had been offered a bicycle bell or a model engine in that moment I should undoubtedly have refused it. Nothing and no one could have parted me from my gleaming bulging treasure to the swelling side of which I clung with an almost sensual joy.

Nothing and no one, that is, except the outraged winner of the race, my thwarted conqueror, who later, in the boot-hole, bore down upon me as I was taking off my running shoes with my prize protected by one arm like a chicken covered by its mother's wing.

"Hi, you, kid! Give that up! That's mine you've got. This is yours."

"No, no!" I cried in an agony of distress. "She gave it to me. It's mine, I tell you, it is mine. She did give it to me!"

But it was true. The purple lady had made a shocking mistake when Mr. Shuttleworth's attention was engaged elsewhere. The true reward of all my hopes and efforts was a light slender thing with a single stem, like a tulip made of silver paper. I anointed it with tears of disappointment.

"Never mind," said the victor magnanimously with his arm around my shoulder. "Perhaps you'll get the big one next year."

I grinned at him gratefully, in some degree comforted but knowing full well that I should never again recapture that moment of triumph and elation. For even if I had ever won the nobler prize, which I never did, that moment which to-day had brought, and which belonged only to to-day, would not return. For it is one of the mercies and perhaps at the same time one of the cruelties of life that you cannot achieve the same height or descend to the same depth twice. Dimly I perceived that in the boot-hole when I gave up my prize with tears and accepted the second best. The joy, the ecstasy, the triumph, or the disappointment, the despair, the bitterness of one moment belong to it alone and cannot be repeated at another moment even in identical circumstances. And circumstances are never identical so we may be even less certain what will be the texture of life but only sure that it will astonish and confound us.

But I have my slender trophy still somewhere. I never won another. For years it stood on my mantelshelf at home and followed me about from place to place receiving gratefully the buttons, golf balls, drawing pins, pieces of string or nails that were from time to time absently dropped into it. Early in its career it had its moments of usefulness for when, ever less frequently and more shamefacedly, I could find a moment to be a king again reviewing his troops or holding court under the beech-tree it formed a useful sort of helmet. But that was many years ago. For many more years it served only to remind me, as perhaps it was intended by its makers to do, how I had once hoped and striven and, at least in part, triumphed. Now I do not quite know where it is nor where is the victory that it commemorates.

VII

WITH the approach of the end of the term and of the holidays
I began to work myself up into a steadily increasing excitement. Long before anybody else I began vociferously and
joyously counting weeks and days, chanting those worn old rhymes
beloved of schoolboys—"This time four weeks where shall I be?"—
and going around with an elated air which did not escape the eye of
Mr. Shuttleworth. He took exception to these unseemly manifestations
of emotion and interviewed me about them in the study. I must practise
self-control, he said. Even if I found life at Downfield so intolerable
that the thought of leaving it made me forget myself it was only good
manners to keep such feelings decently in check. If not, he reminded me
with a sinister movement in the direction of the sofa, there were ways
of enforcing good manners. He would not allow me to unsettle the
whole school by my conduct. But the fact was that he found my joyful
anticipation of approaching freedom unflattering to himself and to the
way of life he ordained for his charges. After these rebukes I was somewhat more subdued but nothing could for long suppress my mounting
fever. Even if I gave less vocal expression to it there was a new brightness in my eye, an increasing inattention and a recklessness which assured
Mr. Shuttleworth that over one small boy at least he cast no spell and
that his mantle was always ready to slip at any moment from at least one
pair of insignificant shoulders.

No homecomings in after years ever exceeded in joy and delight those
of my schooldays. On the last day of every term, just as on Friday
mornings at Miss Grey's, the sun rose more brightly and shone on a
world in which familiar objects had a new reality, an altered significance.
Breakfast on that morning was not simply a dull routine but, as it should
always be, a thanksgiving for a new day. And all the ceremonies that
marked the last day of term and made it a day apart from other days,
the distribution of luggage labels and journey money, the packing of
play-boxes, the visit to Miss Watson to receive clean clothes, were sacred
rites. My immense bowler hat, crammed down over my ears, my Eton
suit and wide Eton collar (surely the most ludicrous costume ever
devised for snobs of tender years), my small Gladstone bag with my
pyjamas and sponge-bag in it, were the robes and regalia that went with
them. How different were my feelings about them on the last day of the
holidays! My mother met me at Charing Cross after a journey in which

the Kentish fields and gathering suburbs of London had an aspect quite different from their aspect on the journey in the reverse direction. How anxiously I stood on the platform at Charing Cross among the crowds disgorged from the train until I saw my mother's figure advancing towards me! Then, regardless of all the rules of conduct and etiquette which prevailed at school, I ran to her and flung myself into her arms. I was already in another world and before me lay long happy sunlit weeks untouched by any shadow. Or so it seemed under my bowler hat at Charing Cross station.

When I got home I wandered around renewing contact with all the familiar things I loved, gaining reassurance from the fact that nothing was seriously changed and that no melancholy decay had set in directly my back was turned. Such small changes as there were showed only that the world still revolved and life still went on though I was not there to see it. For there, in the plot of ground I called my garden, were rising as tender shoots the seeds I had planted last holidays. While I had been away, slowly and subtly, that miracle at least had been working underground. And the nasturtiums I had put in as tiny plants were cavorting madly over everything like a tropical growth, showing a million green discs and red or yellow trumpets, proclaiming by their coarse growth the triumphant progress of life in spite of Mr. Shuttleworth. I had to renew my acquaintance once more with the beech-tree and stand once more gazing upwards into its tent of green in silence in order to let the spell and enchantment come upon me once again. It was the same and yet self-renewing, like the days and nights themselves, for at the beginning of the Easter holidays it was putting forth myriads of sharp sticky buds and bursting into feathery green upon its lower branches. When I returned for the summer holidays it was a huge dome of sombre green but at Christmas the winter daylight fell upon its mossy floor through the fine tracery of its naked boughs. My little bedroom too, with its flowered wall-paper and familiar china ornaments, I found with relief was exactly the same as when I had left it. The library with its own musty leathery smell and the faint indefinable fear that it held after dark, the same. All the same; no change. My world indeed seemed to be a permanently established institution, peopled with unalterable faces, fixed in a setting built to last for ever, lovely and enduring, to be taken for granted and never for a moment thought about. I had no doubts about it at all and if anyone had told me that in ten years it would all have faded away I should not have believed it. Indeed so permanently delightful did my familiar world appear to me that when I met other people whose world was less enchanting, like the boy at school who, it was rumoured, really did live in a row at Leytonstone, or my cousin who lived in a flat over-looking the Underground at Turnham Green, I felt no pity but only unalloyed astonishment that there should be people who had no lawns to run about on nor huge old trees for friends. It was a sweet cheat, my world, when I was not yet nine.

The same, too, as when I had left them remained the faces of those I loved. I searched their features for signs of alteration but could find none. Time seemed to work no change in my grandmother. I always returned to find her the same vigorous little old lady to whom I had bidden a tearful farewell a month or so ago. Her step was as firm and her keen eyes as bright when she came forward to greet me in her black dress and flowered apron as they had been when, wearing the same black dress and apron, she had kissed me good-bye. Only as time went on she seemed to grow a little smaller, but so slowly that I hardly noticed it.

"How well he's looking!" she always said. "Why—he's grown. He's bigger than ever. And how long is he home for now?"

Only in one face I seemed to perceive some alteration, almost imperceptible at first but quickening, greater with each homecoming. For with my sister I was not immediately able to take up the threads where I had dropped them. We greeted each other with a certain shyness and without any demonstration of affection. She accompanied me in silence round the garden, pointing out small changes here and there almost as though they were something she herself had achieved. When we met thus at the beginning of every holidays we each became aware, I think, of something in the look or manner of the other that told us that we were growing up. She indeed was growing up and developing faster than I and I think I was more conscious of a slow change in her than she was of any change in me. In time she was to outstrip me mentally but that time was not yet. She herself soon began to go daily to school and I became increasingly aware that my lordship over her was coming to an end. Though I did not yield my place without a struggle I found myself listening to stories of her exploits at school without that grand patronage to which two years' seniority had entitled me hitherto. She began too to make her own friends and when little girls came to tea I saw that Mary was surrounding herself with a world in which I had no part. So it was with a new diffidence at each homecoming that, after a long rather shy and silent walk round the garden, one of us turned to the other and said, with an air of breaking ice, "Let's play something."

"All right—what?" replied the other with relief.

"Kings and queens."

The holidays had begun. The world of school had dropped from me.

In the summer holidays the garden was ablaze with roses, rhododendrons, azaleas and delphiniums. Constellations of daisies shone on the
dark and light stripes of the lawn, to be eclipsed by the mowing machine
whirring through long afternoons but only to reappear more thickly
than ever. In the evening night-stocks and tobacco plants made sweet
the air and evening primroses shone afar down the broad walks where
bats fluttered, wheeled and vanished. But all these "high midsummer
pomps" we incontinently deserted every year for the sea. The thrill
and delight of this annual pilgrimage quite took away any regret I might
have felt that I should not see the sweet-peas blossom which I had planted
with such care last holidays in a trench full of stolen manure. Without
a qualm I left my canary creeper, coiling its delicate stems around my
trellis work, to twine and blossom unregarded.

Every summer for several years we went to the same little place on the
west coast. We arrived there after a long wearisome train journey which
began as an adventure full of breathless interest but long before its end
became an almost unendurable bore. But when late in the evening we
arrived at the little terminus of the single line we felt indeed that we had
arrived at the very ends of the earth, for those were the days before the
baleful arrival of the internal combustion engine had obliterated the
sense of distance, had destroyed remoteness and spoilt the local character
of all the quiet places in our small island. We seemed to be almost in a
foreign country. The trees and fields themselves were different from
those nearer home. Tamarisks and stunted hawthorns leant backwards
from the wind above stone walls. The houses crouched on the sides of
great hills and the little grey town went tumbling down to where, clearly
visible above the roof-tops, was the sea. There was a clean freshness in
the air blown across fields from great spaces. And here the people too
were different from those at home, speaking with slow burred voices
like the porter who lifted our numerous baggage on to the old four-
wheeler.

"Look!" we cried at every glimpse between the houses. "There's
the sea! The sea!" for all the world as though we had never seen it
before.

We took rooms in a round-fronted old house facing the sea. This
house was always referred to by my mother, and so by us too, as "the
rooms." Some weeks before our departure she would say, "We really
ought to write about those rooms." When we went out on any kind of
expedition she would say, "I have left such-and-such behind at the
rooms," or "I really think we ought to be getting back to the rooms
now." The rooms consisted of a first-floor sitting-room with a curved

bow window overlooking the sea and a back bedroom occupied by my mother and father and my younger sister who was still a baby. There was a double room upstairs for Mary and myself and later two small single rooms when it was held that we were becoming too big to occupy the same bedroom. It was a fine old house built in the Regency period. It had obviously seen better days but it retained still, in its spaciousness and airy dignity, something of the elegance that belonged to that civilized period. The clinging aroma of past meals, the dreary Edwardian furniture and dingy wall-papers could not rob the old house of its arched hallway and excellent curved staircase. Now it seemed to resent the low estate to which it had fallen. Some rich west-country merchant must have built it and occupied it and bred a numerous family in it. Only when the prosperity of the little town declined, presumably, did the gracious old house decline also until at last an unkind fate delivered it into the possession of the anxious and faded Mrs. Pears. She stuck an "Apartments" notice in the graceful fanlight over the door and let out the rooms during the summer.

Mrs. Pears was a thin person of enormous and terrifying refinement. She lived in a forbidden region behind a mysterious door at the back of the hall. Since we were strictly forbidden to do so it was our constant ambition to penetrate beyond it. The door, however, was always kept shut and Mrs Pears only opened it, on entering or leaving her own domain, just wide enough to admit her spare form and never enough to allow inquisitive eyes a glimpse behind it. The poor lady lived in a perpetual state of anxiety arising, so far as we could make out, from two sources. One was the quite understandable fear that we should ask too much, make demands on her time and attention or on the resources of her establishment not covered by the seven guineas a week or so which my parents paid for her hospitality. In time, as she got to know us, this fear seemed to grow less but the sense of anxiety seemed to remain. For there were others in the house besides ourselves. She was constantly emerging from her secret door with anxious questions on her lips and others in her eyes. "Would you be requiring sandwiches this afternoon?" "About coal? Will one scuttle be sufficient in the drawing-room?" By which, it was felt, she really meant, "I hope you won't want sandwiches this afternoon," or "One scuttle of coal is all I think you're entitled to but I'll give you more to oblige and if you insist." But whenever any particularly knotty problem arose between my parents and Mrs. Pears, whenever she felt that her worst fears were about to be confirmed, she shelved all responsibility for the future conduct of her war and placed it on the shoulders of the power behind the throne. With an air of referring the matter to a higher authority she would say, "Well, I shall be obliged to consult my husband." "My husband doesn't really approve of dogs in the rooms." This vague nebulous power known as "my husband" never materialized and was all the more formidable for that But once or twice, when at last we achieved our ambition and penetrated behind the forbidden door on some pretext or other, we caught a glimpse of a morose moustached individual in shirt sleeves sitting at the kitchen table reading a newspaper. Immediately we entered he got up and left the room.

The other anxiety that haunted Mrs. Pears arose from the fear that it should ever for a moment be supposed that she took "guests," as she called them, for any but purely altruistic reasons. She let it be understood in a hundred ways that her social position really made it unnecessary for her to fill her house every year with other people's families and that she only did it for a variety of complicated and not very convincing reasons, because she "liked to have young people in the house" (a taste not shared, she might have added, by "my husband"), because "it put a little jam on the bread and butter, if you understand what I mean." When she said these things, white lies that kept her flag flying as it were, she gave an affected little laugh that immediately spoilt their effect. All her gestures and her speech seemed to convey that she belonged to a state of life higher than that to which it had pleased God to call her. She used elegant words in conversation. She never asked if there were enough coal but inquired if the coal were sufficient. She presumed but never supposed. She would light a fire in the drawing-room "should you so desire." And during an acrimonious discussion, not with my parents but with the family upstairs, one of those unfortunate discussions that constantly disturb the peace of landladies, we heard her voice, acid and raised to an unaccustomed pitch of anger, saying, "Might I presume to inquire whom you are addressing?" Matters affecting charges she would never discuss without first retiring behind her door to consult "my husband." Then she would make light of the matter as though it were completely unimportant and really rather sordid. She always spoke of "my little account" and had a way of pretending to be entirely uninterested when it was paid. However, I do not think she allowed anything to escape her. The sitting-room which we occupied, with its pearly nautilus shells on the fringed mantelpiece, its "First Communion" and "Stag at Bay," and its bamboo palm stands, designed for the sole exclusive purpose of supporting aspidistras, she always insisted upon calling "the drawing-room." We gathered that when we were not there she was accustomed to withdraw into it in well-bred and chaste seclusion.

But no amount of flinging open of windows, a manœuvre practised by my mother from the moment we arrived, could banish that airless smell that told of long months of silence and emptiness. Mrs. Pears clung, in fact, desperately to something that she felt was slipping from her, to her pride. Her life was a constant sad rebellion and her whole bearing a protest. And frequently, by way of registering it, she appeared in the drawing-room for one reason or another in the evening, if we happened to be there, dressed to go out in faded grandeurs as though to show that she too had a life and a position apart from all this of which, of course, we could know nothing and could only catch these occasional privileged glimpses.

Nevertheless Mrs. Pears was a kindly soul and we grew fond of her and regarded her idiosyncrasies as all thrown in with the high tea at six o'clock, the sand in the bath and all the other significant details that went to make up our holiday. We spent a noisy quarrelsome and happy four weeks in her house, clattering up and down the stairs, filling the front hall with buckets and spades, sand-shoes, shells and strips of dried ribbon seaweed. We hung our bathing costumes like processional banners from her windows.

There were other guests in the house besides ourselves, usually holiday visitors also, parents with noisy children whose buckets and spades and sand-shoes and spoils combed from the beach mingled with ours in the front hall. We usually began on terms of faint mutual hostility with these people. When we heard their voices on the stairs we darted into our own rooms and waited until "those people" had passed. But by the end of the first fortnight, as a rule, we had made friends with them and discovered in them unsuspected virtues. My mother would decide that Mrs. So-and-so was really quite a nice person. "I think she's a lady," my mother would say at last, setting the final seal of her approval. And Mary and I, after glaring with hostile eyes at the other children for a week or so, perpetually suspecting them of having designs on our shells and strips of seaweed in the hall, would discover that it was fun to go shrimping with them or to dig ramparts with them against the incoming tide. In the last week or ten days we went for combined picnics with them on the downs above the cliffs and at the end of the month parted from them with vows of eternal friendship. These vows, I am afraid, like most such vows, seldom bore any fruit for these holiday friendships were as fleeting and evanescent as those made on board ship. They began with the same aloofness and mutually hostile glances, ripened into the same warmth and ended with the same affectionate farewells. We departed to our respective homes, to our different worlds, to school, to the daily round and common task, and soon our friends were only a memory. They became "those nice people we met last year." But sometimes there were attempts to renew the acquaintance in other surroundings, to play the match, as it were, on the home ground. Our seaside friends would come over to lunch one Sunday, perhaps, but it was never quite the same. Something was missing and we never knew quite what to say to them. "Now, you children, go out into the garden and play." We wandered about in silence for a bit. None of them seemed to like playing the games we liked playing. They saw nothing funny in any of our jokes. Jokes revived and transplanted into the atmosphere of home fell flat. The beech-tree meant nothing to our guests. They were not very interested in the bulbs coming up in our garden. Then one of the boys would suggest a game of cricket. Mary and I would look at one another in horror. He had intruded the world of school upon our holidays. It was the end.

On the first day of our arrival at Mrs. Pears' Mary and I ran out of the door as soon as we could, across the small esplanade and down the steep shingle beach to the sea. For me it was a different sea, cleaner, wider, vaster, than the sea I wandered beside at school. It was a sea washing another shore upon another planet. It fingered the stones and sighed in just the same way but with another message.

There was a small stone jetty at one end of the esplanade with a lighthouse on the point of it. To this we ran hand in hand to renew our acquaintance for yet another summer with its ancient smells and the sweet decay that lingered in that part of the little town. The jetty enclosed a small harbour in the sweep of its arm and here a fleet of fishing smacks with saucy names lay rocking gently on the murky tide or stranded half upon their sides on the pocked mud. Their shabby sails were furled and their decks were heaped with lobster pots, nets and coils of rope. There was a sprinkling of crab claws, dead shrimps and fish scales everywhere. An "unforgettable unforgotten" smell clung to them.

These ancient vessels belonged to those equally ancient men for whom time seemed long ago to have ceased to be of any account, who stood about on the jetty or sat about on bollards or on steps talking endlessly, puffing blue smoke into the evening air and spitting from time to time. Old Tom, skipper and owner of the *Sally*, was one of these. It was not long before we found him. He was resting his broad rump on a bollard, gazing meditatively at nothing in particular. He, like all his companions, had the gift of sinking into a state of complete abstraction, a total withdrawal of all mental processes, which seems to be characteristic of people who have led a hard physical life. Looking at old

Tom as he sat on his bollard and puffed into the still air you might have thought that he was carved out of wood except for the wreaths of smoke that ascended from his short pipe. Nothing whatever seemed to be going on beneath his peaked cap. A grizzled beard rested on his broad chest, clad in a blue jersey, which lower down merged without any dividing line into a round paunch. No rhythm of breathing seemed to disturb that rotund outline. But occasionally he leant a little sideways to spit, out of the orifice in the middle of the beard, a brown jet into the still water of the harbour and then resumed his Buddha-like contemplation. When we approached him, however, he came magically to life, uncrossed his short stout legs and stood up. He removed the pipe from the middle of his beard and looked down upon us over the curve of his blue-clad paunch.

"Well, well. If it ain't the young lady and gentleman again! Why I believe you've grown, the pair o' you."

Out of the holiday season Tom made a living by putting out lobster pots, by line fishing and by drifting. But during the season he found it more profitable and much easier, as did all his fraternity, to hire the *Sally* out to holiday-makers for mackerel-spinning. This enabled him to spend more time sitting on his bollard contemplating the universe. We were among his regular patrons and often went out in the bay in the *Sally* to return, almost asleep but very happy, after dark with a precious bunch of striped fish caught with enormous skill and still more enormous noise during the afternoon. These we would deliver over to Mrs. Pears to cook for breakfast next day. She would look at them with profound suspicion. "I presume they're eligible," she would say dubiously, meaning that she supposed they were edible. "I'll consult my husband."

These afternoons when we went mackerel-spinning with old Tom, Captain and Leader of the Expedition, were among the best of all during those seaside holidays. My admiration for the captain of the *Sally* was boundless and he typified in my eyes the perfect man of the sea, the real sailor. He was everything that I thought and still think a sailor should be, wise, resourceful, patient, brave. And whenever I read a story of the sea during those years it was old Tom, or old Tom when he was young Tom, who lived in its pages, in *Midshipman Easy*, in *Masterman Ready*, in *Moby Dick*. So, in moments alone, when I thought I was unobserved, I practised spitting, out of windows and over bridges on to passing trains, without ever acquiring the mastery of the art which old Tom possessed. However closely I watched the magic performance I never found out the secret. But most astonishing of all was to see him remove his peaked cap, revealing a smooth dome in the middle of an

aura of grizzled hair, to produce from inside it a quid of tobacco, cigarettes
or matches. These he would presently stow away again inside his cap,
replacing it on the dome so that you would never guess there was anything in it at all.

Every year, we noticed, Tom seemed to be getting a little older.
Every summer he seemed to spend more time sitting on his bollard and
the days when the *Sally* went out grew fewer. The weather became
less and less suitable every year. Fish seemed to grow scarcer and
scarcer in the bay. "Ah, I doubt if it'd be a terrible deal o' good goin'
out to-day. The fishin' be that poor." When my father asked after his
health at the beginning of each holiday old Tom shook his head and
placed his hand on the broad small of his back. "It's this rheumatiz,
sir. Terrible bad this winter it were." He complained of it more each
summer and the last year we ever went to the little west coast town, the
summer of 1914, old Tom was bedridden and the *Sally* was sold to
someone else. We visited him in his cottage and found him sitting up
in a huge brass-knobbed bedstead that almost filled the tiny room, his
beard spread over his thick woollen pyjamas. So now, I am afraid, he is
dead, my wise and patient sailor. But perhaps if I were to meet old Tom
now, the blessed scales having fallen from my eyes, I should see only a
beery and possibly rather sly old man. I hope he sits in Heaven on a
golden bollard gazing abstractedly into a celestial nothingness and only
occasionally plucks the harp strings with his horny tobacco-stained fingers.

When the *Sally* had cleared the jetty the soft breeze filled her russet
sail so that, heaving and creaking gently, she sped like a bird towards
that distant line, decked with tiny plumes of smoke to show where other
questing ships were voyaging like ourselves into the unknown. It was
the limit of all knowledge to which I turned my hopeful eyes and the
faster and farther we sped on the faster and farther it withdrew. Soon the
beach, the town with its rows of toy houses, the cliffs and fields retreated
into the distance, became remote and unreal. The world suddenly shrank
to the size of the *Sally* rocking on the smooth swells that lifted us on their
backs and sped on towards the distant shore. There we could see them
breaking with a faint murmur in a winking line of white. The diminished
line of cliffs took on other and unfamiliar shapes. They opened out to
reveal their secrets, unsuspected caves and tiny bays, places where the
green mantle above them swept suddenly like a skirt down to the water's
edge. Thus, diminutive and green, I thought, must England look to
men going on a long journey beyond that constantly withdrawing line.
Thus must she look to travellers returning with eyes hungry for the sight
of home. So she remains in the hearts of men all over the world. And

this was my discovery, I believe, bobbing in a fishing smack off a little west coast town, absently trailing a mackerel line in the water—that I had a country and that I loved it. Yet still, far away as ever, stood that distant line to seaward with the sunlit clouds arising from it like the towers and pinnacles of a dream city, constantly dissolving and changing into ever newer stranger shapes. Forgetting my fishing line I stood up in the boat and pointed towards it. "Farther out, Tom!" I cried. "I want to go right out to sea!" Then there would be a peremptory tug on the line like a postman's knock and I turned to pull it in breathless with excitement. On the end was a striped glistening beauty which fell wriggling and flapping into the bottom of the boat and lay there among the others until, like them, it was glazed and dull, its glory faded.

We returned after dark when the cliffs had become a darker line drawn across the stars. The sea glowed with chill secret fires and presently the moon came up to hang above us like a pale lamp in the net of heaven. She drew upon the sea a pathway to that line which, as the night came down, drew farther off than ever.

VIII

I F I had been no credit to Mr. Shuttleworth I was even less to the ancient grammar school to which I next graduated.

It had been founded originally for the sons of indigent parents in the reign of one of the Henries, but, apparently, after some centuries the supply of indigent parents ran out. As time went on the sons of other and always less indigent parents gained admittance in increasing numbers. In inverse ratio to the indigence of the pupils the fees of the grammar school went up. All sorts of extras were gradually added to the curriculum and grammar rather faded into the background until at last, behold, it was a school for the fairly well-to-do. Towards the end of Victoria's reign, and in Edward's, the old building with its battlemented gables, mullioned windows, wide draughty passages and tortuous stairs collected to itself other, newer and very much uglier buildings around the expanse of the cricket field. Several other houses, classrooms, a gymnasium, a perfectly hideous chapel, and at last swimming baths and squash courts clustered around the somewhat astonished Tudor structure. It became a public school, it invented a tie and a magazine. People began to admit that they went there quite blatantly without having to explain where it was. But in spite of the tie and the magazine, the school never quite succeeded to the front rank. The fees were still, comparatively speaking, too low. Occasionally it made a bold bid for fame by challenging an aristocrat like Harrow or Winchester, with magnificent fees and maddeningly well-known ties, to a football match. As often as not this impertinence was treated with the contempt it deserved and no reply to the challenge was forthcoming. In those days a very proper and lofty snobbery ruled in such matters. Whether or not this is so to-day I do not know and could scarcely care less. But on one occasion the grammar school did at last succeed in enticing some disdainful young men from Harrow (who arrived wearing strange tassels on their heads) to play the first eleven at football. But the junior supporters of the home side over-enthusiastic, disgraced themselves and gave away the whole show by dancing like dervishes on the touch-line and throwing their straw hats in the air whenever their side scored a goal. This the lofty visitors considered definitely not done and they never came again or invited a return match. The seniors were outraged at this lack of tact and good taste on the part of their juniors. The headmaster stormed up and down the touch-line purple in the face, shouting "Stop that folly! Keep your hats on your heads!" After the match it was mooted in the upper school whether it might not be a good thing if everyone in the lower school were given a beating in order to instil into them good manners and a proper attitude of snobbish respect for a school whose fees were so very much higher than their own. As for me it was the only football match I have ever enjoyed watching.

One of the reasons why the seniors considered themselves worthy to rank with the great was the venerable old age of their establishment. "After all," they said with indignation, "we're older than Harrow and far older than Rugby"—forgetting as they said the words the indigent parents and how comparatively recent were the tie and the magazine. The school made a fetish of its age. When I first went there the original Tudor school house had made no concessions to modernity. It remained original and Tudor. There was no heating in any of the dormitories. Shivering children broke the ice on their basins of water on winter mornings. The sanitary arrangements were extremely Tudor. The passages and classrooms were meeting-places for the winds—with the result that I spent lot of my time in the sick-room. The boys were compelled to wear the most uneconomical and expensive costume imaginable, as well as the most undecorative, a black coat with pepper-and-salt trousers and straw hat. My black coat was grey with dirt and shiny with grease all down the front long before the end of each term. In imitation of more exalted and expensive seats of learning black-coated pupils wore straw boaters summer and winter. It was "done" to carry your hat under your arm with your hand in your trouser pocket so that before long it was a crushed and shapeless mass, dingy and black, held together only by its encircling ribbon. In this condition you carried it about for months, presumably as a sort of sign of your occupation, for it was impossible to wear it and it had long since ceased to bear any kind of resemblance to a hat.

As a part of this age fetish which obsessed those in authority there were innumerable customs and traditions which made pitfalls for unwary timid new boys such as myself at the age of thirteen. Before and after meals we stood in long rows with our backs to the tables in the dining-hall while a prefect intoned from a dais an apparently interminable Latin grace. But during my three years at the school I never succeeded in finding out just what that grace meant. Only the headmaster knew. He listened intently to every word with his head cocked on one side, blinking through enormously thick glasses. But as he was deaf the more daring prefects occasionally (especially towards the end of their last term) played strange and ribald tricks with the sacred words. Suppressed titters ran down the black-coated ranks. But it was not noticeable that the Almighty blessed our lump sago any less—nor any more when the words were correctly spoken. It just remained lump sago.

But it was the small unwritten but inviolable laws which formed, as it were, local hazards in the difficult game that was life for the tender novice. You were expected to know, for instance, that the door leading from the quadrangle, where the big chestnut-tree grew, to the library was for the use of the sixth form only. If you didn't know it at first you soon found out. For the use of this door was a privilege most jealously guarded by those who possessed it. They strolled in and out of their door with a lordly and self-conscious air as though it were the door into paradise. Only the elect, you understood, might enter by it. Any innocent offender caught using the sacred door was savagely punished. Then again it was not "done" for grubby chickens in the lower school to walk about with their hands in their pockets and their coat tails pulled back from the second button. Only the upper school were allowed to walk about in this sophisticated manner. No one had ever said so but it just was so. The upper school saw to it. The third button must be kept fastened in the lower school and the skirts of the coat draped forward with becoming humility. If not one of the "bloods" would come up to you and say, "Good God! What bloody sauce! Don't let me catch you swaggering again. Can't have filthy new bugs swaggering." And in your first term you were not allowed to walk to chapel arm in arm. In your second term you succeeded to this great privilege and you saw to it yourself that it was not usurped by new bugs only just arrived. And no one could explain the origin or purpose of these and many other articles of this unwritten code though now, looking back upon them, I see their purpose plainly enough. It was to make insignificant new boys feel more insignificant, lost and friendless still. It was to impress them with the greatness and dignity of the institution of which they now found themselves members. They were customs which had always been there. They were part of the thing called tradition which is so often allowed to be like sand in the wheels. But their effect on me was not to impress me with anything much except with the stupidity and petty cruelty which they indicated. But the first of their two objects they achieved for they frequently made me feel profoundly miserable. And frequently they made it difficult for me to sit down for several days.

It was all part of tradition, I suppose, that the penal system and general administration of justice had been handed down unchanged from the days of Dr. Arnold. There was only one punishment for any offence and that was a beating. The only modification was that you got a big beating for a big offence and not such a big beating for a small one. As a new boy one was beaten by practically everybody. Masters beat you for failing to give satisfaction in class. Captains of games beat you for inattention on the football or cricket field, or simply for not being good at football or cricket. Captains of classrooms and captains of dormitories beat you and prefects beat you whenever they felt like it and very often without any particular reason. Beating soon lost its significance as a punishment and one began before long to get quite clever at preventing it from hurting. You did this by stuffing things skilfully inside your trousers. Some even went to the length of having double thicknesses sewn in their seats. Or you pretended you had been terribly hurt and straightened up at the very moment of impact. This had to be very artfully done to be convincing.

In most boys a general hatred and contempt for authority was the result of all this. Masters and prefects only differed from one another in that some beat often and others seldom. Some could be provoked more than others, some more easily deceived. Some masters were dreaded for their ferocity or for the pain they knew how to inflict. Others were laughed at because they were full of empty threats or because their beatings failed to hurt. The music master, a mild and gentle old man, beat frequently and quite ineffectually. The way to deal with him was to go through all the antics of being in terrible pain. You grimaced and limped back to your seat holding your behind and then pretended you couldn't sit down. The dear old man would then become so contrite that he gave up beating his class for a whole fortnight and thus you earned for your classmates the right to be as unruly and unkind, after the manner of small boys, as they liked until their master's almost inexhaustible patience at last ran out again. With another master, whose particular line was extreme ferocity and who glared at you down a huge hooked nose, the gambit was to assume abject terror. This was by no means always assumed, but if you appeared frightened enough he seemed to be appeased and let you off comparatively lightly. Another master made ancient and maddeningly familiar jokes whenever he wielded the cane. If suppressed giggles could be heard coming from the flexed figure before him he went on making jokes. The class, in support of their comrade, laughed more and more uproariously until the master, flattered by so much applause, sent the victim back to his seat with his chastisement only half finished. Some masters beat so seldom that it was an event and a subject for discussion by the whole school when they did so. Others were always at it and no one who was wise would attend their classes without blotting paper or something in the seat of his pants. But the master who never beat at all, "on principle" as he said, but gave lines as a punishment instead was generally admitted to be a poor fish and a cad to boot.

In this simple and crude hierarchy we, the black-coated little beetles with the greasy clothes, dirty collars and neckties like pieces of string, looked upon the masters rather as the Ancient Greeks must have looked upon their gods. For us they were remote beings with varying powers. Some had practically unlimited powers and some had very little. Some were more or less benign while others were definitely malign. All had power enough to hurt mortals and all were subject to human weaknesses. From a lofty Olympian impersonality they often became suddenly and disconcertingly personal. They made swift descents upon the earth to visit their wrath, bestow favours or mete out sudden justice. They chose favourites and developed antipathies. And if you were beloved of the gods you were in some respects lucky but apt to be an object of jealous contempt to your fellow-mortals. The prefects were far more personal minor gods. They impinged upon our immediate lives more often and more violently than the dwellers in Olympus. They were more incalculable and capricious and accordingly they were more dreaded. Dressed in a little brief authority they had almost unlimited powers over their diminutive kingdoms. There was no appeal against their wilful edicts and commands. Power was theirs for the first time in their lives. Never again on this earth, one may be fairly certain, did any of those little potentates who ruled over me at that time wield such undisputed power. Never again would they be so little qualified to wear the mantle of authority so suddenly and so early thrust upon their young shoulders.

This was the frightening world I entered one lovely evening in May 1916, a shy, timid and tearful little boy with an unruly thatch of spiky hair, dreamy wide-apart eyes and a sensitive mouth which was ever ready to stretch into a crack-in-a-pie grin like the Cheshire Cat or turn down at the corners in a curve of unutterable woe. I wore a new thick black jacket whose sombre sheen was very soon to be tarnished and whose sleeves would soon retreat up my growing arms leaving knobbly wrists exposed. I had a pair of pepper-and-salt trousers soon to be torn and constantly mended and soon to retreat up my calves leaving thin ankles in wrinkled socks. I had a new straw hat with a dark blue and light blue band but I could not wear it because of the peculiar shape of my head. A small girl once incurred my undying hatred by referring to me as "the boy with the head like a football." Had the

description not been so apt I should not have been so indignant and
should have been able to wear the succession of straw boaters which my
parents were continually buying for me. But each one perched like a
plate and had to be carried under my arm until it disintegrated into a pulp.

That lovely evening I was standing forlornly under the chestnut-tree
in the quadrangle feeling very lost and very near to tears. I had just
bidden my mother good-bye. It was for ever, of course, as it always
seemed to be. I was just thirteen and the first World War was nearly
two years old.

IX

THE first World War, in its early stages, at any rate, meant little to me. It is strange how, as you grow older, your horizon widens out. Your world slowly expands from the crib in which you lie to the room which encompasses it. From this the household takes on a world-wide extent and becomes all there is for you to know until you find yourself in the much vaster world of school. And ever more swiftly the world enlarges and opens out. Like an unrolling bud it shows the canker at its heart. The full depth and sweep of evil is only made known to us by degrees and perhaps we may be thankful that this is so. How could we come all innocent into full knowledge? So, when I was eleven, I had no idea of the horror that had been launched upon the world that warm August day. And yet I do not know if any of my elders, who rejoiced and sang and waved flags, had any idea either. They were innocent about war too. How different it was in 1939! But in those days I was mildly caught up in the excitement of war's outbreak. I remember my mother running into her bedroom with tears in her eyes saying, "Oh, brave little Belgium! Brave, brave little Belgium!" I remember passing long columns of men on my walks at the Shuttleworths'. They sang as they marched and had a rank sweaty smell. They were Kitchener's Army. How was I to know they were all so soon to die? There was a master at the Shuttleworths' during my last two terms there who was always very kind to me. He had a quiet voice and smoked a large pipe. He used to put his hand on my head and say, "Well, Funny-Face?" About six months after this gentle kindly man had left us Mr. Shuttleworth read out a letter from him. He was writing from a place vaguely called "the front." I had a rather confused idea about "the front" then but I knew that it was in France and that the war was there. All men, I understood, who were not decrepit or physically defective, were cowards if they were not there. They were not "doing their bit." "The front" was shown on maps of France as a wavy line. When it bent alarmingly westwards everyone was very anxious and when it bent eastwards, which it did very seldom and then only very little, everyone was jubilant. The papers said there was a great victory. "Picture yours truly," the letter ran, "shaving out of a mug by candle light at five ak-emma, standing ankle deep in mud. It is pouring with rain outside the dug-out and we are expecting the morning strafe at any minute now. It always comes as regular as clockwork with the sunrise." And then the letter added, "PS. Remember me to all at Downfield—especially to little Funny-Face." And when a few weeks later Mr. Shuttleworth told us that the writer of that letter had been killed I buried my head in my locker and wept into the cardboard box containing my caterpillars.

But what I chiefly remember about the early stages of the war was the strange frenzy which possessed my father. In the years before the outbreak he had been colonel of a territorial battalion. The downstairs bedroom where I slept used to be full of military paraphernalia. There was a tin box with a magnificent uniform in it slumbering among moth balls. It was covered with froggings and tassels of braid. There was an odd-shaped box containing a cap of astrakhan fur and, in a drawer, a long crimson plume with a silver base. It was meant to spring upright from the cap like a flame. I used to steal it for dressing-up purposes whenever I dared. There was a shining and beautifully engraved sword in a scabbard in a corner of the wardrobe. I used to pull this out and gaze at it with awe when I could and imagine my father at Balaclava, charging down upon the foe and mowing him down with scythe-like sweeps six heads at a time. There was a less resplendent khaki uniform in the same wardrobe and a pair of high leather riding boots with trees in them. Occasionally on summer Saturday afternoons my father came back early from the City and disappeared into the downstairs bedroom. An hour later he reappeared, after an orgy of grunting and swearing, dressed in this khaki uniform with the riding boots on, and spurs and the sword clanking by his side. He left the bedroom in an incredible confusion. His black frock-coat and pin-stripe trousers lay in a heap on the floor like the discarded skin of a dragonfly. He usually disappeared then for the rest of the day. I would watch his tall figure, suddenly metamorphosed, upright and soldierly, striding away through the trees of the park leaving nursemaids and children agape with admiration. But on one or two occasions I had the proud experience of watching him volleying and thundering in the park itself, drilling his battalion on the green sward between the pond and the oak plantation. Then indeed I saw him in all the pomp and circumstance of glorious war and swelled with pride at being the Colonel's son. He sat very upright on a horse and barked commands in a strange brassy voice quite unlike his usual one. When he shouted the marching ranks of men turned and wheeled and handled their rifles like one man. I thought it must be wonderful to have so much power. And after it was all over for the afternoon the little dining-room filled up with red-faced men in khaki drinking whisky and smoking. The air became blue with smoke. Empty glasses and cigarette ash made a distressing litter which had to be cleared up when they had all gone. They laughed a lot and addressed my father as "Colonel" or "sir." They put their heavy hands on my shoulders and called me "Nipper," said I was a chip of the old block, they were sure, and wouldn't I like to be a soldier like the Guv'nor? I replied shyly that I would, of course, although such a thing had never entered my head or for a moment seemed within the bounds of possibility. In later years, when I discovered that I was not a chip of the old block, or of any particular block that I could recognize, the very last thing that I ever wanted to be was a soldier. And it still is.

In the summer Father used to go off to camp for a week or fortnight with all his military trappings, to return very bronzed and healthy and shaking his head over the negligence of the gardener during his absence. All of this he enjoyed enormously. He loved soldiering. He loved the purely male companionship, the freedom from home ties, the open air and the exercise. Most of all, perhaps, he loved the authority of his position among all those men who called him "sir" and were at his beck and call. Who can blame him? Who does not love a sudden brief taste of power and for a little while to be able to say unto him "Do this" and he doeth it? For him it was all escape.

A year or so before the war broke out Father retired most regretfully from his colonelcy and those thrilling parades in the park ceased. He no longer went to camp and the big collection of fading photographs, which decorated the downstairs bedroom, added no more to their numbers. They showed Father, for a number of successive years, sitting in the middle of rows of his red-faced companions against a background of bell tents. But now someone else sat in that place of honour. The soldiers went to camp, the Saturday parades took place, but without him. The mantle of authority descended on other shoulders and a younger man reigned in his stead. Sometimes he went to regimental dinners or receptions or attended parades as a spectator but from these he came back silent and melancholy, saying, "Ah! Well. Ah! Well." Old Major So-and-so had gone. Young Such-and-such was a captain now. Think of that. It seemed only yesterday he was a raw subaltern. The battalion was obviously going to pieces. The young officers were not what they used to be. Attendance at voluntary parades was falling off. Discipline was not what it was. It all seemed a great pity but there it was.

"You and your old 'costumers'," my mother would say scornfully. She had always been slightly intolerant of my father's military activities sensing, perhaps subconsciously, his escape. It was through a door by which she could not follow. She called it derisively "costuming"; and his fellow soldiers the "costumers," which derived naturally from the uniform to which she always referred as his "costume." "You've left that costume of yours lying on the dressing-room floor. I do wish you'd put it away in the wardrobe." Like most women she looked upon this essentially male activity as a somewhat foolish but harmless game. And now, when he went "costuming" no more, she seemed relieved. "Thank goodness we shan't have any more of those costumers here, thumping about in their great boots."

But when the war broke out my father made himself ready for battle. Metaphorically he girded on the handsome sword which now for two years had rested in its scabbard and its canvas case in a corner of the dressing-room wardrobe. "At any moment now," he said confidently, "I expect I'll get my papers." Bits of military trappings kept reappearing from time to time. On going to bed one evening I would find the high boots in the middle of the floor and father sitting on my bed gazing at them.

"What are you doing with those?" my mother would say.

"Oh, just looking at them to see if they're all right," he would answer. He seemed slightly guilty about it.

Another evening he had his kit-bag out and was rigging his camp bed in the middle of the dressing-room floor. "I might want them very soon," he explained.

"Nonsense, dear. Whatever for?"

"Well, it's just as well to have everything ready. I'm sure to be called up any day now."

"Oh, but surely not, my dear. You're much too old."

"Too old!" he exploded indignantly. "Good heavens! Too old! Dear me, no! They'll be only too glad to have me. They're clamouring for trained officers. Why, even old Randall's gone and Edwards was telling me . . ."

But no call came. Posters appeared on walls showing Kitchener pointing an accusing finger. Bills proclaimed everywhere "Your King and Country need you!" People rushed off and "did their bit." All sorts of improbable people appeared in uniform. On the music halls they sang:

> Oh, we don't want to lose you
> But we think you ought to go,
> For your King and your Country
> Both need you so.

Yet nobody, it seemed, needed an ex-colonel of the South London Rifles, a highly trained soldier and a crack shot, a winner of medals at the Hythe School of Musketry, an expert on field training, a patriot and a gentleman. Nobody thought he ought to go except himself. But it was a long time before he himself realized this. Daily he watched the post with an eagerness he had never displayed before the war, looking for a buff envelope in the slender pile on the hall table. But the British Army retreated from Mons to Le Cateau and from Le Cateau to Ypres without him. The battle of the Marne took place and the winter dragged itself into the spring. On Saturday afternoons that winter the ex-colonel of the South London Rifles would be seen walking alone in Richmond Park, an upright soldierly figure with a stick, watching recruits training on the open space beyond the oak plantation. "Raw stuff," he would say when he returned. "Raw stuff. Now, if I had charge of those lads. . . ."

But what finally pulled the trigger that propelled Father into action was the appearance of an uncle of mine at lunch one Sunday afternoon—a slightly meretricious but resplendent figure in a uniform with red tabs and a red hat. My grandmother kept referring to him as "the Major." "Give the Major some more bread sauce."

"Well, I'm damned," said my father after the uncle had gone clanking out of the gate. And he disappeared to the end of the garden not to reappear until dinner-time.

Next morning we were astonished to see him in uniform at breakfast.

"My dear boy!" said my grandmother. "Why this warlike aspect, pray?"

"Going up to town to see if I can't pull a few strings," he said.

I have learnt since those days the true meaning of that phrase "to pull strings." It was so often used in my class before the war and less and less frequently after it. Now it is hardly ever used at all. Strings have ceased to exist—or almost. In the days of my innocence I used to picture the puller of strings in the act of pulling them. He would be ushered into an august presence over a rich Turkey carpet. When the suave efficient secretary had bowed himself out of the door the presence would rise and hold out his hand.

"Delighted to see you, old fellow. Sit down. Have a cigar. Now what can I do for you? . . ."

"Well, I called, as I happened to be passing, to see you about a little matter of . . . I think it might be a good idea to . . . I suggest . . ."

"Why, certainly, old man. Nothing could be easier. Anything I can do, you know, any time. How's the missus, by the way? . . ."

And, the strings successfully pulled, the cigar half consumed, the puller would be bowed out of the door into the street.

But now I know that to say you are going to pull strings is a polite way, a face-saving way, of saying either that you are going to use undue influence to get something for yourself or for somebody else that cannot be won in open competition, or else it means that you are going to pocket what pride you have left, after the failure in open competition, and frankly beg for it. If you are rich and powerful it usually means the former of these two things. If you are not very rich and not at all powerful and out of a job it means the latter. It means being kept waiting for hours in draughty offices on a hard chair, hat in hand. It means telephoning and receiving no reply. "No, I'm sorry. Mr. So-and-so is out. What name shall I say?" It means suffering the polite boredom of under-clerks and secretaries.

"Mr. So-and-so? Have you an appointment? . . . There's a Mr.—what did you say the name was?—in the office. . . . Yes. . . . Yes, I'll tell him. Mr. So-and-so says he's very busy. Would you mind waiting?" And then, at last, after that wait, after reading a newspaper from front to back, gazing at calendars on the wall, gazing at flies chasing each other round the electric light, sitting first on one buttock and then on the other:

"Good morning. Yes, I think we have met before. Won't you sit down? Oh, excuse me—this damned telephone—— Now, then, what did you say your name was? . . ."

"Well, I was wondering if perhaps you might not be able . . ."

"Ah, well, you see, it's very difficult . . . so many demands . . . such a long list . . . creating a precedent. . . . Good-bye, sorry I can't be of more help."

I once had an uncle, a very just and upright and unbending old man, rich and powerful and at the top of his profession, who was asked to pull strings for one of his nephews. He sternly refused, with profound wisdom, and in doing so incurred the outraged indignation of the nephew's family. "Every tub," he pronounced oracularly, "must stand on its own bottom." How right he was! Thank goodness I have never had to pull strings either for myself or for anybody else. Nor, if I should ever be in a string-pulling position, will I ever do so.

So my father, in his colonel's uniform, went up to London to go through just such a day of waiting and being put off, of being saluted smartly by sentries at doors and orderlies in passages and politely asked to wait. Of waiting in bleak-looking waiting-rooms trying to look like a general about to take part in a staff conference and not like an anxious soldier trying to find a job, pleading to be allowed to fight for his country. Of being treated with bored indifference by men twenty years his junior.

But whatever success he may or may not have had that day in town, to whatever august presences he may or may not have been admitted, he came back that evening confident, tired but cheerful. Any moment now, he had learnt, he would be called upon. They were badly in need of officers with his training and experience.

"So-and-so said he would bring my case before General Sir Some-body Something in person and it wouldn't surprise him a bit if I got a commission within the next few weeks. He said the reason for the delay was probably . . . . You see, the trouble apparently is . . ."

The boots and the camp bed reappeared. Leather straps and belts began to be draped over chairs again in the dressing-room, newly polished. They had vanished back to their cupboards in these last disheartening months. But now once more, like the equipment of an army about to strike camp, they were mustered and checked and contemplated afresh with a new eagerness.

"But how silly you are, dear," said my mother with cold logic. "Why must you go at all? You have your business and your family. It seems so absurd to go and throw it all up. . . ."

Yet how could a soldier explain that stir of the blood that comes from the sight and sound of marching men? It was "the dim drums throbbing in the hills half heard." How explain in mere words why, when young men go off to war, with throats bared and arms swinging to the stamp of feet, the hearts of old soldiers beat higher and they buckle on their swords? To them it is the same as for the sailor when he sees the masts and funnels above the roof tops and that wide airiness that presages the sea.

But the winter became the spring again. Snowdrops appeared once more beside patches of old snow. Tender green fingers, war or no war, began pricking upwards through the softening earth. Crocuses burnt like little flames beneath the chestnut-tree in the front garden and after them the daffodils heralded the spring of 1915 with fanfares of tiny trumpets. They brought in the battles of Loos and Arras. They brought in death for hundreds of thousands of young men who wished for nothing better than to see them come many times more. But for my father, the idle warrior fuming in his tent, they brought nothing. Their frail trumpets sounded no call to arms. They withered, turned brown and sank back into the earth again with those rousing notes unsounded.

Back to sleep again with them went the boots, the polished straps, the camp bed, the uniform.

Father wrote, about the time that the roses were coming out, to General Sir Somebody Something. "Just as well to jog the old boy's memory," he said. Weeks later a buff envelope appeared on the hall table. My father, coming in from the garden, saw it lying there and made a brave display of nonchalance, casually picked it up from its tray and then waited a suitable time before opening it. When he did so it was with careless deliberation but with a light in his eye. The letter was a printed form with a date filled in by hand.

"I am instructed to acknowledge the receipt of your letter of May 23rd, 1915, which is receiving attention."

But it came at last when he had almost given up hope towards the end of that summer. He was summoned to an interview at the War Office. He departed in his uniform, which he had strenuously polished overnight and neatly laid out ready for the morning. When he left to catch the train his step was young and light like that of a man twenty years younger.

"Well," he said to his anxiously waiting family circle on his return. "It's come. I'm off on Saturday for a three months' course at Grantham." He spoke with an air of tragedy like one who had long feared the worst but hoped for the best. Now that the worst had come it must be bravely faced, his manner implied. But the new spring in his step, the light in his eye and his cheerful whistling in unguarded moments, when he was packing his tin box, for instance, implied something quite different. There was peace and joy in his heart. Honour was served.

In three months' time, on a winter's day at the beginning of 1916, we stood on the platform and waved good-bye to him. He was going to the front. There were tears in my mother's eyes when the train pulled out. "You may never see your daddy again, my darling," she said and kissed me. To me this seemed incredible. Before he went he had given me his silver watch. "In case anything happens to me. As a memento, dear boy." I grinned and said, "O-o-oh! Thank you, Daddy!" It was an unexpected and beautiful present but it had no other significance for me at the time. Now I was astonished to see my mother in tears on the platform. I had never seen her so moved about my father before. I did not know that she had joined the ranks of those who suffer in war, rich and poor alike, the same dread, the same torture of anxiety, the same loss—the wives, mothers and sweethearts who have hallowed the soil of England with their tears for centuries. War is crueller to women than to men. For them it has no glory but only waiting, striving, praying, a sense of impotence, frustration and futility.

And as is so often the case it was, in the last analysis, my mother and not father who suffered from the patriotic fervour which spurred him so insistently into battle. The sacrifice was hers. He thoroughly enjoyed his war. He was in the second battle of the Somme and had "a pretty thin time," with all that that entailed, at Mametz Wood. He loved it. He was lion-heartedly brave to the point of foolhardiness. It was said that the men thought the world of him. We heard stories of how it was impossible to prevent him from exposing himself needlessly to the enemy and how he was constantly obtruding a bald head above the parapet for enemy snipers to take pot shots at. Occasionally he came home for a few days' leave looking bronzed and well and somehow more handsome than I had remembered him or have ever seen him since. And behind the lines there was the hectic gaiety to be found there in those years— Paris, Amiens, the jolly male companions, French wine and French women. For him it was all pure escape. It was liberty. Probably for the first, perhaps for the only, time in his life, he lived his days to the full. He drank them to the dregs. The horror of the war, the tragedy of it, the beastliness and cruelty of it, seemed to pass him by. And when, a quarter of a century later, the second World War burst upon my generation and found him an old man with white hair, he lifted his glass in September 1939 and said, "I'd go like a shot but I'm too old—too old. Well, here's to the memory of it all." And he really was too old this time.

It was mother who suffered. Father had been a partner in a well-known firm of solicitors in the City. When he "went to the war," as everyone said in those days as though it was a remote sort of thing that didn't touch our home life much, he gave up his share in the partnership. All my mother had with which to educate a family of four growing children was the pay of a non-substantive major, drawing captain's pay. Before the war was another year older there was a prospective fifth member of the family.

It was because of the very non-substantive pay that my father drew for "doing his bit," and the somewhat more substantive amount that he spent while doing it, that I never became a budding Old Marlburian or Old Carthusian or Old Wykehamist, as had been originally intended. I cannot say that I think I am any worse for this alteration of the stars in their courses. I wore the lesser tie with exactly the same lack of distinction with which I should certainly have graced a more famous one. But it was because of Father's patriotic ardour, because of his

93

martial fervour and his urge to do his bit, and because of his triumphant
fulfilment of it at last, that I stood that summer's evening in 1916 tearfully under a chestnut-tree in the quadrangle, feeling like one cast adrift
upon a great ocean in a frail and untrustworthy boat.

X

THE ties which bound me to my family circle were a part of myself. I was not consciously aware of their existence. One could, I suppose, call that intimate sharing of emotions by the name of love. But it was more as though I shared a common bloodstream like an unborn child. Spiritually, perhaps, I was unborn. I was like a young shoot upon a tree, feeling tremors from the smallest breeze that stirred the older branches. When any member of the family was in distress I too felt that unhappiness. No conspiracy "not to say anything in front of the children" had any hope of success because I felt everything in my blood like an animal. It was not necessary to tell me if anything was amiss. I knew. And when, as happened on one or two occasions, I had seen my mother in tears as a result of an acrimonious passage with my grandmother, I had run to my bedroom and flung myself down weeping on my bed because her tears were mine also. When she was displeased with me I endured agonies of self-hatred and remorse. At the beginning of each holiday I returned from the Shuttleworths' with a clean slate, as it were, and filled with high resolves. This time I would not transgress nor offend against the unwritten laws of the household. I would not run past the kitchen door when the servants were at meals. I would not come into the house with dirty shoes. I would not step on the flower beds or steal gooseberries. I would not quarrel with Mary or "get up to mischief" or be "tiresome." But alas! for the frailty of human nature! I had seldom been at home long before I fell again, found myself engaged in a violent but brief battle with Mary or was "tiresome" in some way or other. "Really it is too bad of you," my mother would say. "You've only been home two days and you're being as tiresome as you know how to be already." The storm passed, the crime was expiated by an hour or two of close confinement to my room, the anger cooled but I was left with a gnawing self-disgust and contempt for my own weakness. It persisted long after my mother's momentary annoyance had been forgotten. Thus, it seemed, some invisible cord still bound me to her. Time slowly, though never completely, dissolved it. My spiritual birth was slow and the labour pains were severe. Terrible gusts of reasonless anger and bitter quarrels about nothing were the outward and visible sign of the process. Indeed as I grew older and approached adolescence, that time when a boy's life is filled with so many strange and unexplained nightmares, my relationship to my family became increasingly angry. Stormy scenes burst like squalls upon the calm surface of life, born out of our power to hurt one another and out of our very oneness. They passed as quickly as they came. But they meant that without knowing it I was waging my spiritual War of Independence.

With my sister I shared the common dream-world of childhood. I had a sort of dominion over her in it and she was my partner, sometimes my shadow. She became an increasingly unwilling and recalcitrant shadow. Slowly she eluded me and escaped into her own life. I found myself, on a day to which I can give no date, alone with my own dreams. For her who once shared them they ceased to have any appeal. When she went to school she began to weave around herself a world of her own and my power over her declined. She too had made her Declaration of Independence.

It was then, when I was beginning to steer my own tiny boat on the wide ocean of life, that I found myself standing deserted under the chestnut-tree in the quadrangle at my public school. I thought that life had come to an end. It had always been so in moments of separation. The more I grew away spiritually from those I loved the more heartrending became physical separation from them. It was like the sudden cessation of a familiar pain. And yet I did not know as I stood there under the chestnut-tree, a small lonely figure in my new black suit, that life was only just beginning. I was awakening. Hitherto I had been like an embryo slumbering within its shell, like an egg unaware of the other eggs around me. Soon the first cracks in the shell would appear and a strange formless thing would look out with its bright cautious eye at the other eggs softly splitting all around it. Soon it would begin to stand, hesitant and trembling, on its two legs—legs thin and frail, of doubtful value as a means of support, but indubitably its own.

It was a somewhat incongruous egg on which my emerging eye first lit. Circumstances drew me towards it. It happened to be cracking, in its own ponderous way, next to me in the nest.

The nest was the long dormitory where I and a dozen others slept. There were six hard little beds down each side of it and a rather larger one, dignified by wooden knobs, in the corner. This was the prefect's bed. The knobs denoted authority and at its foot was a washstand for the great man to wash in. At the end of the room was a bay filled with casement windows and a row of twelve basins in which the rest of us washed, or, on winter mornings, broke the ice and wetted the tips of our fingers. Down one side of the room was another row of casement windows and there was a door at each end so that the room was a passage.

It was white and bare and scrubbed. It had a comfortless penitential air with its bare boards and its high ceiling supported by beams and struts. Yet I remember it not unkindly for its healing darkness had hidden the laughter and tears and covert prayers of many generations of boys since the days of that later Henry. It often hid mine. It was a nest in which brood after brood of oddly assorted eggs had opened releasing a long procession of hopefuls into the world, some to rise and some to sink, some ugly ducklings, a few swans. And in those days, as in these, some to die untimely so that the next brood might hatch in peace and safety. I remember that long unadorned room because from my hard little bed I could look through the diamond casements opposite at the green mountain of the chestnut-tree. Or I could turn on my bed on to my left side and look through the windows at the end of the room. There I could see the battlemented gables of the other wing of the house, rose red or heavily mantled with ivy, and the fluted chimney pots above them, no two the same. The cedar-trees in the Headmaster's garden waved their flat branches against the sunset, entangling the moon and evening star. And if, on summer evenings, you knelt on the shelf that held the row of basins below these windows and cautiously peeped out you could see the Headmaster and his wife walking in their twilight garden, picking off the dead heads of roses. The Headmaster's rich fruity voice floated up to you with the scent of night stocks and tobacco plants. He seemed no longer formidable.

On my first evening I went up to the dormitory early. I had attended evening prayers in the great echoing schoolroom and, in the half-hour that followed before the bell rang us to bed, I had stood alone among a boisterous noisy crowd of boys. They swirled around me like a tide. No one took any particular notice of me. I felt very lonely. Someone extremely grand, with hands in pockets and coat tails pulled back as far as possible from the lowest button, sauntered up to me with a lordly air and said, "Hullo, you a new bug?" I confessed that I was.

"Well, what's your filthy name?"

I told him.

"Good God! Is it really? I say, you men, here's a new bug with a funny name. Spell it again."

I spelt it again gravely, challengingly, staring defiantly back at the ring of faces which had suddenly surrounded me. But they only burst out laughing and turned away. They melted into the swirling throng and, to my great relief, forgot me.

So I wandered upstairs to the dormitory. It would be quiet up there

G

at any rate for a little while. On each bed was a bowler hat, a pair of gloves, and a Gladstone bag—the travelling accoutrements, as it were, of the owner of the bed. These were whisked away from each boy as he arrived and he would not wear them again until he put them on, like a victor's helmet and shield, for his triumphal journey home, an occasion that now seemed inconceivably remote. My new bowler hat, with my new bag and gloves, lay on one of the beds, the one next to the large bed in the corner with the knobs. From the bag I began to unpack the things skilfully stowed away in it only that morning by my mother. My pyjamas, the ones with the blue stripe. I had watched her choose them, fold them up and pack them in. "I'll send the ones with the red stripe to the laundry, dear, and post them on to you. I've packed the others in your trunk." There they were in the bag exactly as she had folded them. Taking them out was like disturbing in the chill of winter a chrysalis that went to sleep in summer. I ought to leave them there, I felt, until I could unpack them again at home. There was my new sponge bag bought at Boots' the previous afternoon. It seemed an age ago in a different world. I took the things out of the bag one by one and laid them on the bed, trophies from my mother's successful shopping foray of the previous afternoon. I had been at home among loved scenes and faces when I had last set eyes on these things. How alone and lost I felt now as I beheld them again! I tortured myself with silly and profitless reflections such as these and they brought on a paroxysm of home sickness. I kept turning the knife in my own wound. Melancholy tears began to drip on to my pyjamas with the blue stripe and on to my new silk sponge bag.

"What are you blubbing about?"

A harsh croaking voice interrupted my sad reflections. It was a voice just about to break and so uncontrollable that its owner never knew whether it would come out as an uneven bass or a cracked falsetto or both. The noise it made signified that its owner was in the very act of achieving manhood. It went with the down that had to be shaved, with great ceremony, from his cheeks about once in three weeks. It went with the slight darkness of hair that was beginning to appear on his chest. And it went with the vague uneasy stirrings inside him which expressed themselves in a violent but unconscious sadism. Lester was a bully and he chose me as a victim. He set to work with scientific cruelty and considerable ingenuity to make my life a misery from the moment he saw me dropping crocodile tears upon the contents of my Gladstone bag. I was an easy prey. I was very much smaller and younger than he was. I was much more timid and a new boy. He had reached the beginning of his third term and would soon be allowed to walk about with his coat tails pulled back. I noticed, through the tears into which I frequently dissolved, that my enemy never made his attacks upon me unless he was quite certain of having the crowd with him. But this he was nearly always sure of, for he had made himself feared and the others followed him like sheep rather than fall foul of him.

The years divide us but my gorge rises at the memory of the first of my enemies even now. Time with its healing hands would, you might have thought, have healed the wounds we inflicted on one another in our youth with our brittle weapons. Yet they still ache.

"We don't allow milkers in this dorm," he said. "And anyway you're on the wrong bed. That's yours." He pointed to the bed with the knobs that stood in the corner.

I looked with intense distaste into the greenish eyes glaring balefully at me across my bed. They were fringed with sparse almost invisible lashes.

"That's the pre's bed," I said.

"Oh, so you'd call me a liar would you? I won't take an insult like that from a stinking new bug. You wait. Just you wait, that's all."

There was a sound of a stampede on the stone stairs outside, a shouting and scuffling in the passage and what seemed to be a mob burst into the room. In reality there were only eleven boys but from the noise there might have been a thousand. They rushed to their beds and began throwing things out of their bags, pillow fighting, jumping on to each other's beds and shouting in loud assured voices in an odd language that I was to become used to as the weeks went on.

"I say, bags I the basin at this end. Who's the pre this term?"

"Old Cheese, I think. He had Eight Bedders last term."

"I say, good egg!"

"What, that navvy! Oh, he's awful."

"He bloody well isn't. I think he's jolly decent."

"Oh, we all know he's got a push for you. That was the inter-house scandal of last term. He's awful. He's a navvy and he's pi as hell."

"I say, men," said my enemy. "Here's a bloody new bug. He won't believe he's been given the big bed. Doesn't know when he's lucky. Thinks I'm a liar too. Sauce!" He came threateningly towards me. "That's what that is. Bloody sauce! We don't allow sauce from new bugs."

The others followed him across the room and made a hostile circle round my bed.

"You'd better look out, you know," said one. "If the pre comes up and finds you in the wrong bed there'll be an awful row. Old Cheese is a bit of a beefer. I wouldn't care for six of the best from old Cheese, would you?" A shout of laughter greeted this apparently very witty remark. They began to throw the things I had just unpacked on to the other bed. One of them pulled hold of my tie, which was part loosened round my neck. It tore with a rending sound. I struck out wildly at my assailant. There was a sudden blinding flash of light that blotted out the world and I sank on to the floor whimpering with surprise and pain.

But one boy did not join in this exciting sport of baiting the new bug. A large angular youth, wearing steel-rimmed glasses which I never saw him take off all the time I knew him, was sitting on his bed slowly undressing. When the others gathered round me he went on undressing. Each garment, as he took it off, he folded precisely and neatly and laid upon the chair beside his bed. He seemed so aloof and detached from the rest that I came to a swift decision. Like many of my swift decisions since then it was the wrong one. As soon as I had recovered from the pain and astonishment of the blow I had received I shouted thickly at the ring of enemies around me, "You're all liars! You are! That's the pre over there!" And I pointed to the aloof figure pulling on its pyjamas on the other side of the room. This was greeted by a shout of laughter.

"That's a good one! Bland, old bean, have you heard the latest? You're a pre, old boy! Pretty good in your second term, what?"

Bland was so much older, apparently, than any of the other boys in the room that this fearful blunder of mine was understandable. I had seen him unpack shaving brush and razor and place them on the shelf above his bed. He wore a turned-down stiff collar instead of the wide Eton variety which the rest of us wore. He had hair on his chest. No one but a prefect, I thought, could show so many signs of manhood. But I had no sooner spoken than I realized that I had made a mistake which I should not live down for weeks, if ever. But Bland himself seemed to see nothing funny or unnatural about it. He got into bed and sat with his knees drawn up to his rocky chin. He looked at me across the room through his steel-rimmed glasses and smiled.

"Take no notice of them," he said. "That's your bed, the one where your things were. The big one's for the pre. He'll be up in a minute so I'd get undressed if I were you."

He picked up a book from the cupboard beside his bed, and, turning so as to get as much light as possible from the single gas lamp, he began to read. His room-mates ceased to exist for him.

There was a disappointed silence. Everybody felt let down. They had been robbed of the exquisite moment when the prefect should come in and find me in his grand bed with the knobs.

"That's right, Bland. Go and spoil the whole show. You are a wart I must say," said my enemy peevishly.

But Bland took no notice and went on reading.

From that day there was an unspoken alliance between myself and Bland. In due course it ripened into an incongruous friendship but it was some weeks before we went about together.

There was a certain formality about this business of "going about together." It was a kind of contract, strangely analogous to another more binding contract made later in life.

The long ragged procession of boys that wound out of the school gate every Sunday morning and down the hill to the ugly red brick chapel was made up of pairs and groups of three. There were the Prefects and the Bloods walking arm in arm, their squashed straw hats beneath their elbows, their coat tails magnificently pulled back from the first button. There were the juniors also arm in arm but with the skirts of their coats more modestly arranged. There were the new boys, first termers, not walking arm in arm and their hands dangling outside their pockets. Only a few walked singly and alone. It was considered odd and slightly shameful to walk to chapel alone. It was like being an old maid. It meant that you had no friends. No one wanted you. And for the first few weeks of my first term I went to chapel all alone, a solitary little figure slipping along in the rear of the crowd. So also did Bland but he seemed to prefer it. He always carried a book under his arm and wore his hat, to be different from the others, on his head.

"Who do you go about with?" said a lofty but not unkindly Blood to me one day.

"No one," I confessed.

"Good God! You poor kid," said the Blood with quite genuine surprise and pity. I decided that my state of single blessedness must cease at once. I began to look wistfully on my way to chapel at the aloof figure of Bland ambling along with his book under his arm. Should I dare? But he seemed to have no wish for any society but his own. He never noticed me or returned my glances.

The social disgrace of going to chapel all alone meant nothing to Bland who seemed to move in a world of his own. But it made me feel conspicuous and ashamed. Even in those days I was self-conscious and afraid of doing the wrong thing. Like all people who have this somewhat cowardly respect for conventions and who conform to them mainly through fear I have always lived in a state of ineffectual rebellion against them. I have always admired, mingling distaste and envy with my admiration, those independent spirits who flout the conventions, or those elect who simply do not know that they exist. So, as I went to chapel Sunday after Sunday alone, I felt ashamed and envied Bland for his unawareness. Years later I went to dinner in Australia and sat next to a man who did not know that the port should circulate with the sun. When I pointed this out he laughed and said, "What a lot of phooey!" and passed it the other way. I should never have had the courage—nor, I may add in extenuation, the bad manners. I felt for the man at dinner the same horror-struck admiration that I felt for Bland ambling along to chapel blissfully alone with a book under his arm and his hat challengingly on his head. He was unaware of my existence or of anybody's existence. I should never dare to ask him.

One evening in the dormitory Lester organized a sort of pogrom against me. There was probably no reason for it. Most likely he decided that I must be persecuted for being myself. Lester would have made a good German, I think. In fact I think Germany must be a country where all young men have Lester's attractive mental make-up. As usual he organized all the others, except Bland, against me and they held a conference about the kind of torture which they would make me undergo the following evening. It was decided that I should run the gauntlet. This meant that two rows of boys formed up on each side of the dormitory while the victim ran between them wearing only a pair of trunks. As he passed he was struck on the back with wetted and knotted towels.

"Right!" pronounced Lester, when this decision had been reached. "Wait till to-morrow then. I owe you something for sauce. We all owe you something for sauce. We don't allow sauce in this dorm." On the morrow I passed a day of dread waiting for this event. In all sorts of incongruous moments I found myself praying fervently. "Please don't let them do it."

"Wait till this evening, you little milker," said Lester during the morning break.

"My God, we'll give it you to-night," he said again over the luncheon table.

As the day went on and the moment approached I found an unaccustomed resolution growing up inside me. I would kill Lester that evening. I would murder him rather than submit. Loathing such as I have never felt since began to take the place of fear. If I went baldheaded for that hated face, I thought, he would probably run. I knew inside myself that my tormentor was a coward, like all tormentors.

I changed my prayers. Eyebrows must have been raised in Heaven when my new prayers ascended, for instead of "Please don't let them do it," there now arrived, "Give me strength to do for him." "Oh, God, please let me bash his face in."

When the bell rang us up to bed that evening I was as grimly resolved as a soldier going into battle. There was no fear, only determination.

"Now then," said Lester when we came into the dormitory. "Get your towels ready, you men. Get undressed, stinker. Now we're going to teach you a thing or two." He dipped his towel in his basin and knotted it, brandishing it under my nose.

"Take your bloody clothes off," he repeated and came close to me. It was the moment. I hit him across the face with my braces. He sprang back with his hands up to guard his face on which was a look of unutterable astonishment. The eleven other boys seemed to be frozen by astonishment into a moment's immobility. And then the Headmaster came into the room.

The Head was a dear old man of strict nonconformist views. His passions were Nonconformity, collecting beetles and the happiness and morality of his boys. He wore a black clerical suit, green with age, every day all the year round. With it went a white nonconforming bow tie. Other manifestations of his views were the extreme triteness of his sermons and the hideousness of the chapel where the Almighty and I never came into any sort of contact during my three years of attendance under its roof. And as to beetles I recall even now the feeling of suffocation that used to overcome me during the lectures the Head used to deliver from time to time. He would display before our drooping eyes box after box of dead husks like seeds, pierced through their middles with slender pins upon cards printed in minute letters. He had a habit of carrying these things about with him. Once a week he made rather dreaded descents upon the lower school bearing, as if on a platter, great indigestible hunks of Ovid and Livy. He was a great believer in these as a means of educating the young. He would begin these sessions by producing from his pocket a husk transfixed upon a pin.

"Now then," he would say in his rich and rather unctuous voice, "let us see which boy can use his powers of observation. Head boy, what do you notice about this interesting specimen?"

And each boy in turn would take the thing and rack his brains to find something which distinguished it from other husks which the Headmaster had produced on other occasions.

"Well, well," he would say finally in a tone of grieved exasperation.

"Can no boy see those hairs on the first pair of walking legs with which he cleans his mouth parts? Fie, fie! Eyes to see and yet blind! Blind! Ah well, let us turn to the classics."

And, hanging our diminished heads in shame, we turned not without relief to the performances of Hannibal and his elephants.

But the greatest of all the Headmaster's interests, to his honour, was the happiness and morality of his boys, especially their morality. His life was one of perpetual investigation and research, rather methodless and ineffectual. He was continually going about among the boys, trying "to get to know them," asking them rather anxious questions and honestly believing their answers. One would find oneself suddenly the victim of a cross-examination in the middle of the playground or on the cricket field, a fatherly hand laid on one's shoulder and dim eyes peering down at one out of immensely thick glasses. One hated these sudden interviews, of course, and lied magnificently, aching to tear oneself away. Perhaps it was because he was a little deaf and very short-sighted, and because everybody lied to him as a matter of course, that he never thought to correct the abuses that flourished under his very nose. Instead he decreed that there should be no separate studies because that meant "locked doors with mischief going on behind them," and no surplices in chapel because that meant popery which led straight to hell. But further than these two moral safeguards he seemed unable to go and for the rest limped about on his stout stick buttonholing boys and peering anxiously down at them through his thick spectacles.

"Are you happy, my boy? Are you quite sure? Good! Good! Well, make the most of your youth. It's the best time of your life, you know, and will soon be gone."

And the small boy, who probably prayed nightly for the end of this uncomfortable youth of his, lied handsomely and said, "Yessir. Oh, sir, yessir, thank you, sir. Quite happy, sir," and fled, thankful to be free of these unwelcome attentions.

Periodically, in quest of truth, the Headmaster made the round of the dormitories before the prefects, who were privileged to go to bed an hour later than the other boys, came up the back staircase from their sixth-form room. In each the Head stayed for a while to talk to the boys and say "Good night." He would seat himself on a chair under the gas-light and draw a reluctant pyjama-clad figure towards him. Very often on these evening rounds he picked on me, perhaps because I looked small and insignificant and fey. He would place his arm around my waist and draw me to him, peering through his thick glasses into my face which was then about on a level with the shining dome of his head.

"And how is this little man this evening, eh? Still enjoying life? Good, good."

Dear kindly old man! When at last he did discover the truth it broke his heart. For at last his patient researches bore their bitter fruit. He found out at last that many of his boys were not happy. This was when one of them, hating his school so much that he could bear it no longer, tried to run away. He discovered too that they were not particularly moral, not at least any more so than other boys in spite of no studies and no surplices. Mischief went on even though there were no locked doors to conceal it. And when his investigations reached this melancholy conclusion he packed up his beetles and his chunks of Ovid and Livy and retired to a country parsonage. There in a little while he died.

On this evening he came into the dormitory and found me standing by my bed hot and flushed and on the verge of tears, my braces clutched in my hand like a whip. Lester, hotter and more flushed, stood opposite me with a weal across his face. The group broke up instantly and sheepishly and each boy began to undress, trying to appear as though caught in the very act of doing so.

"What is all this?" said the Headmaster from the threshold. "What is going on here?" He sat on my bed and drew me towards him by the arm. "Not fighting, my little man, are you?"

"Oh no, sir."

"'The soft answer turneth away wrath,' you know."

"Yessir."

"'Let not the sun go down upon thy wrath.' Never go to bed in anger for you'll wake up in sorrow. Are you sure you were not fighting?"

"Oh, sir, no, sir. I mean, yessir."

"They're not bullying you, I trust."

"Oh no, sir."

"And you're quite happy? Still enjoying life?"

"Oh yes, sir. Thank you, sir."

I was choking back the tears of rage which came welling up as an aftermath of my emotion. I was still trembling. But, obeying instincts and traditions older than I knew, I lied as bravely and handsomely as I could.

"Yessir, very happy, thank you, sir. Oh, sir, yessir."

"Good! Good!" said the Headmaster. "'Behold, how blessed a thing it is, brethren, to dwell together in unity.' Well, I think it will be a fine day for the match to-morrow. . . ." He stayed, talking about cricket, for a little while. We undressed and got into bed as he was talking to us. Presently he rose and went out of the room. His big shoulders shut out my view of the cedar-trees for a few seconds.

"Good night all," said the Headmaster.

"Good night, sir. Good night, sir," piped a dozen voices from the two rows of beds.

We heard his footsteps echoing down the passage.

There was silence for some minutes.

"Saved by the whistle this time, you little milker," said a familiar voice presently. "Wait till to-morrow night. Just wait, that's all. I'll pay you back for that all right, see if I don't."

There was another silence.

"Who votes for doubling the sentence?" Lester went on remorselessly. His voice was thick and trembling with spite. "Who votes for teaching the little wart a lesson?"

"Leave the kid alone," said Bland's voice in a new tone.

"What's that?"

"You heard what I said. In case you didn't I said 'Leave the kid alone.'"

"You're not sticking up for him are you?"

"Yes, if you want to know."

"You don't mean to say you like him."

"Yes, I do. Damned good little chap."

There was a gasp of astonishment followed by a long disconcerted pause.

"Well . . . Let him just wait, that's all," said Lester at last, somewhat lamely however.

But curiously enough nothing happened the next evening nor the next. Indeed after that surprising opposition, coming from such a strange quarter, I was bullied very much less. Boys are odd creatures. Like sheep they will run in any direction at a bark. Now it seemed that Lester had overshot the mark and they decided that I was quite decent after all while Lester was rather a stinker himself. Evidently he himself felt the change and realized that he no longer had the crowd with him. A week or so later he came up to me when I was alone in the quadrangle.

"I say," he said. "Shall we make it up? I'll be decent to you for the rest of the term if you'll do some of my prep for me."

But I refused the olive branch so invitingly held out.

"Right," he said. "Just wait, then. That's all. Just wait."

In a hundred little ways, no doubt, he repaid me for the snub but he could not rob me of the satisfaction of having administered it.

To Bland for his sudden intervention on my behalf I was boundlessly grateful. His shaving gear and his turned-down collar apparently gave him some measure of authority over the others. That act of kindness is over twenty years old now and the author of it is dead. He was killed in the war soon after he left school. But his defence of a small boy in the dormitory that summer evening is not forgotten. It is part of the sum total of his immortality. For the first time in my life I felt a sudden rush of emotion, of gratitude and affection for someone outside my immediate family circle.

Presently there was a sound of lordly voices in the passage outside. "Good night, Hiscock. Good night, Croft Ma. Good night."

The prefect came in.

"All very quiet here," he said. "What's up?"

Nothing was up. I was almost asleep watching the cedar-trees waving their arms against the stars. I was thanking Bland and the Almighty jointly under the sheets. My guardian angel had done his stuff. I made a great resolution. To-morrow I would ask Bland to go to chapel with me.

XI

ON Sunday afternoons for the rest of that term two somewhat ill-matched figures might have been seen wandering about fields and lanes rich with summer flowers and busy with the traffic of insects. One of the pair was tall and gaunt. He walked with his head bent and his eyes, behind their steel-rimmed glasses, always on the ground. He seemed to see nothing of the bright landscape around him. His hands were often clasped behind his back, trailing an ash stick so that its point traced an uncertain line in the dusty road. Now and then he made an explanatory gesture as though expounding something. Whatever it may have been that he was expounding it seemed to make little impression on the other member of the pair who was much younger. His wide-apart eyes wandered ceaselessly over his surroundings as though anxious not to miss anything. He was paying, I am afraid, very little attention to the learned discourse his companion was pouring into his ear.

On summer evenings also these two could have been seen walking about the cricket field accompanied by their lengthening shadows. The air was filled with the sound of boys shouting at the nets and the hard tap of ball against bat. Swallows wheeled overhead and each blade of grass became etched with deepening shadows. Still they walked and still the elder one talked on until at last the bell from the octagonal tower called them in with its insistent toneless note.

It was a strange and short-lived friendship which Bland and I formed. Long after we parted company it continued to exist in the form of that intangible alliance which had arisen between us in the dormitory. Whenever we met we would smile at each other and exchange a few trivial words which meant that we mutually agreed that our attempt at friendship had been a failure through no fault of either of us. We realized our incompatibility. It was foolish to have begun it. It was based on a foundation that was too slender and too frail to support a relationship between two human beings—even young and rather hungry ones such as we were. For my part there had been only the wish for companionship of some sort, any sort, as a means of escape from loneliness, from discreditable solitude. I had only wanted to have someone to go about with. Bland at first was as delighted to have a companion as I had been. It was a new experience for him. He had found an audience. Inner fires, unperceived by anyone, had been burning within him, ready at a touch to explode into a sort of verbal conflagration. He was like a dammed-up river ready at any moment to overflow its banks. Mine was the hand that opened the sluice gates. Mine the head over which poured that ponderous flood of eloquence, suddenly released and rejoicing to run its course. There were moments when I felt myself drowning in it. Its course was in at one ear and out at the other. That made no difference. It flowed on rejoicing.

Lucky Bland! Life for him had no problems, presented no difficulties. He had settled and arranged it all. Regardless of the incalculable hand of Fate, which so often upsets the best laid schemes of all of us, he had determined upon the path his life was to follow and knew already the goal that lay at the end of it. It shone before him like the Holy Grail. To my feckless intelligence it always appeared a singularly dingy and unattractive goal, a Grail with no magic to lure on any man. For it was a B.Sc. degree at a provincial university. And the passion which spurred him on towards it was an absorbing interest in biology to the exclusion of every other interest. He was inhuman. Nothing else appeared to hold any colour or attraction at all. It was biology that he poured forth into my inattentive ear during our walks about the lanes and fields on Sunday afternoons and while pacing the cricket field on fine evenings. He told me about heredity, environment, variation, species, acquired characteristics, hormones. For him these were the whole of life. I suffered from a surfeit of evolution and was desperately bored long before the end of that summer term. And yet how strange that it should have been I and not Bland who did eventually become a biologist—albeit a poor one! Bland meant to leave school in a term or two, he told me, for a provincial university. He would take his degree there. After that he would take a teaching post, he thought, and so be able to devote some years to research. He had the lines of his research already mapped out. And yet all the time, "there the antic sat" and grinned while he told me of these humble hopes, walking in the evening beneath the wheeling swallows. For he did none of the things he had planned so carefully. He left at the end of his third term not for the university and his B.Sc. degree but for the blood and muck of the trenches in France. There he was blown to bits. So much for evolution, heredity and hormones.

But a long while before he left I am afraid my polite boredom became too evident even for me to conceal.

"I don't think you're really very interested are you?" he said one day, looking up in a hurt manner from the ground on which his eyes had been fixed. "I don't believe you've been listening."

"Oh yes, I have," I lied like a coward. "Go on."

But we both knew that something had come to an end.

After that Bland began more and more to seek the society of a mild fair youth with glasses whom I had often seen him with lately. More often in the evening this boy walked about the cricket field with us. I began to play the part of gooseberry then.

One Sunday morning Bland came out of the school-house door deep in conversation with his new friend. I was waiting for him in the quadrangle. The chapel bell was ringing tinnily in the distance.

"Coming to chapel?" I said. "The bell's been ringing some time."

"Sorry. I'm going with Anderson this morning," said Bland hastily and somewhat guiltily. And without glancing at me or hesitating the two of them walked on out of the gate and down the hill towards the chapel. It was over. And I once again, but this time not without a slight feeling of relief, found myself going to chapel disgracefully alone.

Towards the end of the term there was always a pleasant relaxation of discipline. For one thing there were the exams. These were invested with a certain amount of mysterious ceremony. Masters made dark references to them weeks in advance and hinted at the never very clearly defined consequences of failing to answer the teasing questions which would confront us. Weeks in advance, too, if you happened to be left alone for a moment unattended in a master's study, you might, by craning over the desk, shuffling stealthily a pace or two nearer, by swiftly edging the corner of a sheet of paper out of the way, or deftly altering the position of a book, manage to get a glimpse of those piles of hectographed sheets with the blue ink scarcely dry on them. After that you could go about with a mysterious air as though in possession of great secrets. You made sly references to what you knew. If you were unscrupulous enough and had been able to gather enough illicit information you might even sell or barter your knowledge. I enjoyed the exams because they meant the end of the term. The hours in the classroom under the eye of the master fled quickly by. Outside was the noise of rooks in the elm-trees and inside the scratching of thirty busy pens. The sunlight dappled the window pane. Years later, when I was sitting for other and more critical exams, I remembered with regret those at school. With what joy I had explained, with reference to the context, how Shakespeare showed his contempt for the mob! How I had spread myself on "My Favourite Sport"! With what gusto I threw myself into "A Walking Tour in June"! I, who loathed nearly all sports and had never been for a walking tour in my life! I have still never been for a walking tour but I am afraid I could not do such justice to the subject now! But I never could fill tanks or paper rooms and had no conception where two trains of different speeds would meet if one left Paddington at one time while the other left Penzance at another. And when at last I had put down my final thought about walking in June ("Give me a good pair of stout boots," I ended once, "and I will walk with you to the sunset." Little liar—I had been reading Hilaire Belloc and was in the Beer and Sussex School for a moment), or had at last come regretfully to the conclusion that C would never be able to finish the job in the time that B had taken, the master at his high desk straightened himself and said with a weary sigh, "You have five minutes more." I had forgotten his presence. In five minutes' time he came round, wearily, as though the mental effort of the whole class had been his, and distributed pieces of string with which we tied together the result of about twelve weeks' education. We never saw our papers again and I often wondered what happened to those literary masterpieces of mine. At subsequent exams next day, and during the remaining days of the term, we saw the masters at their desks poring over sheafs of paper, crossing out and marking in blue pencil with pursed lips and contracted brows. We guessed that they were walking down summer lanes with us, outpaced by our enormous and entirely fabulous boots, filling our sadly empty tanks and papering our half-bare rooms. Only once did one of my literary creations return to haunt me like an evil ghost. I shall never forgive the master who, in a moment of cruel and thoughtless indiscretion, liberated it. I wrote an essay on "Spring." Over the paper I had lost myself in a poetic dream. The allotted hour sped past and I was in a dream for a long time after I had handed my masterpiece in. It began, "There are three spokes in the wheel of time—seedtime, blossoming and harvest." Next day, in the classroom, the master, to my horror, dragged my most secret thoughts, the shy flowering of my muse, into the ugly light of day. He held a discussion of our essay papers during which I wanted the earth to open and swallow me. He read my essay through from beginning to end. "Now that," he said, laying my paper aside, oblivious of the titters that came from all parts of the room, "is just the kind of thing I've been looking for. That's what I want to see from all of you." There was a loud burst of laughter which astonished that good man though it should not have, for he was as likely to get that kind of thing from the rest of his class as he was to persuade me to paper rooms or fill tanks. "Who ever heard of a wheel with three spokes?" they said in the dormitory that evening. "Bloody funny sort of wheel!" I was consigned to the very depths in public opinion. I was damned by my poetic flights. Everybody's worst fears were confirmed. For nobody capable of writing such outrageous nonsense could be anything but a milker. If I had been any good at games it might have been different.

But after the exams were over all the masters, who had charge of our souls, evidently thought they had done their best or worst, and rested from their labours like the Almighty after the Creation. They suddenly lost interest in our souls. After all they were not very important. So, on the last few days of the term, they came into class with an exhausted air as though they had fought a long and fruitless battle. "Well," they would say, "we won't do any grammar" (or maths or geometry or whatever it was they had been trying to instil into us) "this morning. You can read if you want to." We all knew this was going to happen and had come prepared. We had magazines or detective stories or novels stuffed into our pockets or beneath our coats or between the leaves of our exercise books. On the word these appeared like magic. Even the noisiest class became strangely quiet on the last few days of the term.

I read greedily with a concentration I never brought to any other occupation. When reading I drifted off into that shadowy dream world where I seemed to spend so much of my time. I frequently floated off into it also when I was supposed to be filling my imaginary tanks, playing cricket or listening to the Headmaster's sermons. The familiar inhabitants of this other world accompanied me on my walks on Sunday afternoons. They spoke to me when I was trying to listen to Bland's discourses about biology. Perhaps it was because I lived so much in my imagination that my favourite reading in those days were highly imaginative novels like the early romances of H. G. Wells, Jules Verne and Rider Haggard. Especially Rider Haggard. I developed an extraordinary passion for that prolific writer and I think that during the years I was at school I must have read almost every book he produced. Some of the better-known ones, such as *King Solomon's Mines* and *She,* I read three or four times over. Allan Quatermain was my hero—Heaven knows why, for if I had ever met him I am sure I should have been bored to death. However, I do not think my choice of a favourite author was a bad one. He led me into scenes of colour and splendour whose brightness still glows in my memory. But some time ago I tried to read *She* again and could have wept with disappointment when I found I could not do it. Allan Quatermain and Sir Henry Curtis and Captain Good, R.N., even old Umslopogaas himself, had lost their glamour. As soon as I found the spell was broken I put *She* away. I could not endure that these splendid figures of my youth should fade. I knew that they themselves must be exactly the same as they were thirty years ago since the printed word does not change. It was the shades of the prison house. It was I who had changed.

But there was one master at least whose care for our youthful souls did not apparently cease when the exams were over. Into his gentle hands my ripening intellect passed in my first term. He was one of the few schoolmasters to whom my memory turns now with affection and respect. He had a gentle manner and a sorrowful voice which he never raised. He maintained order in his class without ever, so far as I can remember, resorting to that ruthless wielding of the stick that so many of his colleagues found necessary. He was very tall and thin and wore a pair of pince-nez that perched precariously on the end of his long nose. Down this nose he would gaze at a miscreant with one pale sad eye and one glass one which was exactly the same colour as its fellow but fixed, expressionless and unwinking. Sometimes he would be seen to place his handkerchief to this eye and keep it there for some seconds. It was said that, when he did this, mysterious manœuvres with the glass eye took place behind the cover of the handkerchief. He was thought to be removing it and turning it round so that when he took the hand-kerchief away again the glass eye was the other way up. No one was ever able to detect any difference afterwards, but whenever he put his handkerchief to his eye the whole class might have been seen to look up furtively from its books with sudden rapt attention. Bobbie had an air of perpetual sorrow for the sins and follies of small boys and seemed always about to burst into tears on their account. "Next boy," he would say in class, letting his asymmetrical regard travel down the rows in front of him, "Next. And the next boy. Well, next then." And so more and more tearfully down to the boy who sat ignominiously at the bottom—not infrequently myself. "Well, then. Tell them, top," he would appeal sweeping his single eye back up the class again. And, when the top boy failed him also, all the grief and despair in the world were in his voice, as though he had been utterly and finally let down. "Oh, my dear boy. How often have I told you—the verb at the end of the sentence." The boys imitated him ceaselessly, laughed at him behind his back, respected him and loved him. It was said that he had been a magnificent athlete in his youth, a champion runner, fives player and a rugger blue. No one had ever seen him show the slightest sign of athletic activity and he displayed only a mild fatherly interest in inter-house matches and sports. But when a man in late middle age earns the love of the young he must bear, like a cross, a reputation for youthful prowess. When asked about it he only smiled and shook his head. They said he lost his eye when playing rugger for Cambridge but no one really knew the truth about it. Bobbie left the school for an honourable retirement at the end of my last term. When the taxi that took him and his wife to the station turned out of the school gate the boys pursued it down the drive and down the hill past the chapel, climbing on to the running boards and shouting "Good-bye, sir! Good-bye and good luck! Come back soon! Good old Bobbie!" Inside Bobbie held his handkerchief to both his eyes. He was really weeping. Perhaps for the sins and follies of an old man who loved boys.

It was the last period of the last Saturday morning of my first summer term—an hour usually devoted to Bobbie's English class. Most of the class were bored to death by the study of the treasures of their own language. Indeed who would not be, for it was made uninteresting enough? We paraphrased great chunks of Shakespeare, very often passages that I find difficult even now, such as Richard the Second's soliloquy in his cell or Hamlet's broodings over the skull of Yorick. We analysed the ponderous sentences of Gibbon. We wrestled with the Anglo-German of Thomas Carlyle. We learnt slabs of Milton parrot fashion. The result was that English Literature—with a capital L— became a sweat and a bore. Any Friday evening during the term boys might have been seen pacing up and down the quadrangle with measured tread, as though taking part in an imaginary funeral procession, their heads bent and their eyes fixed on grubby dog-eared books. Their lips moved as though in prayer. Occasionally they raised their eyes to heaven while their lips continued to move in some mysterious incantation. What strange act of devotion, what mystic preparation was this? What indeed? They were preparing for Bobbie's English class next day. For the following morning one or two of them, chosen at random by the high priest, would be called upon to rise from his seat and haltingly repeat:

> Once more, O ye laurels, and once more,
> Ye myrtles brown, with ivy never sere,—um—
> I come to pluck your berries harsh and crude,
> And—er—with forced fingers rude
> Shatter your—shatter your——

And while he stumbled on those around him waited like hungry wolves for a hesitant pause. "Sir! Oh, sir! Please, sir!" they hissed with raised hands at the first sign of uncertainty. The classroom sounded like a cage full of snakes.

"Well, then, tell him, next boy—next—next."

"Please, sir—'Leaves', sir. 'Shatter your leaves before the mellowing year.'"

And he would begin with shame to take a lower place.

This too was my introduction to the Elysian Fields of poetry and like all the rest I regarded them as a desert waste. Many years of this sort of thing at academies for young gentlemen had produced a state of mind in young gentlemen exceedingly hostile to poetry and literature and everything that went with them. Poetry was effeminate balderdash. Anyone with a taste for poetry was automatically regarded with deep suspicion. He was suspected of being a cissy. Anybody who could string words together himself was obviously beyond the pale. Hence the persecution that descended on me as a result of my flight of fancy about spring. "He'll be writing bloody poetry next," they said. I myself learnt to regard poetry as something of a bore and I could see no charm in the difficult slabs of Milton and Shakespeare I was forced to swallow and spew up again in class.

So we felt nothing but relief on that last Saturday morning when the English period came round and we knew we should not be called upon, for once, to stand up and give a ponderous and meaningless recitation. Forestalling events we came into class with our favourite story-books in our pockets, with detective magazines inside our exercise books. I had my latest Rider Haggard. I was in the middle of *Nada the Lily* and itched to hear the tramp of T'Chaka's impis once again.

Imagine, then, our bored consternation when Bobbie, gazing sorrowfully at us for a moment over the top of his glasses, smiled gently and said:

"There'll be no lesson to-day. Put your books on one side. I'm going to read some poetry to you."

Poetry! And on the last Saturday morning of the term! Could there be a greater refinement of cruelty than that? No words could express our contempt and dislike for Bobbie in that moment. We gasped and stared blankly at one another. This was too much.

In a quiet, even, sorrowful voice Bobbie began to read Matthew Arnold's *Sohrab and Rustum*. Before he had gone very far I had forgotten *Nada the Lily*. I was listening to a new and strange music. The classroom with its ink-stained desks and its blackboard covered with yesterday's vulgar fractions faded from before my eyes. The listening boys, some attentive and some bored, took on the shape of tents pitched upon a great waste of sand under the blazing sun. All the distance that stretched before my mind's eye was filled with a host of dark-skinned strangely accoutred warriors, watching and silent. In a square cleared in their midst the lovely youth lay gasping on the ground,

> Like some rich hyacinth, which by the scythe
> Of an unskilful gardener has been cut,
> Mowing the garden grass plots near its bed,
> And lies, a fragrant tower of purple bloom,
> On the mown dying grass.

His blood flowed out from his white side and clotted on the sand— a dark question mark draining out his life. Over him his father, huge and dark and bearded, who had just cut down his own son in mortal combat, knelt weeping. His sword and shield were cast away. He held the boy's drooping head upon his arm. Silently and in sorrow the warriors turned away in twos and threes and went back to their tents. The sun went down and their camp fires came out and glowed upon the plain. They left the father in the growing darkness weeping for his son. Soon the host of Heaven shone passionless upon the dead boy and the strong man undone by grief.

> But the majestic river floated on
> Out of the mist and hum of that low land,
> Into the frosty starlight, and there moved
> Rejoicing through the hushed Chorasmian waste,
> Under the solitary moon: . . . till at last
> The longed-for dash of waves is heard, and wide
> His luminous home of waters opens, bright
> And tranquil, from whose floor the new-bathed stars
> Emerge, and shine upon the Aral Sea.

He ceased. The night desert and the stars faded from my sight. The tents once more took the form of boys sitting, black-coated and slumped in attitudes of boredom or resignation, at their stained desks. The white dead boy and the old warrior vanished. But there, on the card-board cover of *Nada the Lily*, were the tears I had shed for them, hiding my face with my hands. There was silence for a few minutes. Only a blind cord tapped against the window. Nothing seemed to move but the sunlight through the leaves of a plane-tree outside.

Suddenly there was an uproar. The outburst of shouting and whistling of boys suddenly released from class, the slamming of desks, the clatter of books gathered up. They were trooping out of the room. I still sat there unable to move.

"Christ! What a bore! Why, you've been blubbing, you bloody milker. What the hell have you been blubbing about?" It was Lester.

On the way down the stone stairs someone put his arm in mine.

"That was grand wasn't it? Bobbie reads beautifully. I'm so glad you liked it. I did too."

XII

I HAD made a new friend. The following day was Sunday and the last of my long first summer term. As a rule on Sunday afternoons we had to spend an hour and a half learning a chapter from the New Testament and writing home those laborious letters which our parents would read the next morning, often not knowing whether to laugh or cry over them. But on the last Sunday of the term we were excused this penance. Our parents would so soon see us in the flesh that there was no point in our writing and the masters were eager to excuse us in order to escape the painful duty of reading our blotted and misspelt letters. All the sunny hours until supper-time were, therefore, ours for us to wander in. It was the custom on this last Sunday of the summer term, if the weather was fine, for almost the whole school to walk to a river about five miles away. A gentle stream wound slowly through flat fields among willow-trees and, where the water ran deep and cool, the boys bathed naked. Bathing "with nothing on" was a special luxury reserved for this one day. It was a treat much looked forward to—and, in any case, who can doubt that there is particular joy in bathing and running about in long soft grass naked? "You *must* come," said my new friend. "You can bathe with nothing on." I was delighted because I had feared that, owing to the regrettable defection of Bland, I should be unable to go. One could not very well go alone—though goodness knows why. I dare say it was not done. So that afternoon, charmed that my company should be desired by somebody, I found myself on my way there with a new companion under a serene blue sky, as nearly perfectly happy as I think I have ever been in my life. Ahead of us and behind us went in twos and threes the black insect figures of other boys, small in the distance, for nearly the whole school was in migration on that lovely day.

Although we had only known one another for twenty-four hours Ronald and I seemed to be in sympathy at once. This was a new experience for me. I had never before found anyone I could talk to without reserve. This time the flow of talk was mine. It was silly enough chatter, no doubt, and at times I seemed to be listening in a detached sort of way to the sound of my own voice running on. We made plans for the holidays, promised to meet during them though knowing that we never would, and swore to be friends in the following term. There was a feeling of happy finality abroad that afternoon, as there is at the end of term, as when a ship sights land at the end of a long and arduous voyage.

"Let's be friends, shall we?" said Ronald.

"Yes, let's."

"All right. That's a bargain."

Then he stopped suddenly and looked at me. We were in a lane bordered by meadow-sweet and yellow iris. Ronald took me by the arm and said, in a hushed conspiratorial whisper:

"I say, can you keep a secret? Can you?"

"Yes," I lied.

"All right then. I'll tell you something, but you must swear not to tell a soul."

Ronald's face was like a bird's egg, oval and covered with freckles. In the front of the egg a pair of grey eyes were set obliquely so as to give him a curious faun-like look. "Like a goat," the unkind said. His pointed ears stuck out on either side of his head and added to his satyr-like appearance. There was something mysterious and dreamy about him, not altogether of this world, but of what world, and whether or not it was a better world than the one to which I belonged myself, I never could quite decide. You noticed that he seldom looked at you directly and if you held his oblique eyes they usually dropped before your gaze as do the eyes of an animal. One of Ronald's strange characteristics was his way of appearing suddenly and silently beside you as though he had materialized out of the air and of disappearing again as suddenly.

I felt there was something a little mysterious about him altogether, something to which I could not put a name. And yet, because he did not seem quite to belong to this world, his company was for me a delightful escape. I think mine was the same for him. As we walked to the river each tried to give the other a glimpse of the private world he lived in. And without success, for these dreams cannot be shared. I could convey no real idea of the scenes which made up the world of my imagination or of the beings that inhabited it. Neither could Ronald communicate much of his kingdom to me. But, though neither could understand much of the magic language of the other, yet the fact that we each did have a private world into which we could withdraw, and which was dearer to us than the visible world, drew us together. We were like two patients sharing the same disease and comparing notes in the doctor's waiting-room. We exchanged experiences. We walked along describing the imaginary splendours with which each surrounded himself and often we would pause to look at one another and laugh, amused and yet slightly ashamed, almost guilty. We were confessing things we had never dared to admit to anyone but ourselves.

"If the others only knew——" I said.

"Yes, if they knew——"

Like me Ronald was unhappy at school, but he was unhappy for a different reason. He was sturdy and independent. It was his salvation to be moderately good at games so that he could probably have made as many friends as he wished. But he repelled all advances.

"They're all so dull," he said. "And oh! how ugly!"

He hated school because life there was ugly. This had not consciously occurred to me before, though I must have been unconsciously aware of it. With Ronald's eyes I suddenly saw that it was so and became suddenly and rebelliously aware of it. I perceived that we were all dressed alike in the dingiest and ugliest clothes imaginable. Our lives were modelled on ungracious lines, more like life in a penitentiary than a school. We sat in gaunt and hideous classrooms learning dull lessons, taught by mostly negative, bored and uninspired masters. Our religion, which ought to have filled our lives with light and beauty, was as trite and unattractive as it could possibly be made. For Ronald life at school was almost physically painful. He had an intense perception of beauty and felt it as a physical sensation. As an equally intense but opposite sensation he felt ugliness in the marrow of his bones. "It's so hideous it makes me ache," he would say of something which offended him. The ugly red-brick chapel with its deal pews and its red and yellow chequered windows afflicted him with such depression that he went to all manner of lengths to avoid going there. He would come out of Sunday morning's service in a state of irritability and gloom. On the other hand a thing of beauty made him cry out with ecstasy. He felt that creeping sensation up the spine and that sudden rush of tears which all of us know in embarrassing moments, but which some experience more frequently than others. And on this summer's day, when we came to a turn in the lane where, from a low hill, we could see the river wandering amid its flowery levels to the blue distance beyond, Ronald stopped and exclaimed:

"Oh, God! How lovely!" as though he felt it as a sharp physical pang.

It was then that he said:

"Let's be friends, shall we?"

"Yes, let's."

"I say, can you keep a secret? *Can* you?"

I said "Yes." It was untrue. For with me the closest secrets have always been unsafe. For directly I am entrusted with an intimate or closely guarded piece of information, something not shared by others, a fatal sense of elation comes over me. I begin to feel superior in my newly acquired knowledge. From that moment a stream of veiled hints and allusions keeps slipping from me against my will and better judgment. They lead at last and inevitably to my quite guilelessly, and almost without my knowing it, giving the whole secret away. I swear myself to the deepest secrecy knowing that this is going to happen. I know, while vowing myself to silence, that before very long the secret will be a secret no longer. It will be shared by everyone with whom I have come into contact since the secret became mine. Each, of course, will be sworn to silence by the most sacred vows. So now, when Ronald asked me earnestly, "Can you keep a secret?" I felt that fatal elation coming over me, that sense of privileged importance which is one of the pleasures of the confidant. When Ronald said, "Swear on your oath you won't breathe a word," I drew in my breath and nodded.

"I swear" I forswore myself without a blush, itching with curiosity to hear what this dread secret might be.

"I write poetry," whispered Ronald into my ear. Only the meadow-sweet heard it beside myself and the yellow iris in the ditch.

"Oh." I felt considerably deflated. I had somehow been expecting something much more than this, though what I had been expecting I was not sure. Something slightly scandalous I had perhaps half hoped. That Ronald's father was a shopkeeper. That his mother wore a wig or had false teeth. Or that he was "illegitimate," whatever that meant. But this revelation gave me no sense of elation but instead quite a different feeling. It gave me a sudden sense of not being alone, like a ship which suddenly sees another ship far off on the horizon and realizes that in that immensity of ocean there are others travelling towards some harbour like herself.

"So do I," I answered.

"*Do* you?" said Ronald eagerly. "Do you *really*? I'm so glad. You must show me. What do you write?"

I was silent for a while. Should I dare? Should I cast discretion to the winds, make a clean breast of it, come out into the open and so on? If so Ronald would be the first living soul to whom I entrusted this secret, as closely guarded as the one he had imparted to me.

"I'm writing a play," I said at last, like one admitting to a secret vice. "But don't you tell anyone either. Promise?"

He promised and so far as I know he kept the promise.

This was indeed something I had never yet shared with anyone, a dream I had always kept to myself, my dream of immortality. I cherished secret literary ambitions. Among the immortals, I believed, there was already a throne, my throne, labelled "Reserved." None of my family knew of these aspirations yet, though eventually they came to know about them. As yet my dream remained bound between the pages of a black exercise book. I was afraid that uncomprehending laughter might kill it for I suspected that it was a frail and delicate thing. It might wilt and die in the first puff of the chill wind of scorn that blew upon it. And I knew what a gale would blow too. "All this scribbling, my dear," I could hear my grandmother saying. "What a pity he doesn't get something useful to do." And my formidable brother, now a sub-lieutenant on active service, blowing blasts of icy derision upon my tender plant—"What a lot of rot! You great ass!" So I hid my black exercise book and took it from its hiding-place only by stealth, secretly, like a miser with his gold. At home I hid it in the library behind dusty volumes which I knew were never moved, or in drawers beneath things which had lain untouched for many years. When everyone else was out or safely in bed I took the exercise book into my bedroom, which was near the library, and covered its pages with an almost illegible scrawl, with eloquent blots and with erasions. At the end of the holidays I packed it at the bottom of my trunk, slipping it in at the last moment under shirts and pyjamas neatly stowed there by my mother. Each time I put it there it had grown a little nearer to its triumphant but still far distant conclusion. I had drawn a little nearer to my throne. But at school the exercise book lay for weeks at the bottom of my locker untouched. There were so few moments when I could bring it out unobserved, still fewer when I could write anything in it. Some inquisitive or malicious eye, I thought, would be sure to notice that I was busy with something which was obviously neither a letter nor a lesson. They might suspect that I was writing poetry, openly and in broad daylight. I did not dare stand condemned of such an offence. To have expressed unorthodox views about the spring in an essay had cost me unpleasantness enough.

This sort of double life, that I had been leading for some time when I confessed it to Ronald, had its origin long ago. The seeds of the tender plant which was my literary dream had been sown on winter evenings when my mother read to us. On one day of the week only, on Sundays, as though to mark the holiness of the day, a fire used to be lit in the drawing-room. Only on this day, or when visitors were present, was the drawing-room used for the purpose for which it was intended, for withdrawing. It gave a special texture to the day, just as did Church and roast beef. On these evenings, with Mary and myself sitting on either side of her, my mother read two pious little books which told stories of the Old Testament in language that was simple almost to the point of being fatuous. She read *Great Events in History*, *Treasure Island* and *Tanglewood Tales*. It was the last that captured my imagination. I can recall those evenings as though they were only yesterday. The fire of cedar logs threw sparks up the wide chimney and shone golden upon the yellow wall-paper. The flames danced again in the satinwood furniture, glowed upon my mother's dress and upon her face bent towards the book. The oil lamp upon the table by her side presided quietly like a large unsteady yellow moon. From time to time she had to pause in her reading to check the thin pencil of black smoke that wreathed serpentine from the top of the glass chimney. The scent of burning cedarwood and potpourri filled the room and combined to produce that stuffy aromatic smell that I have always associated ever since those days with drawing-rooms and of hours spent withdrawn into them. I sat with my hands clasping my knees, voyaging in my imagination with Theseus to slay the Minotaur and with Perseus on his winged sandals to capture the head of the Medusa, the most dreadful of the Gorgons, who had serpents for hair. But it was not until many months afterwards that my love and admiration for Perseus flowered into the shilling exercise book and I began my long, arduous but secret journey towards the stars. The story of Perseus and his winged sandals began to take shape as a monumental play in blank verse. It ran into many acts and scenes, but I never reached the stars. Perhaps the wings of my sandals were of wax. Perhaps I flew too near the sun, like Icarus, and my wings melted.

When I made my confession to Ronald, the first living soul to whom I had ever breathed a word about Perseus, the pages of the black exercise book were nearly filled with a scrawl which no one but the proud author could possibly have read. Blots spawned over them like amoebae of ink. Whole pages and lines ruthlessly scored out bore witness to the pangs that accompanied the birth of this immense composition—my *magnum opus*. Slowly it grew on lonely walks. Ideas leapt at me in the bath and immobilized me suddenly while the soapy water grew cold around my limbs and my hands idled with the sponge. Visions crowded upon me during lessons so that my spirit, floating away with my Muse, left my body sitting vacant at my desk, an empty husk. Rolling iambic pentameters flooded out the vulgar fractions on the page before me. During French grammar the hat of the female gardener became the sandals of my brave hero and the pen of my aunt his sword. And weary masters, whose minds, of course, could not rise above vulgar fractions and the pen of my aunt, puckered their foreheads and wrote in my report at the end of the term—"Poor. Could do better. Does not concentrate." It was true, for what was the hat of the female gardener to me when I was flying through space beside Perseus on his winged feet?

Alas! I have long ago lost that priceless manuscript. It cost me so much pain. It began, long before I was half-way through it, to assume Wagnerian proportions. Tremendous music ought to have been written for it. Yet, after all my dreams and all my hours of abstraction, I never finished it. I lost interest in it about Act Twelve, Scene Sixteen. It was less than half-way through even then. Now even the memory of my thunderous periods has gone and the stage directions are all that I can remember. But even about them there was a certain sweep and grandeur. All the resources of Covent Garden and the Metropolitan Opera House could scarcely have done justice to them. For the technicalities of stage management and production meant no more to me than they did to Wagner. Like that great master I brushed them aside. For instance, the opening scene disclosed the Lady Danäe, nursing the infant Perseus, in an oak chest tossing upon the foaming billows. She, poor dear, had been cast adrift thus in a moment of pique by a disagreeable and narrow-minded father. "Act One, Scene One," the stage direction ran. "A Stormy Sea. Danäe discovered in Oak Chest nursing the Infant Perseus. Danäe (sings) . . ." It was brave of her to sing in such circumstances but I forget just what she sang . And the last scene, before my Muse became discouraged and left her hero to his fate, was—"The Open Sky. Enter Perseus on Winged Sandals, with Shield and Head of Medusa in Sling."

But there my Muse forsook him. Perseus, having rescued Andromeda from the dragon in a scene of high drama, running into pages of blank verse, sped on to consult the three Ugly Sisters in their icy fastness as to the best way of disposing of the Medusa, the most dreadful of the Gorgons with serpents for hair. For whosoever looked upon the Medusa was instantly turned to stone. The three Ugly Sisters had one eye, one ear and one tooth between them. They advised Perseus to descend upon the Gorgons while they slept and to cut off the Medusa's head while looking upward into his shield. This he did and, with the loathsome head, covered with hissing serpents, in a sling, he soared into the air upon his sandals. But the other two Gorgons awoke from their sleep and pursued him on wings of brass, shrieking in fury. And there, in mid-air, pursued by ghoulish foes, my Muse abandoned her brave hero. For all I know they are still pursuing him. And it was all Ronald's fault.

But as I lay naked on the grass beside the river Perseus was not yet forsaken. The air was filled with shouts of boys bathing. They made a frieze of Attic shapes upon the green landscape. The sun threw back a million lesser suns from the broken water of the pool and gleamed upon white bodies. I told my companion all that I had hoped and dreamed for Perseus, reliving all my birth pangs. It sounded a little ridiculous as I told it for I could not really convey anything of the aches it had caused me nor of the height of my literary aspirations. I could not really confess to that ivory throne among the immortals which shone before me so clearly that I seemed to have my feet already upon its lowest step. But when we returned to the school I went to my locker and stealthily dug the book out from below the Latin Primer and my shabby writing case, the cigarette-card album and the half-eaten cake nearly a fortnight old. After prayers I overtook Ronald in the passage. With an air of conspiracy I thrust the book into his hand.

"Here. Quick! Take it home with you and read it in the hols. But for God's sake don't let anyone else see it."

"I say, may I really? Thanks awfully!" said Ronald and disappeared with Perseus, the child of my imagination and my dreams, under his arm.

So Ronald became the first member of my reading public. He was the foundation member, so to speak. The thought that someone was really reading the result of so much striving and travail on my part ran through those holidays like a bright thread from day to day. I tasted the joy of being read which is one of the compensations of writing. It was like the thrill of facing an audience which actors know. And I was indeed as excited as an author awaiting his first review or an actor after his first night. Already imaginary words of praise had begun to sound sweetly in my ears, Ronald's words—"Oh! It's great! It really is. Do finish it—you simply must." So each day during the holidays I went to bed thinking, "I wonder how far he's got now!" When I got up in the morning I thought, "I wonder how far he'll get to-day." And when at length the end of the holidays came the usual melancholy of that occasion was mitigated by my eagerness to see Ronald again and hear his praise of Perseus.

It was that very satisfaction of mine, had I but known, that was my hero's undoing. I have learnt since that no written words exist which can properly express what one feels. The more intensely one feels the more vain is the attempt to translate those feelings to paper. The greatness of poets lies simply in that, that they do find words for what ordinary men feel but cannot express. For us lesser mortals discontent and dissatisfaction and a sense of frustration are all that writing brings. Not even words of praise can overcome them. I have learnt how dangerous it is to feel satisfied with a manuscript. But in those days I had not yet learnt it.

It was not quite dark when I got out of the train at the station on the first day of the next term. I caught sight of Ronald farther up the train at the other end of the platform.

"Hallo, Ronald!"

"Hallo, Dick. Walking up?"

"Yes."

"How stunning—let's walk up together. Isn't it awful being back again? Wonder what dorm we'll be in. Have a good hols?"

We walked up the hill to the school along a path that took us between the gardens of villas, on to a country road and then downhill through fields. From the top of this hill you could see in the distance the gaunt roofs, battlemented gables and the octagonal clock tower of the school among trees. It was the sad decline of a day in early autumn.

We talked of the holidays, of another summer of youth gone past. As always on these occasions a horrid and inconvenient lump stuck in my throat and made it difficult to talk of my vanished happiness. We each hoped the other had had a decent time. Ronald said he had been to Ireland where his father went to fish. He told me about the little inn beside the lake and the blue mountains behind it. "It gave me a topping idea for a new poem, Dick. I must read you some of it when we get in. You *should* go there, you know. It's not like any other country in the world. But then I'm Irish myself so perhaps I'm prejudiced. And what sort of hols did you have?"

"Oh, all right. We went to Devonshire again."

"How lovely. Do any fishing?"

"Yes—oh, yes. We did—a bit."

But not a word about Perseus. As Ronald talked on about Ireland, and about his own inspiration, Perseus began to shrink. It was like those disconcerting dreams I used to have in those days in which objects in the room, or the dim square of light formed by the window, seemed to retreat into the distance and grow farther and farther away and smaller and smaller. The lump in my throat felt as though it were going to choke me. I wanted desperately somehow to turn the conversation round to the subject uppermost in my mind, to catch Perseus by the hem of his garment before he vanished altogether out of reach, but strangely enough I could not bring myself to mention him. I became inhibited as though the words were jostling one another to pass my lips but had all stuck in my throat. This disability sometimes assails me even now.

It was not until we were almost at the school gates that at last I swallowed the lump in my throat and, assuming as casual a manner as I knew how, gulped out:

"Oh, by the way, Ronald, did you—did you, by any chance, read my—that thing I gave you last term?"

And waited with beating heart for his reply.

"What? . . . Oh, Lord! Do you know, I'm afraid I didn't. I clean forgot all about it. I'm so awfully sorry. It's still in my playbox. But still, I will read it . . . I will, really. Honestly, I will. I really didn't have time during the hols."

"Oh . . . Well, never mind. Don't bother."

My hero died in that moment and there were never any reviews, no audience, no encores. Instead of which there came flooding over me the realization, all this time dammed up and held back, that this was the beginning of the term and I was back at school. In bed, after lights were out, I mourned for Perseus in loneliness and desolation. I was the only mourner. He was buried by the morning and with him were buried my hopes and aspirations. And my throne among the immortals is vacant yet. But one never knows.

XIII

"THERE," said my grandmother, hastening with short quick steps, her eyes, as they always were when she walked, upon the ground, "that's the second bell."

The carillon had ceased in the square Victorian-Gothic tower, which overlooked the gardens of the well-to-do. There was a minute or two of silence which the blackbirds filled with hymns of their own. Then the bell began again on a single more insistent note. It was five minutes to eleven. From all directions along the shady suburban streets the faithful were converging upon the church, summoned somewhat more urgently now by the monotone of the bell that tolled above the trees.

In the high, arched, over-decorated interior the congregation were settling into their pews. Through the green baize west door we entered —my grandmother, my mother, Mary and I—and settled into ours. Our pew was marked by visiting cards—my grandmother's, my mother's and my father's—in metal holders at the end of the narrow shelf which held prayer-books and hymn-books. My father's name was included, I suppose, out of courtesy for he had never been known to make use of his seat in the pew. These cards proclaimed our indisputable right to that much space in God's house. After all, we had paid for it. The house was God's but the pew was ours. And if, as sometimes happened, we arrived to find our pew occupied, there was some indignant whispering and shuffling and hostile staring. Sometimes even the frock-coated churchwardens had to come forward and make sibilant apologies and explanations. Then, the battle won and the intruders routed, we could settle down to the comfortable, rather drowsy business of worship. There was a ritual about this. My grandmother entered the pew first, making in the aisle a genuflection to the altar as she did so. I stood behind her, hat in hand, wondering shyly whether perhaps I ought not to make some similar obeisance, but feeling too self-conscious to do so. I edged into the pew and sat down between my grandmother and my mother. Mary sat on the other side of my mother at the end of the pew. On alternate Sundays we exchanged positions and quarrelled on the way to church about whose turn it was to sit in the middle. After some manœuvring with umbrellas, hassocks and hymn-books, we all four knelt on our hassocks and covered our faces with our hands. Every member of the congregation did this as a preliminary. It was the correct procedure, part of the "way to behave in church." Knowing how to "behave in church" was one of the signs of being well-bred, I had been told, and so I did the same as everyone else, though I am afraid that nothing much happened during those few moments. I looked between my fingers at the elaborate grain of the deal shelf in front of me and at the pattern on the coat of the lady in front. She, I was often shocked to notice, was not really kneeling at all but only pretending to kneel. Her behind was still resting on the edge of the pew. I noticed with disapproval that quite a lot of grown-up people did this and came to the conclusion that they were not very well-bred and hadn't been told about it when they were young.

After a few moments in the kneeling position, we sat back in our pews and waited. The interior of the church was dim and vaguely Gothic. It was suffused by a red and blue and golden light which shone through melancholy bearded figures in the windows who raised two fingers in perpetual benediction and gazed down upon us in irremediable sorrow. There was much ironwork everywhere in the form of screens and rails and hanging constellations of lights. Iron curled into leaves and effloresced into stiff little flowers with gilded centres, fleurs-de-lys and roses. There was much gleaming brass. A brass eagle bore the Book upon its wings. A brass cross by the parson's chair took the light of the hanging constellations. A cross and candlesticks of brass gleamed high upon the altar behind a brass rail. There, in quietness of their own, a row of tall white candles waxed and waned, six remote and virginal stars beneath the great east window. Above where I sat trefoil pillars of polished granite shot up into the gloomy roof and there spread branches which joined and crossed, with little stone roses at their intersections, so high above my head that if I looked up at them my mother touched me gently on the knee with her gloved hand. I was not behaving.

Architecturally, perhaps, the church was bad, over-elaborate and sham. But to me it was exceedingly beautiful, familiar, dear and holy. It was all that it should be. It was Church—with a capital C. I knew all the sorrowful, gentle figures in the windows by name and every Sunday felt devout and humble before those six pale and distant stars.

The faithful, who sat delicately coughing and fidgeting all around me, were also part of that Sunday performance known as Church. And with Church, marking Sunday as a day apart, went clean clothes, my Eton suit, roast beef and rhubarb tart and a fire in the drawing-room. For Church my grandmother always wore a hat with feathers on it, furs and things that swung and glittered. She emanated a pleasant Sunday smell of eau-de-Cologne, camphor and leather. So did my mother. So did all the other ladies though few of them had hats with feathers on them. And I was clean and proudly uncomfortable in my Eton suit and white collar. All the other male members of the congregation, both young and old, looked proudly, self-consciously clean, pressed and uncomfortable. It was part of Sunday.

There was a subdued expectancy in these minutes of waiting though what was expected, apart from the entry of the choir and the two clergymen, it would have been difficult to say. Certainly no one was anticipating any alarming or inconvenient manifestations of divine power. If any had taken place there would have been general consternation and disapproval. It would have made us late for lunch. Through the shuffling of feet, the muffled whispering and smothered coughing the organ, invisible but vibrant, maintained a continuous melodious hum —a sound indissolubly associated in one's mind with Church.

Presently the bell, tolling faintly above the branches of the stone forest, stopped. There was a moment's silence. Then the organ boomed from its many pipes that looked like rows of gigantic inverted pencils. Everyone stood up and I became suddenly conscious of backs in front of me, of tassels of fur, and buns of hair and hats. From a side door in the chancel a procession of black and white robed figures emerged, little ones in front and larger ones behind. Their hair was brushed and their collars were clean. Their eyes, behind spectacles more often than not, had a devout and downcast look. I was aware of boots below their black skirts for somehow one half-expected them to move on wheels. The procession divided at the chancel steps, opening out right and left into the choir stalls below the rows of inverted pencils. It disclosed in so doing the vicar and his curate in their surplices and stoles. The vicar was a large man with grey hair and a red face, a healthy outdoors man, very fond of gardening and cricket. His frail, tired little wife sat in the front pew beneath the pulpit with five of her seven offspring, over which her hands fluttered throughout the service, hushing, admonishing, fussing. The curate was a pale young man with a bald head and spectacles. Now the vicar took up his position in his stall where gleamed the cross of brass. He clasped his hands in front of him and turned his large red face, like a healthy and remarkably unspiritual beetroot, towards the congregation.

"When," he intoned in his mellifluous voice, "the wicked man turneth away from his wickedness that he hath committed, and doeth that which is lawful and right, he shall save his soul alive."

Ah, when! . . . The familiar proceedings had begun.

It was always the same. All my life it has been the same, whether it was in the dim many-coloured interior of that church many years ago, or in the red-brick chapel at school, or on board ship in time of war with ranks of sailors cleaned and shining for Sunday divisions. Always those same prayers in their lovely language, so right, so appropriate, so pleasant in the sight of God, but yet so often galloped through or swallowed and mispronounced so as to become an offence to the ear. The same oriental savage old psalms with chants much too difficult for the congregation, and words that could only be fitted in by means of surprising rushes at the verses, several words strung together and disgorged at one breath. The same hymns too, in which the congregation joined with a gusto sometimes unsuited to the sentiment or manfully strove with unexpected intricacies of melody and phrasing. And the same sermons. Always among all this there has returned to me that smell of eau-de-Cologne and camphor and leather. In my imagination my hand has stolen into my mother's muff for it was thus I used to sit during the lessons and during the vicar's sermons. I see again those aspiring trees of polished granite, the lianes and tendrils of ironwork, the constellations of lights, the sorrowful figures in red and blue robes with their fingers raised in perpetual benediction. It is like a calm, broad untroubled river flowing through life; something that was, is and ever shall be.

And yet it has always been Church, with a capital C. It has never seemed to have any real relation to life. That has always been part of its beauty and its charm. It never seemed to have anything to do with me. I was just there, watching it and breathing its comforting easeful atmosphere. It brought me, and still brings me, a strange peace, like gentle hands upon the forehead. So remote, indeed, did it seem from life as it is actually lived, at any time except between eleven and twelve-thirty on Sunday mornings, that I could contemplate without astonishment the two old Misses Easton, comfortable and well fed, in their shapeless hats, bending their eyes devoutly upon, "My wounds stink and are corrupt through my foolishness. I am brought into so great trouble and misery that I go mourning all day long." Equally as a matter of course at school I joined with two hundred odd other innocents to repeat, in that cataract of words inseparable from the psalms, "Behold, I was shapen in wickedness and in sin hath my mother conceived me." Without astonishment because, quite obviously, such words could not possibly relate to me or to the Misses Easton. They were just part of Church. There was the same remoteness too about the sermons. Those which the vicar preached in his ornate pulpit differed little from those of the Headmaster in the chapel at school. Or, indeed, from any that I have listened to a thousand times since. There was always the strange feeling that they were inapplicable. It seemed to communicate itself to the whole congregation for hardly anyone was really listening and the sigh of relief when the preacher turned to the east and ascribed, as was most justly due, all might, majesty, dominion, power, was almost audible. It was as if the well-meaning and kindly gentleman, six feet above correction, were striving to make himself understood in a language which his hearers had forgotten. Indeed, perhaps he was. But one reason for this, I think, was possibly the strange trick which clergymen have of complicating simple passages from the scriptures. There seems, in fact, to be a sort of lowest common denominator of sermons, the simple text, which has to be juggled with as one juggles with vulgar fractions, until it comes to mean something quite different from what it seems to means, and much more obscure.

This lack of human contact in the pulpit, the savagely poetic but improbable words of the psalms, the incongruous religiosity of most of the hymns as well as the distortion of most of the prayers, so that they sounded like a too familiar and oft repeated recitation without any true significance, all combined to make Church a thing quite apart from life, something detached as if railed off, as it were, by that very ironwork and gleaming brass which I admired so much. It was a pleasant Sunday anodyne distinct from the life which I resumed with my Sunday lunch. And this effect was heightened by what seemed to be an undue emphasis on a wickedness of which I was not in the least conscious and a contrition I never felt.

It never occurred to me that Church could ever be different from this. I knew in a vague sort of way that there were other kinds of Church in which a different order of things prevailed. For instance, there was High Church and there was Low. Sometimes I heard people say that they found the service at such and such a church too high or too low but I never quite knew what that meant. And my father used this as an excuse for never going to church at all. "Too low for me," he would say. "Don't like low church services. Never go to 'em." And he would disappear on Sunday mornings down the garden in his oldest clothes and remain there until lunch-time. As a matter of course the church we went to was Church of England. I knew that there was a Roman Catholic Church because history was full of the dreadful things the "Catholics" had done, though they never seemed to do them nowadays. All the Catholics I met seemed to be ordinary people like my own family and not in the least given to burning and massacring. And yet there seemed to be a slightly sinister significance about the word "Catholic." I had heard it said, in a mysterious whisper, of some new arrivals in the neighbourhood, "I believe they're R.C.'s." This was followed by the reply, "Oh, I see," with pursed lips and a comprehending look. And an uncle of mine had performed a manœuvre known as "Going over to Rome," which was considered by the family to be a rather discreditable proceeding and was always spoken of in subdued tones. Then again, as it were at the other end of the scale, there was something called "Chapel" to which the servants belonged. This was a very lowly and undecorative form of Church. Most of the people who lived down the hill by the main road made up this vast but somehow obscure community. They could be seen on Sunday evenings, if one ever happened to be that way at that time, emerging from their unpretentious temples from which came a low droning sound. Nobody whom one knew was chapel.

I find it difficult to recall what sort of impression I gained from my religious teaching and what seeds of belief, if any, were being sown in those days in the shallow and unfruitful soil of my brain. At school I must have gathered very little for my only memory is one of mild boredom. It was divinity, which was just another lesson—"divvers"—like French or Maths or Stinks—and a particularly irritating one because it broke into Sunday afternoon. Curiously enough, however, I was fairly good at "divvers" and almost ran the risk of being labelled "pi," which was liable to befall anybody who, as I did, became expert at the journeys of St. Paul and could enumerate the kings of Israel and Judah in chronological order. And much good that accomplishment has done me!

Such religious teaching as I did absorb came to me sporadically at home. It came, as it should, at my mother's knee, though the plant that finally flowered from these seeds was a strange one. On Sunday evenings by the fireside my mother read to Mary and me, sitting on either side of her, from two little books called *Line upon Line* and *Peep of Day*. They told the stories of the Old and New Testaments in simple language. *Line upon Line* dealt with the Old Testament. It was, I suppose, a little essay in self-deception, for although it was obviously most sincerely and devoutly written yet, in the stories which it told with such an air of piety and reverence, the chief characters cheated and betrayed one another, lied, stole and even murdered. And the Deity who ruled their destinies, as petty and spiteful as His subjects, wreaked frightful vengeance upon them as well for small transgressions, such as offering up a sacrifice whose smoke did not ascend straight to heaven, as for more grave ones such as murdering one's brother. There is something old and almost primeval about our reverence for these stories, like the reverence and awe of the Greeks for their frail and human gods. I loved these old fables and found them deeply satisfying. I listened enraptured, letting them soak into my blood so that they became part of me as they have of all who profess and call themselves Christians. But they gave me a somewhat distorted conception of the Almighty. He was presented to me, as to thousands of other Christian children, as an omnipotent and vindictive old gentleman who, mercifully, had long ago ceased to function. He seemed now to have lost that power of sudden disconcerting intervention in the affairs of His subject mortals. For which, I thought, we must all be truly thankful. For all the evidences of His power, it seemed, had to be dug up out of the remote and fabulous past. All His interests and activities apparently centred round a small corner of the Levant, where a poor nomadic people, remarkable chiefly for their longevity and their habit of relying entirely on their Deity to fight their battles for them by means of miracles, inhabited tents in the desert and were as false and unstable as primitive human beings may be expected to be. At the end of each story in *Line upon Line* there was appended a series of naïve questions, somewhat as follows:

Q. If I gave you some wood, some nails and a hammer, could you make a box?

A. Yes, I think I could.

Q. But without the wood, the nails and the hammer could you still make a box?

A. No, I certainly could not.

Q. Quite right. You could not. But God could make a box out of nothing.

To which the reply, not in the book certainly but not far from my mind, was, "Well, perhaps He could but He never does."

So that religion all seemed to be something fabulous and concerned with things that happened very very long ago. And though I loved these stories they remained for me fairy stories, slightly enhanced by a faint gleam of truth. Nor did I ever really believe in that omnipotent vengeful God or imagine that He ever intervened in human affairs. The evidence seemed too much to the contrary.

The other little book, *Peep of Day*, told the New Testament stories in the same simple language but for some reason it failed to capture my imagination to the same extent as *Line upon Line*. The Central Figure remained nebulous.

And yet I prayed frequently when I was young and often when alone tried to materialize that sad and gentle spirit as I tried later to conjure back the loved spirit of grandmother after her death. And sometimes

I thought I had succeeded though I never could be quite sure. I still pray, though to what and to whom I do not know. Perhaps to the brooding spirit that must have been born out of centuries of human thought and hope and prayer. The prayers begin, as they began thirty years ago, "Oh God." Sometimes I think, as I thought then, that they are answered and I burn anew with faith until the next one falls apparently on deaf ears. Then, false and fickle, I say to myself, "There is no God."

One day in my second term at school the Headmaster sent for me. A prefect called to me across the quadrangle:

"Hi, you! The Head wants you in his study at the double."

Astonished, and remembering previous interviews in studies, I went with misgiving. The old man was sitting behind his desk which was as usual littered with papers. Shelves of books and high cabinets of drawers full of beetles surrounded him on all sides. The room smelt of leather and, for some reason, decaying apples. Through the windows I could see the garden sinking into its winter sleep. No more roses now, only dead leaves lying in heaps or falling singly with a dry rustle. I entered somewhat timidly, wondering what crime I was about to answer for.

But the Head beamed kindly through his thick glasses.

"Well, my little man. Still happy?"

"Oh, yes, sir. Quite, sir. Thank you, sir."

So this was to be another of those cross-examinations.

"How old are you?"

"Fourteen, sir."

"Have you been confirmed?"

"No, sir."

"Do you want to be?"

I had no idea. It had never occurred to me that one ever actually wanted to be confirmed. One just was confirmed. It was one of life's milestones, an inevitable thing that just happened in the course of time, like being born, baptized, married. Like coming of age, like dying. And it was "the thing." Everyone did it. But that one should decide for oneself whether it should happen or not was a new idea. I hesitated.

"You know what it means, of course?" continued the Headmaster.

Did I? I knew that when I was baptized my godfathers had promised and vowed three things in my name. The time must arrive when I must take those vows upon myself. One of my godfathers was a kindly and extremely wealthy man who had made a lot of money in South America. I bore his Christian name as my second name and my parents, I think, had vaguely hoped—I wonder what they had hoped. Anyhow two or three times a year I was taken to see him in his lovely house which was an oasis in a desert of brick on the outskirts of London. These visits were always remarkable for me because on these occasions, and on these occasions only, I was known by my second Christian name, which was also his. I was always taken to see him in the billiard-room where he lay on the sofa with a book. He was a handsome regal old gentleman with a pointed beard and was a more or less permanent invalid, able to move about only very slowly with the aid of a rubber-tipped stick.

"Ah, yes. Now let me see. And who is this young man?"

"This is Downes, Father. Downes, you know. Your godson."

"Ah, to be sure, to be sure. And how is Downes?"

And, fishing with some effort in his pocket, he would produce a sovereign and give it to me.

"There!" said my mother ecstatically with an excellent imitation of delighted surprise, "Isn't that lovely? Really that's too good of you. Now you must thank your godfather very nicely." Which I did and was then led out of the presence into the spacious drawing-room where there was tea. As I left the billiard-room I would see my godfather, out of the corner of my eye, taking up his book.

My other godfather was an uncle who had gone to Canada some years before my earliest memories. There he had "made good." I had only once seen him and could scarcely remember what he looked like. He had given me a silver bowl as a christening present and once a year, at Christmas, I was reminded of him by the appearance of his bowl in the middle of the table filled with crystallized fruits. But this godfather, I rather feared, had forgotten my existence.

Nevertheless these two gentlemen, so I understood, had undertaken to be responsible for all my misdoings until I was confirmed when I should be responsible for them myself. I cannot say that I thought this burden lay very heavily on the shoulders of either of them. Now, it appeared, I must relieve them of it and assume that burden myself.

"Oh yes, sir. I know what it means," I said.

"And do you wish to be confirmed?"

"Oh yes, sir."

"Good. I'm beginning my confirmation classes in about a fortnight," said the Headmaster. "I shall write and tell your parents that you wish to join. I'm glad you've taken this decision."

And I left, relieved that the interview should have concerned a matter so harmless and of so little moment compared with most interviews I had had in headmasters' studies. I came away, too, feeling that I had made a wise decision which the Head viewed with favour, for some reason comprehensible only to headmasters.

But the same day Ronald was summoned into the study and asked the same question. The result in his case, however, was startling and the interview a somewhat unhappy one.

"No, sir," was Ronald's reply.

The Headmaster appeared dumbfounded and there was a moment's embarrassing silence. Such a reply to this particular question was evidently something outside his experience.

"Do you mean to tell me," he said at length, gazing at Ronald over the top of his glasses, "that you don't wish to become a communicating member of the Church?"

"No, sir."

"Do you know what you're saying?"

"Yes, sir."

"What are your reasons?"

"I wish to become a Roman Catholic," said Ronald.

The Headmaster was horrified. Papism—for him it was the road to hell. Was he nurturing a viper in his bosom? He rose from his desk and strode up and down the room, his hands behind his back.

"This is very serious," he said. "Very serious. It needs deep thought. You should think this over very carefully. You must search your heart thoroughly. I will give you another week for reflection. At the end of that time I hope, I will not say I expect—I hope, that you will have come to a different decision. Meanwhile, I think I had better write to your parents. They already know about this, of course?"

"I don't know, sir."

"You don't know? Haven't you said anything to them about this?"

"No, sir."

"Dear me, dear me. And what do you suppose they would say if they knew?"

"I don't think they would say anything."

"Oh, come, come. Do you mean to infer they would have no objection?"

"No, I don't think so, sir."

"I see. Most extraordinary. Well, I think it my duty to write to them. As you know we do not look with favour upon the Roman persuasion here. I shall write to your parents. Meanwhile I shall give you another week to consider what I can only describe as a most unfortunate decision."

If Ronald had confessed to a dreadful disease the Headmaster could

137

not have been more horrified. In fact, in the Head's eyes, he had confessed to one, for he was suffering from the insidious disease of heresy.

But there was no need for Ronald to think it over. That week was waste of time. He had arrived at this conclusion, which so shocked the Headmaster, by a process much more sure and compelling in such a connection than any amount of thought, through his instincts and emotions. For, unlike me, Ronald was instinctively deeply religious in an intense and emotional way. He had a personal God and believed the Bible literally. For him the miracles were fact beyond argument. Not beyond reason, as Chesterton has said, but beyond ratiocination. He believed that his God did intervene actively in the affairs of mankind, and, believing that, there was nothing unreasonable to him in supposing that God could irrupt into the profound and inflexible verities of science even to the extent of making the sun to stand still or of bringing about a virgin birth. His was a mystic and unshakeable faith, and I am bound to say that he, as are all others like him, was strengthened and made happy by it. In later life no doubt he found it a rod to lean upon which agnostics such as myself sadly lack, and even, indeed, sometimes cry out for. And, like many emotional spirits, he was drawn towards the Roman Catholic Church by its very mysticism, by its colour, its magic and its glamour, and by the triumphs in art and music which the human spirit has achieved in its name. But a burning desire to make converts possessed him. He itched to proselytize. And, since I was his new-found friend, his greatest wish at this time was to convert me. He found it hard going, I am afraid. He talked to me earnestly about it and pressed upon me little leather-bound books, his "pi-books," as the other boys called them. I had never before met anyone who felt at all strongly on this subject which I somehow conceived as being reserved for clergymen. One just took it all for granted. I was a shallow little boy and grossly lazy intellectually, as I still am. I hated having to think about things. I do not care for it much even now and would far rather other and more gifted people thought for me. But as Ronald talked about the glamour and mystery of his church and the perpetual wonder of the Mass I was forced to reflect in a dim sort of way about what he was saying. I was surprised to find myself shrinking from it. I found I did not want to imagine Church as anything other than I already knew it, something holy and remote from life, but very, very familiar, something filled with a peace that was mine alone. So the scent of eau-de-Cologne and camphor and leather, long loved and recognized, like the smell of earth and fields far out at sea, came back to me with a strength of which I had never thought them capable. The sorrowful figures with hands upraised, the homely sweet words I already knew, leapt into my mind, as they do now, from some recess where they must have lodged deep without my knowing, —"Grant us the kindly fruits of the earth so that in due time we may enjoy them." "The Author of Peace and Lover of Concord, whose service is perfect freedom." "Let your light so shine before men." All these came pouring into my mind in a torrent. I found that Church— with a capital C—had become part of me. It was and is in my blood. So I never read those little books which Ronald left by my bedside or slipped into my locker, and though I dare say this was largely due to laziness it was not entirely so. It was the tall pillars branching above my head and those gentle figures with their perpetual benediction.

The Headmaster held his Confirmation classes in one of the class-rooms. He held them without Ronald but with me. Ronald's father had written, to the further disgust of the Head, that his son might please himself, and Ronald, in the Head's eyes, was consigned to eternal damnation. "In other words," Ronald explained, "my old man doesn't care a damn. He hasn't been inside a church himself for twenty years."

So one evening a week I and about fifteen others gathered in one of the classrooms and were excused prep. The Headmaster seated himself on a chair in front of us, not on the dais beside the desk but on the floor of the room, in order, we thought, to make us feel more at home, to impart an air of intimacy to the proceedings. At first we rather enjoyed the novelty of these sessions, although they usually began, as any session with the Head was apt to, with an embarrassing few minutes over a dead beetle. Also they were a means of escaping prep once a week. This gave us a sense of importance and of being slightly apart from the others. If the absence of any of us from prep were noticed on these evenings the answer, to which there was no effective reply, was "Confirmation class, sir." And if, the following day, we were called upon to translate or to recite something we were supposed to have learnt the previous evening, the same effective retort provided a means of escape. Thus we were distinguished from the common herd who still had to do prep or to get up and construe or recite while we listened.

"Lucky blighter!" the others whispered. "Wish I could go to Confirmaggers again myself."

After the Head had disposed of the beetle and lamented, rather more gently than usual, our obtuseness and lack of understanding of beetles, he began to talk. He talked for about three-quarters of an hour in the chapel variation of his voice, a slight additional unction reserved, apparently, for religious occasions. He kept his chin sunk upon his white nonconformist tie as he always did when he said prayers. A short prayer ended the proceedings and we had to turn round and kneel in our desks with our elbows on the seat, an act of almost acrobatic difficulty. Then we were released and went clattering down the stone stairs, glorying in the abandonment of having done no prep. And I very much doubt if any of the fifteen of us gave the matter another thought for a week, except to pipe "Confirmation, sir!" in a tone of evil triumph when asked for our prep next day.

But after six or seven of these evenings I began to enjoy them less. A suspicion began to grow that nothing at all was happening to me. These talks, the Head explained unctuously, were meant to prepare us for the Laying on of Hands, an outward and visible sign of an inward and spiritual grace. And, after each class, when I was in bed and the dormitory was silent, I tried to make myself feel prepared for grace. I failed. Nothing seemed to come. I usually fell asleep in the attempt and dreamt that I was at home under the beech-tree. I never heard anyone discuss the subject and no one seemed to take it very seriously. I once tried to open a discussion with a member of the class but could get no more out of him than that he couldn't see why we shouldn't have a real Bishop, like last year, instead of only a Suffragan which wasn't the same thing at all. I began to get the idea that neither I nor any of the others had a notion of what the Head was talking about. The light . . . the word . . . the entry of the Holy Ghost. "You see that gas jet," he explained as we gazed at the bubbling gas mantel above our heads, "you can imagine God like that. The power, the light and the heat, three in one. None can exist without the other." We were empty vessels into which the Word was about to be poured like a refreshing stream. The Church was the trunk of a tree of which God was the root and we the branches. And so on. And soon I began to wonder whether the Head, for all the unction of his voice, really believed this either. Perhaps it was the very unction with which he told us all these things which made me begin to doubt whether he really believed them.

I wrote to my mother secretly: "Need I be confirmed? I don't think I want to after all."

Apart from my doubts and the feeling of emptiness there was another and more earthly consideration which was turning me against the approaching event. It was being presented to me as a kind of public performance on my part. I began to dread it. I had stage fright. It was to be something I had to do in front of an audience, one which I imagined would be about as hostile and critical as any could be, an audience of my own school mates. The chapel would be filled with unforgiving eyes. The Headmaster began to introduce into his talks a great deal about procedure and deportment until soon they seemed to be more important than anything else connected with the ceremony. Later there were to be rehearsals in the empty chapel. The occasion, in fact, began to assume frightening proportions. I conceived a dislike for the whole business and wrote again more urgently as though I were about to undergo a critical surgical operation.

The Headmaster sent for me again about a week before the event. All preparations and arrangements had already been made for it. He was less benign this time. A wave of disapproval seemed to advance towards me across the disarray of books and papers on his table, where I caught sight of a letter in my mother's writing. He did not ask me if I were happy.

"Your mother writes that you do not wish to be confirmed after all," he said.

"Yes, sir," I replied feeling small and guilty.

"I understand you do not feel prepared yet to receive grace."

The use of that somehow incongruous expression made me immediately feel relieved and guilty no longer.

"Yes, sir. I mean—no, sir."

"I do not, of course, wish to press you, although I think you might have arrived at this decision sooner. It would have saved a very great deal of inconvenience since I must now tell the Bishop there will be another candidate less and we have lost two already through sickness. However, this is a decision you must, of course, make for yourself. I think, perhaps, it would be better to leave the matter until you are a little older. You may go."

As I left the study disapproval followed me out of the room.

My mother had written that I did not really seem to understand the confirmation classes. She could hardly have said anything more unfortunate and when I learnt of it, a long time afterwards, I understood the full measure of disapproval I had earned from the Headmaster. I had indeed fallen from grace. He was gravely disappointed in me. He never again asked me if I were happy, never again stopped me in the quadrangle and placed his hand upon my shoulder. He never again drew me towards him affectionately in the dormitory. And for this I was not altogether sorry. At the end of the term he wrote in my report, under the heading "Comments"—"He is in danger of becoming a dull and uninteresting boy."

XIV

RONALD vanished. I never properly understood why or how. It was as though he had been spirited away. It seemed to be somehow part of a general upheaval which took place one winter term and which shook our little world to its foundations. I hovered only on the fringe of the general whirlpool and was never very clear what it was all about. It drew into its vortex several familiar figures and Ronald, apparently, among them. However, I got a certain amount of rather pleasurable excitement out of the rumours and counter-rumours that flew about, and a sense of heightened importance from handing them on, slightly enlarged. I enjoyed the diminutive part in the drama that was allotted to me. Rumour said that several boys had been expelled.

It was considered a shameful thing to be expelled. It meant that you had committed an offence so heinous that not even a beating, that universal panacea, would meet the case. You were sent home in secret, without ceremony and with dishonour. Nevertheless, I used to reflect, you were sent home. It meant that never again could you go to school because no school would ever accept you, though whether that was altogether a bad thing I was not so sure.

Ronald's bed in the dormitory was empty one night and his household gods—his little pi-books, his volume of Keats and the photograph of his mother when young (one presumed)—had disappeared. The bed continued empty and the place that was his knew him no more. All inquiries as to his whereabouts only elicited a mysterious silence. And, when the Headmaster came up to the dormitory one evening and I was rash enough to ask him directly where my friend had gone, an astonishing, an unprecedented thing happened. The old man boxed my ears and strode out of the room.

I had lost a friend again. But I was no longer so alone as I would have been if this had happened a few terms earlier, for slowly, and despite my many handicaps, I had begun to make other friends and other contacts. My circle was enlarging. Further I am sorry to admit that my friendship with Ronald was beginning to cool off just a little. After all the company of a genius is bound to be exhausting and exhausted I was becoming.

I had no doubt whatever that Ronald was a literary genius. Neither had he. In the early days of our friendship I abandoned myself to wholehearted admiration of his literary prowess. No brighter star had ever shone in my sky. For hours during our walks about the fields and lanes

I listened with content to the recital of his compositions. They grew longer and longer and more and more ambitious. My admiration and rapture were considerably enhanced by the fact that I understood hardly anything he wrote. For the more ambitious his efforts grew the more loftily obscure they became. The more obscure they were the more I was entranced.

"You probably won't understand this," the genius would say magnificently. "But I may as well read it to you."

And read it he did, always being careful that there was no one near but me, his humble admirer, to overhear him. In the warm sun of my admiration and flattery Ronald's belief in his own splendour as a star in the literary firmament grew steadily. It became a conviction. He was soon very vain. His was the throne among the immortals now and I gave up all attempts to compete for it. I began to look on Perseus with awakened eyes. How paltry an offering, I thought.

Needless to say Ronald was not a genius at all but an immature schoolboy like myself. He had a flair for rhyme and a seeing eye. Everything he wrote, as was natural, was derivative, a copy of whatever he was reading at the time, and he read extensively. "Now this is rather Byronic, don't you think?" he would say, and "Doesn't this put you in mind of Browning?" Of course I thought so, and of course it did—only it was much, much better. Only slowly did I begin to feel slightly fatigued by the company of such enormous genius, slightly out of breath and unable quite to keep up. So I began to seek the company of others who were less uncomfortably brilliant, more on my own level. Slowly, after this, I began to suspect my idol of having feet of clay. I think perhaps he disappeared just in time.

However, no friendship is without profit and one never comes away empty-handed from contact with any human being. Ronald pricked for me, in the dark veil which education was wrapping around me, a pinhole through which I looked into a magic country. For I began to read other things than those which flowed from the apparently inexhaustible springs of Ronald's inspiration. I began to read them on my own account, in spite of Bobbie's English lessons, at first to see if they compared at all with Ronald's and presently for their own sake. I think Ronald began to diminish in stature for me from the day when I read the "Ode to the Nightingale" in the little volume of Keats by his bedside.

Although I have never been a wide reader of poetry I did thus acquire, largely from the time of my school friendship with Ronald, a love for a few English poets. I learnt to listen to the voice of my country singing, a voice as soft and gentle, it seemed, as her green fields. The number of voices has grown slightly with the years but not really very much. I have forgotten more than I have remembered. Yet what I do remember is very dear to me. It is filled with "the wistfulness that is the past" like the memories of my old home. Indeed certain lines and certain words bring to my mind an image of tenderness and beauty that is hardly to be borne. The magic of words is inseparable from their meaning and lies in the infinite variety and inflections of meaning they convey. They must call up in my mind such an image otherwise they have no more value for me than the noise made by a child with two sticks on a drum. Oddly enough the same words always call up in my mind the same image. It is, I suppose, my own peculiar vision. It remains the same however often I repeat the words and no one else can share it. And so it must be for each one of us. When we say:

> Marshalled under moons of harvest
> Stand still all night the sheaves,

there arises in the mind's eye a picture complete in every detail. For me it is always the same one. The same sheaves I see stacked in that very field, silent in the moonlight. Only I know that brooding quiet and that suspense for only my ghost has walked by moonlight across those nameless uplands. No one else has been there—not even the author himself. They were other fields he trod.

Some passages are so full of this compelling music and call up so powerful an image that they run in my head like a tune. For days together I cannot get them out of my head and I repeat them over and over again to myself as one might hum constantly a snatch of song. They accompany me through the humdrum waking hours and fill them at each repetition with the same fugitive vision.

> It was the nightingale, and not the lark,
> That pierced the fearful hollow of thine ear;
> Nightly she sings on yon pomegranate tree.

And wherever I am, whatever I may be doing, I am again at that same tall window, looking upon a twilight garden. From the same tree upon a grass plot the bird sings and two lovers lift their heads from their unending embrace to listen. It is always so. And no doubt that is the reason why my masters' verdicts were so often, "Does not concentrate." And why when I left school and went into business in the City I was a dismal failure. I was listening to the nightingales. And now, nearly in middle life, "still are my pleasant voices, my nightingales awake."

Yet to much poetry I must confess that I have remained deaf, as I have to much music, and now I think there is little likelihood of my ears being opened further. Although when I say:

Ere the high lawns appeared
under the opening eyelids of the morn—

or listen to the "Emperor Concerto" there comes that thrill of joy and that extraordinary sense of completeness and fulfilment which, as Somerset Maugham says, all beauty brings, yet in my case the number of such experiences is limited. I have read and heard a good deal but forgotten more. I look through a tiny peep-hole into Heaven. Perhaps if Ronald had not unaccountably vanished from my sight at that critical moment I should now have a wider view. On the other hand, perhaps it is as well that he vanished when he did. Disillusionment was setting in. I was slowly making the desolating discovery that my friend was not a genius after all. "Laughter holding both his sides" was beginning to be present on our walks and was uncomfortably close when Ronald said, "I don't suppose you'll understand it, but I may as well read it." I had to admit the possibility that he might be, what I now realize he must have been, a vain and self-opinionated boy. But it was largely my fault that he was so. Many years afterwards I found in a bookshop, and bought, a thin volume of verses bearing a well-remembered name long buried in the mists of time. What distant echoes came to me as I read! But the admiration I had once felt was gone, even though I could understand, if anything, less than I had those many years ago the slick and workmanlike lines. So perhaps it was as well that Ronald vanished when he did. It was as though he died and it was, after all, a timely death.

How diligently one may search for truth and yet not find it, even though it seems to be plain enough to others! All the Headmaster's patient inquiries, all his peering into childish eyes and laying of paternal hands on thin shoulders, failed to reveal to him that there were boys who were not deliriously happy under his rule. Nor could all his puritanism make little angels of them. This harsh truth was only brought home to him when one of the boys ran away. Certain other facts about life in the little world he ruled over apparently came to light at the same time. It was a cruel and bitter blow. And because it was so sudden and blinding the truth had an explosive effect. Our world blew up as though a bomb had landed in its midst.

The boy ran away from school because he was unhappy. I was unhappy myself at times too. I would not go back to school for all the wealth in the world. One of the compensations about being no longer young is that life has ceased to be frightening—anyhow, not as alarming as it was at school. It is no longer a sort of continuous obstacle race. The days no longer bring an apparently unending series of hazards to be surmounted and ordeals to be endured. They follow one another more smoothly. I was fortunate at school in that I carried about with me an inward happiness. I felt the beauty of my youthful world more subconsciously but, I think, more keenly than I feel that of my world of later years. My capacity for enjoyment was greater. That sense of fulfilment was easier to attain. Life was more of an affair of contrasts, brilliant high-lights and sombre shadows, and I had that realm of the imagination into which I was constantly retiring. Nevertheless, in my happiest moments, and they were not a few and usually came when I was alone or with Ronald, there was always some fly in my ointment, something just ahead to be got over somehow. Beyond each of these hazards I seemed to see the days stretching ahead unclouded and serene. But other mountains and new precipices, it seemed, were always leaping up before me out of nothing. On the other hand, in the dark moments there were gleams of sunshine of my own manufacture. I was never utterly miserable nor utterly alone. So that at the worst I only toyed in a vague sort of way with the idea of running away. I comforted myself with pictures of the horror and consternation it would cause the authorities if I did so, but I knew in my heart I had not the courage. For one thing it meant setting the whole giant apparatus of authority at defiance. Most of us when we are young have a deep awe of authority as such. Kindly old clergymen are terrible deities armed with mysterious powers. Amiable policemen, who cultivate their allotments and enjoy their pint of mild, embody the merciless machinery of government. I should never have dared to pit myself against these majestic forces. Nor should I ever have dared to launch myself alone into that vast world beyond the school gates. Though at one time my own home and its environs had been all of the world I knew, my horizon had now enlarged somewhat to embrace the school with its neighbouring fields and lanes. But beyond them were other fields and other lanes stretching into the distance over the familiar skyline, unknown and therefore forbidding, hostile. Beyond the village and the cross-roads on the hill wound other roads shimmering into unknown distances, dwindling down to nightmare perspectives of hedge and telegraph pole, overshadowed by unfamiliar trees. Beyond them were undiscovered hills. Odd that so gentle and English a landscape should have been so full of nameless terrors. I should never have dared to set out, like Childe Roland, upon such an adventure into the unknown. Therefore I rather admired the boy who ran away for the excellent reason that he was unhappy. I was sorry for him too. The terrors that dwelt in the fields beyond the horizon were evidently nothing to those he must have been enduring in our midst. He had done a desperate and defiant thing, something I did not dare do. He had put the all-powerful authorities in a fine flutter, as I had often vainly imagined myself fluttering them. Yet even so, I reflected more soberly and in justification of my own lack of prowess, he was found after three days wandering cold and hungry on a common ten miles away. He was glad when they found him.

On the day when the boy who ran away was found exhausted and very hungry on the common the Headmaster announced at morning prayers that he wished to see the whole school in the junior schoolroom at noon. We knew that something big was impending because it was only on the gravest occasions that the whole school was assembled and addressed by the Head. This meant that the hour of lessons before lunch would be cut short so it was an ill wind that blew nobody good. There was a feeling of expectancy, slightly pleasurable, when we took our places in the schoolroom and watched the boys from the other houses troop in. They crowded in until there was scarcely a square inch vacant in the great bare room. They stood packed along the wall spaces and sat jammed together like sardines in the rows of desks. All the masters were present, sitting in the front rows and looking solemn and portentous. Of the three raised desks that faced us under the windows the middle one was vacant for the Headmaster. The senior housemasters occupied the others. Bobbie was one of these, viewed as a mournful bust from where I sat with Ronald next to me, since I could only see his head and shoulders above the edge of the desk. He seemed about to burst into tears. In the very front under the central desk was a bench occupied by only four boys, the prisoners at the bar. They sat there, as prisoners might in the dock, conscious of being the centre of interest but apprehensive, nervous, fidgeting. We peered at them with morbid interest, those at the back craning their necks to get a better view as a crowd cranes and peers forward at a street accident to get a better view of the victim. I watched each one of the four narrowly to see how he behaved. One of them was Lester, my old enemy. Although he had long ago ceased to bother me he was evidently still at it. He

looked a little frightened and furtive now, I thought, but pleased to be
the centre of attraction and to be occupying so much of the centre of
the stage. He fingered his tie and kept glancing sideways around him
searching for a friendly eye. He would have liked to grin or wink at
somebody, anybody really—even me, perhaps—to show that he didn't
care and was not ashamed. He wanted to find in a grin or a wink returned
some hint of sympathy and support, like a hand stretched out to clasp.
But all the eyes avoided his or returned blank stares which implied
betrayal and desertion. Had he been older he might have known they
would. Next to him was a small red-faced boy with jet black hair and
bright brown eyes, a gamin whose face was alive with mischief but not
with malice. He liked tormenting small boys for the same reason that
all of us in our time have enjoyed pulling the legs off flies or chopping
the heads off wasps. It was fun to see them buzz around in futile circles.
But as often he furiously defended one who had an instant earlier been
his victim, charging at the enemy with head down and fists whirling so
that his timorous hangers-on were in constant and perilous uncertainty
as to which side he would be on next. One never knew with him. He
seemed to be always fighting and was always in conflict with authority
with which his life was a ceaseless one-sided battle. I have no doubt
it still is. There was no sign of either fear or shame about him as he sat
in front of us, a prisoner at the bar awaiting sentence. His hands were
clasped, his elbows resting on his knees, while his eyes, bright and
defiant as ever, gazed at the floor between his feet and looked neither to
right nor to left, seeking no support and asking no favours. The third
prisoner had sandy hair and pale eyes and a quiff of hair that stood
straight up from his forehead. He was trembling a little and looked,
I noticed with clandestine glee, not far from tears. Could such a
thing be possible—he, who had so often jeered at me because mine
came easily? I do not remember the fourth prisoner but I searched all
their faces eagerly for tears, that ultimate confession of weakness, as I
once saw some small boys at a boxing match eagerly looking for blood.
As blood was part of the show then so tears were part of the show now.
I wanted to see how soon these formidable figures, whom I myself had
feared, these arms of the unwritten law, would be reduced to the common
ground of tears. For tears were like death. They were the leveller to
which we could all be reduced at last, some soon, some late. Then all
dignity and grandeur fled away. They deserted you. It was no use
pretending any more.

The subdued buzz of conversation in the big room fell silent when
the housemasters took their places. Presently, after a hushed expectant

interval, the Headmaster came in wearing his mortar-board and gown. We all stood.

"You may be seated," said the Headmaster.

He took his stand behind the central desk, looking around upon his audience for a moment or two in silence.

"Yesterday afternoon," he said, "one of my boys—your schoolfellows—was found wandering in a desolate place ten miles away from here. He was found by the police. He was utterly tired out and hungry. He had run away from the school because he found life here, among you, no longer tolerable. You can imagine what sort of a step this was for a schoolboy to take. We naturally felt it our duty to try to get his story from him and I must tell you that it was only with the very greatest difficulty that we were able to induce him to tell us what had driven him to take the step he did. He told us only with extreme reluctance. I am glad myself to think that one of my boys should have shrunk from betraying his schoolmates, even in the face of such temptation and such pressure as we eventually had to bring to bear upon him. However, the boy's parents and I have now wrung from him the fact that his life was made a misery for him during the two months he has been here. You, who are supposed to be Britishers and gentlemen, drove him out from among you. I wish every single one of you in this room to bear a share of this disgrace. On the other hand our inquiries have brought to light the names of certain prime instigators in what I can only call this systematic persecution. They are the names of the four boys you see sitting here in front of you. I have called you together to let you see them. They have disgraced the name of your school, your name, and brought dishonour upon it. Before you all I am going to administer justice by inflicting a public punishment upon these four boys. Will the Captain of the School please fetch the instrument?" the Head concluded. "It is in the library."

I dare say all that the Head had told us was true. No doubt it was disgraceful. But my pity and sneaking admiration for the boy who ran away evaporated as I listened to this somewhat ponderous address. For he had committed the unforgivable offence. He had sneaked. I also, I thought, had been through this and no one had been publicly or privately chastised on my behalf. I had stuck it and had not sneaked. Nor, I boasted to myself, would any amount of pressure have made me do so. I wonder.

But he was an unattractive boy, insignificant and grubby, one of those beings whose misfortune it is to arouse the bully in others. You meet these people constantly throughout life but you learn to be careful of them. You learn to regard their dependence, their horrible humility and dimness, their lack of spirit as so many traps to ensnare you into a betrayal of your better self. You exercise upon yourself a continual brake because you know that if you let your impatience get out of hand it might burst the barriers of adult reserve and make you presently ashamed. But when you are a schoolboy you have not acquired reserve, you have no dignity, no shame. If your easy antipathies are aroused you let them rip and lack of resistance on the part of your enemy goads you to further fury. You keep on until his miserable spirit is aroused. But the boy who ran away had little spirit, or so I thought until at last, driven to a frenzy, he showed what spirit he had by being found on a common ten miles away hungry and tired out. Boys are merciless but life at school is only life in miniature and that is merciless too. I myself often assisted in what the Headmaster called "this systematic persecution" because I was merciless also and because, no doubt, I was cowardly and treacherous. I wanted to be on the popular side. More stalwart figures than I have shown that weakness in the life of which school is a miniature. So, when the others were at the game, I often joined them and added my horrid shrill piping to the general chorus—"Pff! What a stink! Oh! No wonder! Look who's here! Why don't you wash?" But our poor victim lacked those inner springs of happiness which had helped me not so much to resist but to remain not utterly cast down. He had no reserves in himself. He gave way to orgies of self-abasement and self-pity. The more he abased himself the more fun it was for his tormentors. But sometimes I would come upon him alone in the changing-room or in the lavatory, weeping bitterly. There, among the sweaty clothes and old socks, he would retire to weep his heart out. Then I would feel a stab of remorse. On one occasion I found him thus and put a hand on his shoulder.

"It's all right," I said, gently but awkwardly, for it obviously wasn't all right at all. "It's only fun, you know."

But he would not be comforted by me, which was hardly surprising, and only sobbed all the more with his thin shoulders shaking and his face buried in the tail of someone's cricket shirt.

"Oh! Go away! Go away! For God's sake leave me alone! Oh, please leave me alone!"

And I went away feeling now the first pricks of shame. I do not think I joined with the crowd so much after that. When he ran away I secretly admired him.

In the few minutes of silence, while the Captain of the School was out of the room, the Headmaster kept his eyes on the desk. He drummed gently on its edge with his fingers. Once or twice he cleared his throat, lifting his hand each time to his mouth with a wave of his black-gowned sleeve, like a huge bird flapping its wings. The rows of boys looked fixedly at him and from him to the four prisoners at the bar, as a jury looks anxiously from the judge to the dock for a hint to help them to a verdict. Presently the prefect returned with a long and formidable cane. He carried it reverently like a mace-bearer.

The Headmaster spoke the name of each of the four prisoners who, in his turn, stepped to the desk, bent forward and received six sharp cuts across the backside. The Headmaster favoured vertical rather than oblique or horizontal strokes and the cane made a satisfying swishing sound through the air at each cut. When the turn of the fourth prisoner came the executioner, I thought, was showing signs of fatigue. He was breathing a little heavily. Obviously he was not sorry when he had dealt out the full two dozen. A little short of breath he handed the instrument back to the prefect.

"Take it back to my study," he said and paused for a few moments to recover.

I had seen, and suffered, so many executions both public and private that this present occasion rather lacked novelty, as indeed it did for all of us. It was distinguished only by the pomp and ceremony with which it was carried out. The execution itself was probably a good deal less severe than many others we had witnessed on less portentous occasions. One felt that on such an occasion as this some heavier punishment would have been more fitting. A mere beating, only different from others in being administered by the Head, was not really enough. Now, if they could have been bastinadoed or burnt at the stake, for instance——

"I have publicly punished these four boys," the Head resumed, fixing them with a severe look as they sat writhing from the smart of the blows they had just received, "because, in the first place, I did not wish to bring the name of the school into disrepute by expelling them. Secondly, because I think and hope that the dishonour of this occasion will remain with them and be a lesson to them and to any other boy who may have thought of following their example. Let them remember who it was who said 'Whosoever hath done this unto the least of these my little ones, the same hath done it also unto Me.' But let me conclude with this warning. If any cases of deliberate bullying come before me again, I will instantly expel the culprits, no matter who or how many they may be."

Then he left the desk and, with his gown flowing, swept from the room.

On the faces of the four culprits I looked for signs of proper repentance and shame. I looked for tears but saw none. Lester's bearing was nearest to a confession that he was a mortal boy like the rest of us, that his soul could be reached through the seat of his trousers. He writhed slightly as he sat and, with pursed lips, was evidently forcing back the tears. He fidgeted more nervously with his tie. The black-haired boy was again gazing at the floor between his knees but his eyes seemed to have retreated into his head where they burnt like coals and were quite dry. The other two were sitting a little delicately on their smarting posteriors but all their eyes were dry and unrepentant.

When the audience broke up and began trooping out of the room, little circles of admirers crowded round the four.

"I say! Did it hurt?"

"Were you padded?"

"By Jove! You stuck it jolly well!"

"Christmas! I wouldn't care for six with that thing."

"What was it like?"

They had become heroes. There was no dishonour: there was admiration, almost envy. There was no feeling of sympathy for the boy who ran away. He was a sneak anyhow. The Headmaster's justice had miscarried; all his words were forgotten, if they had not indeed fallen on deaf ears. My sense of the Headmaster's failure was complete.

Two days later Bobbie sent for me in his room overlooking the quadrangle. It was as much a housemaster's room as the Headmaster's study was a headmaster's room. It was the room of a man all of whose later years had been dedicated to youth. Photographs of boys who had left, boys now launched into life, stood thickly upon the mantelpiece. Under their faces, grave or gay, were sprawled their not quite mature signatures. Some, the later ones, were in uniform for they had been launched not so much into life as into death. Some of those English faces were already trampled into Flanders mud. On the walls were groups—photographs of football and cricket teams. You could pick out the same boys among those rows, arms folded, frowning ferociously. There were etchings of Oxford colleges—Magdalen Tower, Christ Church Quadrangle. Along one wall a pair of oars was suspended crosswise, varnished and decorated with names in gilt lettering, a tasselled cap at their intersection. There was a roll-topped desk, an overfilled bookcase, a rack of pipes, shabbily comfortable arm-chairs, the Hermes of Praxiteles. Bobbie stood in front of the fire slowly filling a pipe from a pouch, my favourite master, of whom I was not afraid, a man loved by the young like Socrates.

"Come in and sit down," he said, looking mournfully over his glasses and continuing to fill his pipe. He struck a match and lit it, puffing slowly. Clouds of grey smoke ascended and hung about his head. He waved the match in the air to extinguish it and threw it into the fire.

"I have sent for you, my boy," he said at last, "because I want to talk to you. I think you have moral courage. No—don't say anything. I am getting an old man, you know, and when a man who has been a schoolmaster as long as I have reaches my age—well, he is not such a fool as he looks." And he smiled, pausing to perform that baffling manœuvre with his glass eye.

"Now, I think you might be able to help me. I want you to use the influence which I believe you have. I believe it because I keep my eyes open. But I do not, as some people are kind enough to suggest, go about spying on the boys in my house. I do not set traps for them either. All I do is to ask boys, who I think capable of being an influence for good in the house, to use that influence as much as they can. Do you understand?"

"Yes, sir. Thank you, sir." I had no idea what he was talking about.

"Now I want you to help me to improve the tone of this house. There is a good deal going on here that must stop. I need not enlarge on it. You know what I mean. I want you to use your influence and the moral courage I believe you to have to help in checking it. Will you do that?"

"Oh, yes, sir," I said, flattered and eager, but totally in the dark.

"Good, I felt sure you would. I shall be very grateful. I've spoken to several other boys on this subject but I think it better not to tell you who they are. Thank you, my boy, that will be all for the present. And, er—do you remember any of your *Hamlet*?"

"Yes, sir. I think so, sir."

"Well then, repeat from 'The friends thou hast and their adoption tried.'"

I stood up and put my hands behind me in the Shakespearean attitude of schoolboys.

> "'The friends thou hast and their adoption tried,
> Grapple them to thy soul with hoops of steel:
> But do not dull thy palm with entertainment
> Of each new-hatched, unfledged comrade. Beware—'"

"Very good, my boy. You may go—and don't forget what Polonius said. It is very sound advice."

Outside in the passage I stopped dead, pondering. This was the most mysterious interview I had ever had. Somehow I thought it must be connected with the public execution I had witnessed the other day, but yet I could not quite make it fit. I was by no means innocent myself in that direction. An influence for good? Moral courage? What on earth did it all mean? I was utterly mystified but at the same time glowing with pride and satisfied vanity that my favourite master should have said these flattering things about me. I had moral courage and I was an influence for good. I must be if Bobbie said so. And yet I was no good at games. I was not much good in class. And yet—well, whatever it was all about I had that. With my breast swelling, my head high, I went down to the schoolroom and tried to exude a beneficial influence.

"What did Bobbie want you for?"

"Aha!" I said with a baffling air of mystery and self-importance. "Wouldn't you like to know?"

I wrote home to my mother the following Sunday, "The house-master said I had Moral Courage and was an Influence for Good. I don't quite know what he meant but that's what he said."

"I am so glad your housemaster thinks so well of you," Mother replied. "Moral courage is sometimes more useful than the other sort, you know."

For several days after this I went about like a sleuth, my ears pricked, my eyes (so I thought) sharp as rapiers. My Influence exuded from me at every pore, if only someone could have noticed it. I looked eagerly for some opportunity to use my Moral Courage. Yet life continued its apparently even tenor. Nothing happened which could possibly give occasion for the use of my remarkable gifts. How, I wondered, could I improve the tone of the house? In the first place, what was it anyway? And in the second, what was wrong with it? Life seemed to be exactly the same as before.

No—not quite. Two evenings later Ronald said:

"Will you always remember me?"

"Why, yes. Of course."

"I hope so."

"Why do you say that?"

"Oh, nothing."

Next day he vanished.

Three days later, when the Head came into the dormitory, I said: "Please, sir. What's happened to Ronald, sir?"

An astonishing thing happened. The Head took two steps towards me, gripped me by the shoulders and boxed my ears.

"Mind your own business!" he said, and strode out of the room.

Perhaps, I reflected, I had too much moral courage.

XV

ALONG khaki column wound out of the school gates and down the hill. It was about the oddest collection of soldiers who ever struggled into the King's uniform. It began well enough with Company Sergeant-Major Taylor but it tapered away, like one of the prehistoric reptiles, to a laughable and pathetic tail. The tail was Corporal Thomas's section.

At the head of the column was the band with its drums led by the company sergeant-major. It was so martial in appearance that it drew a murmur of applause from the little knot of people who had gathered at the gate to see the O.T.C. march away. But they smiled when the tail of the procession passed them for these were the smallest and the youngest soldiers, half the size of those in front. They looked like goblins. They seemed all head and feet because their peaked caps and their boots were so much too big. They stepped out with exaggerated strides in their efforts to keep up, lips pursed with the gallant exertions they were making beneath the weight of rifles that seemed like tree-trunks.

Sergeant-Major Taylor swung out of the gate and down the hill at the head of his company. His chest was thrown out as though trying to burst his shining buttons. His boots gleamed as only a professional soldier can make them gleam. So did his glossy leather belt. His puttees were exactly rolled to a fraction of an inch with the point directed backwards on the outside of the calf precisely where it should be. He carried a silver-headed malacca cane under his arm.

"Company! Right whe-e-el!"

Above the rhythmic beat of two hundred boots his voice could be heard like a trumpet diminishing down the hill.

"Left! Left! Left-right-left! Pick 'em up there!"

Then, when clear of the gates, the band struck up and drowned it. It drowned all other sounds, the tramp of marching feet, the sound of voices from the people gathered by the roadside, the whisper of hoar frost falling from the bare branches of the elms, the note of the clock striking seven on a cold winter's morning. It drowned them all in the clatter of the kettledrums and the fifes.

Sergeant-Major Taylor, who was such a splendid figure on these occasions, was not at all awe-inspiring out of uniform. He was known as "Old Tails." No one could remember the time when his genial fatherly presence had not presided behind the counter in the tuck-shop and in the store. Every day at the same hours for many years he had dealt out buns and chocolate and ginger beer to succeeding generations. Boys pressed clamouring round the counter where he stood surrounded by these delicacies, their necks craned and hands outstretched, holding their money—twopence, threepence, even sixpence if they were rich. They were like hungry young birds, piping to be fed, and he was St. Francis, feeding them with buns and ginger beer and talking to them in the language they understood.

"Ginger beer and two buns please, Tails!"

"One bun and a plain bar and a ginger, Tails!"

"Hurry up, Tails, can't you? I've been here for hours. Two buns, please!"

"Now then, young gentlemen!" Tails kept saying from among his buns and bottles. "You've got all your lives before you. There's no hurry, gentlemen! No hurry at all! One bun and a plain bar? Fourpence. Thank you! Sixpence and two's change! Next gentleman! One ginger and two nut bars? Ninepence. A bob and three's change! I thank you. Don't push! You'll all get served in your turn. There's no call to push. And now the next gentleman? . . . "

The store, where Tails also ruled, reminded you of a Wild West serial with its wooden counter and shelves filled with an orderly disorder of caps, shirts, shoes in boxes, belts and coloured sports clothes. Old Tails had presided with easy geniality behind its counter for more years than any of his young customers could remember.

And no one could recall the day which had not been heralded from dormitory to dormitory and passage to passage by Old Tails with his terrible bell. For years its awakening clangour had shattered youthful dreams and ushered in days eagerly anticipated or fearfully dreaded, wet or fine. It brought them all with equal cruel impartiality. Every morning he strode into each room, ringing his bell and shouting in a voice of brass;

"Good morning, gentlemen! Good morning, gentleMEN! Come along now, please! Rise and shine! Half-past six and freezing hard. Come along now, gentlemen!"

The corpse-like figures in the beds stirred. A few sat up. A voice or two said faintly, "'Morning, Tails!" And then we heard his bell less loudly in other rooms along the passage, dealing roughly with the dreams of others, and his kindly but unwelcome voice; "Good morning, gentleMEN! Come along now, please!"

Tails was a fatherly and much-loved old soldier who had fought in the Boer War and several other minor remoter wars on the fringes of the Empire, which he had served faithfully and with pride before he retired and became the rough but genial father to us all. On most days of the week he wore shirt-sleeves and a baize apron, but his boots beneath the apron never lost their professional gloss. His ruddy face shone with health and good humour. There was a fresh scrubbed look about it. His white hair and moustache were always neatly clipped and brushed. But when the Corps paraded once a week he came again into his glory as a soldier with a row of ribbons on his chest. He issued his commands with a bark which had been heard on many parade grounds under many suns. Now he was in the evening of life and was too old for service, to his great chagrin, but according to his lights, he was doing his best to turn the young gentlemen into soldiers of the King. He was fitting them for the blood bath into which he would have eagerly plunged himself with all the unreflecting pride and devotion of an old soldier. He cursed his luck at missing it and envied us what he called "our chance."

"Finest life in the world—a soldier," he would tell us. "You young gentlemen don't know how lucky you are, comin' out for officers in the King's Army. Wish I had your chance. You wouldn't find me here long. I'd be back with the regiment to-morrow if I had my way. But as it is I'm a-goin' to teach you young gentlemen to be soldiers. Teach you to shoot straight and keep a stiff upper lip. Teach you that no British soldier ever got a wound in the back, that a British officer thinks of his men first and hisself last, never hits a brave enemy when he's down. Teach you to fear God but no man, honour the King, die for your country and keep your rifle clean."

All those gallant and upright illusions were his, the illusions of an old soldier who had never seen the war as it really was. He was of the school which, at the beginning of the war, had ordered "Officers should attend to their swords." He had a hard job with me, I'm afraid.

Old Tails, in his baize apron or barking in his sergeant-major's uniform, had watched several generations of young gentlemen, as he called them, pass through the school. There was a sameness about them all. They began as humble new bugs, glad of his rough kindness and sound advice. They became "bloods," splendid in their own eyes with turned-down collars and their coat tails pulled back. Then they would address him with familiar friendliness, pat him on his bald head and call him "Old Tails." Later they became prefects and adopted a lordly manner. "Oh, I say, Tails! Just oil my cricket bat for me, will you?" Many, from the humble beginnings he could remember, had become captains of the school, captains of their houses, captains of games, superb creatures, far above all others, who dined with the Headmaster and had their names in gilt letters in the dining hall. Cups bearing their names shone above the high table. He had watched them go out into life with the shrill applause of their admirers ringing in their ears. Years later he had welcomed them back with a laugh and a handshake. They were slightly paunchy now, not so light of step, with eyes less bright. They were growing bald and their hair was grey above the temples. They were unaffectedly glad to find Old Tails still there. And, strangely enough, glad once more to listen to his sound advice and grip that firm steady hand.

"Well, if it isn't Old Tails! Still the same as ever? Remember me?"

"Why, of course I do, sir. '07 you left wasn't it?"

"Dear me, yes. How time flies!"

After the sergeant-major in the procession on that cold morning came the band, making a stirring noise. The big drum in the middle seemed to overpower its bearer so that he leaned backwards under its bulk as he marched. With the full reach of his arm he could scarcely hit the centre. Over the smaller drums the sticks crossed and twirled. On the kettledrums they beat a deafening tattoo and rose repeatedly to the horizontal, level with eyes fixed in a stare of concentration. Cheeks, on which the down was just beginning to appear, bulged like balloons behind the bugles and the fifes. Behind the band came the three platoons, marching at the slope, eyes ahead, arms swinging like pistons to shoulder level, rhythmically in step. At the head of each platoon went the platoon commander—an English master, who thought about syntax and subordinate clauses on other days: a science master, at other times occupied with the specific heat of metals and the manufacture of marsh gas: a mathematics master ordinarily steeped in vulgar fractions. Now they were magically transformed into officers with peaked caps and swagger sticks. But somehow the most startling transformation of all was the company commander who stood by the side of the road with two pips on his sleeve and his swagger cane under his arm, his Sam Browne belt immaculately polished. Under the peaked cap the face that watched the files march past was melancholy and sorrowful. As Corporal Thomas's section passed him, struggling gallantly to keep up, the commanding officer removed his pince-nez and applied his handkerchief to his left eye. Was it to hide a smile? Perhaps he was thinking how young and little they were to be trained to die.

For the war was beginning to draw closer to the skinny little boys who made up Corporal Thomas's section, of whom I was one. It had at first been only something quite distant and remote which caused inexplicable worry to grown-up people. It made for a certain air of excitement and sent long columns of men marching down the road singing. Then there was the night when eight pyjama-clad figures had watched from the dormitory window the searchlights probing the sky. The long fingers stopped wheeling and met to hold in their intersection a small cigar-shaped object very high up and far away. Little points of light winked round it. Then it had suddenly become a small plume of flame and sank slowly below the level of the trees. Watching it sink slowly down one of the eight little boys, realizing that there were men inside it, drew in his breath and said "Oo—ooh!" Food became worse and scarcer at school and potatoes vanished. Growing boys felt hungrier and ran more often to the tuck-shop where Old Tails had less and less to sell. And now the war was drawing closer still, for they wore, after a fashion, the King's uniform. But it was not so close to the section as it was to Corporal Thomas himself, who was seventeen and would soon be called up, or to Sergeant Croft, who was the school captain and was leaving for the army at the end of that term. Yet close enough to make some at least of Corporal Thomas's section feel that they were being caught up in something vast and terrible from which there was no escape. In the breast of one of them a slight cold chill had begun to make itself felt, the first beginnings of a fear never expressed but never very far off, which grew and took shape as the months went by. "If the war lasts another eighteen months longer——" people said. And later, "Soon!" they said.

It was a cold, still, winter morning. The sky was pale and clear where a young moon floated, but the distances were veiled in a white mist. Hoar frost outlined the skeletons of the trees and fell with a dry occasional rustle to the ground. Telegraph wires looped from post to post in curtseying perspectives of white. A heavy fall of snow three days ago had partly thawed and then frozen again so that the roads were covered with a glassy film. Old dirty snow lay thickly heaped upon the roadside. In fields and gardens it lay untrodden but with a hard crust upon it. It was thin and patchy like an old cloth upon the swell of hills, worn into holes through which the frozen grass protruded like an old man's hair. The iron-bound winter landscape looked as though no green thing could ever sprout from it again. As we tramped through the village the smoke stood straight up from the chimneys and lay heavily above the roof-tops. A few women, opening their doors for the morning milk, looked up to see the army pass and smiled when they saw it. What funny little soldiers, they were thinking! A postman on his morning rounds dismounted from his bicycle and leaned upon the saddle to watch us go by. A dog or two ran out and barked. There were no other signs of life and a deep peace still lay over the village which had not yet properly awoken from its sleep. When we had gone through it on our way to the railway station the fields lay broad and silent about us under their tattered snow.

Corporal Thomas's section slipped and slithered in their clodhopping boots. Their breath soon began to puff from their pinched faces like steam from an engine. Drops hung from their noses. Onto the fingers that held the rifle butts the cold clamped invisible pincers. Long before the army reached the railway station Corporal Thomas's section was almost crying with the pain of clasping the cold metal. Suddenly one of the section, carried away by his unruly steel-shod boots, slipped and fell upon the road with a clatter of arms. He became a helpless khaki bundle in the middle of the road, unable to rise.

"Now then, Number Four! What the hell do you think you're playing at?" said the corporal angrily. "Get up there! Come on, get up!"

The bundle struggled to its feet and picked up its rifle. Running gingerly, his face pinched with cold and his nose dripping, Number Four caught up with the rest of the section and fell in once more with its exaggerated stride.

Corporal Thomas was a Welsh boy with soft brown eyes and a gentle manner into which he tried hard to infuse an artificial harshness when addressing his section. He conceived it to be soldierly to do so. But, however hard he tried, he found it difficult to keep the amused twinkle out of his eye or to keep his lips from betraying signs of unsoldierly amusement at the performances of what were, for convenience, known as "his men." He had an unenviable job. Into his care and tutelage came all the new recruits to the corps, the little hobgoblins with the enormous heads, projecting ears and unwieldy feet. He tried to make them form fours and march swinging their arms to their shoulders. After innumerable attempts he had some success at this but all his efforts could not make them cut their hair or polish their buttons. Their puttees came unrolled and entangled their feet as they marched. Their tunics were gathered into folds beneath the belts which encircled their little waists. Weighed down by their rifles they did arms drill under his sharp orders on the cricket field, but all his tutoring and repeated demonstrations could not make them handle their rifles smartly.

"Squad! Ser—lope hipe! One—two—three—as-you-were! Number Four! Don't crawl up your rifle like a slug! Bring it up smartly. Now watch me! Here, give me your rifle. Now look! One. Two. Three. Hit the bloody thing about as though you meant it. Now again —Squad! Ser—lope hipe! One—two—three—Oh, God!"

The last words would escape from him wearily after the tenth demonstration. But it was of no use for Number Four had difficulty in even lifting the rifle. Doing anything with it smartly was out of the question. And often, after twenty minutes' patient soldierly barking, the corporal would drop his harsh N.C.O.'s manner and smile wearily.

"Oh, all right. Never mind."

He could keep it up no longer.

On this particular day the miniature army, so varied and ill assorted, was about to take part in a special parade in the neighbouring market town. After an exciting journey by train, in a specially reserved coach, it would march ceremoniously, with the band playing, through the town, to the military barracks. There it would parade with other units from other schools. It would be inspected by a famous but superannuated general and then march past him. After that it would witness a mock battle and bayonet drill by troops undergoing training in the barracks —real soldiers being fattened for Moloch in the grim brick forcing-house upon the hill.

We had been practising our part in this performance for weeks, with all the necessary marching and countermarching, upon the cricket field. Bobbie, in his incongruous disguise as our commanding officer, had yesterday given us an address. On our smartness and bearing, he told us, depended the prestige of our unit and the honour of our school in the eyes of other units from other schools. We rose to the occasion. Put thus upon our mettle we had devoted hours to polishing our buttons in the schoolroom, shouting and whistling as we did so. Even the worst of Corporal Thomas's section made buttons shine and straps gleam. Those who usually blacked their boots with ink out of the desks used boot-polish, begged, borrowed or stolen, in the cause. Even Number Four made quite a show with his buttons. When the science master, who was the platoon commander, inspected us in the cold early morning before we started off, he stopped opposite me in mild astonishment. There was pleased surprise in his eye as it ran over my ill-fitting uniform.

"Very good leather, Number Four," he said, and passed on.

But it was for Bobbie's sake that I had rubbed it into that mahogany gloss. I did not want to let him down in the eyes of other Bobbies disguised as C.O.s from other schools. Nor did I want to bring upon his gentle head the displeasure of that famous, though superannuated, general.

The market town was up and about when we formed up in the station yard. Thin lines of passers-by, the idle and the curious, already numerous even at that early hour, stood on the pavement edge as the column

wound into the main street. The road was like glass beneath our feet
and still the smoke stood straight up into the cold air from all the chimneys. Sergeant-Major Taylor visibly impressed the crowd. How conscious he was of their admiring gaze! He threw out his chest even
further and shouted "Company! Right whe-e-el!" As we went up
the High Street the band played. People came out of shops and ran from
the side streets as people always do when soldiers are marching—even
little boys playing at soldiers. But a faint ripple of laughter ran along
the pavement edge, like the wash of a boat along the river bank, when
Corporal Thomas's section passed, struggling manfully along in the
rear. Urchins gathered and fell in step with us, marching along beside
us to the sound of the drums.

"Hi, soldier! What size hats d'yer wear?" they piped.

But in the middle of the High Street disaster overtook Number Four.
It marred the effect of the display. For he lost control of his boots once
more and fell, this time in full view of the crowd, with a clatter upon the
road. The tail of the procession passed on and left him lying, a helpless
bundle again, in the middle of the street. Corporal Thomas detached
himself and ran back, but before he could reach Number Four two kindly
women had run out from the pavement and lifted the bundle to its feet.
For them, in the instant that he fell, Number Four had ceased to be a
soldier marching and had become a little boy in boots much too big.
So do all women, watching their sons go off to war, remember them.

"Come on, Number Four! What the hell's the matter with you?"
said Corporal Thomas, his face flushed with anger and embarrassment.
"Pull yourself together for God's sake."

"I can't help it, Thomas," I said miserably, forgetting that he was a
corporal. "I can't help it. I slipped."

"Poor little soldier!" said the women. "There, there! It's a shame,
so it is."

Corporal Thomas was less sympathetic. He took me roughly by
the arm and dragged me slithering along with him to rejoin the rest of
the column, which was by now far down the street. The noise of the
band had grown faint in the distance. A swirl of followers had joined
in the rear of the procession and had closed in behind it. We had to
pass through them without dignity in order to catch up. As for Number
Four he felt keenly both the humiliation of being dragged along in this
unceremonious way and the greater disgrace of being picked up by the
two kind women.

"If you let us down I'll tan your backside when we get back!" said
the corporal suddenly dropping all pretence of being a soldier. He

elbowed his way through the crowd dragging the sad figure of Number Four with him.

"Now fall in! And for God's sake pull yourself together!"

But all my good intentions, my gleaming leather and glittering buttons, could avail nothing against those fatal boots. The march became a desperate battle to keep them under control. Sometimes I felt them slide away from under me and my heart was in my mouth for fear that I should do it again. First one foot and then the other would shoot into the air. I staggered under my rifle, but, lips tight with effort, breathless, managed to recover.

The science master fell back and said angrily;

"Corporal Thomas! Can't you make your section march properly?"

"Keep on your feet there, Number Four! March up there!" said the corporal obediently. "Left! Left! Left-right-left!"

"You wait till we get back!" whispered the others.

The hideousness of military architecture oppresses the soul. I have often wondered who designed those lines of prison-like buildings that crown our garrison towns. What mental qualifications were required of the architects of soldiers' dwellings in years gone by? Contempt for the men who were to live in them? A coldness of spirit, a lack of love for your fellow-men, so that the buildings you designed should deny as much to the mind as to the body? For what raw recruit could pass within those grim portals, flanked by sentries, without feeling that he was going to jail, to servitude rather than service, not to be released until he was too old to be of use either to the machine within or the world without?

Lines of gaunt and forbidding buildings such as these surrounded us on that winter morning. Under the stress of war they had spawned around themselves a rash of wooden huts, cookhouses and latrines, for the multitudes who came there to be schooled in the new arts of war. In their midst was a large open space with a raised dais where two flags hung limply from poles. On this stood the imposing figure of the famous but superannuated general, with Bobbie and three or four others, to take the salute as we marched past. He was a stout man with a white moustache. A red band decorated his cap and there were red tabs on his lapels. On his breast, among rows of other ribbons, were the V.C. and the D.S.O. He was Old Tails removed a few steps further up the scale. I kept wondering what he was like at home and imagining what sort of a home it could be—full of obedient children, guns and well-trained spaniels, I thought. I diverted myself by picturing him with nothing on, stripped of his military splendour, an old man with a paunch, varicose veins and flat buttocks. When he inspected us he had walked down the ranks unsmiling as we stood stiffly to attention. Only our eyes, refusing discipline, followed his progress towards each one of us down the line. When he came to me I saw the firm but slightly petulant lips under the white moustache and marked his cold, unemotional, blue eyes, set in little rolls of loose flesh. He looked into no faces and caught no eye but regarded only buttons, leather and equipment. His glance passed without a glimmer of human interest from one figure to the next in the ranks before him. For him we were troops and not human beings, certainly not little boys desperately trying to look like soldiers. We were future officers, units in the merciless machine that was forcing out thousands like us. How dreadful, I thought, if, during the march past, I were to lose control of my boots again and fall in front of him, metamorphosed suddenly and indecently before his eyes from a potential officer into a silly little boy. Would he come forward, like those motherly women, and say "Poor little soldier"? No! A light of cold displeasure would come into his eye. He would turn to Bobbie, fuming, and say, "Confound your company, sir! You've spoilt the whole parade!" And Bobbie would feel terribly embarrassed, remembering about moral courage. Next day the general would dictate a scathing report about "D" Company. And I should have disgraced the whole school, several schools, the whole British Army in the making, the Expeditionary Force of 1919. I should have lost the war.

As we advanced in line abreast across the parade ground, waiting for the words "Eyes left!", I strove desperately to control my boots. I prayed to them as Perseus must have prayed, and possibly was still praying, to his sandals. The film of ice on the ground, trampled over before me by many feet, had mercifully thawed a little. It gave a foothold. Thankfully I felt my feet under control.

"Company! E—yes left!"

Opposite the dais where the general stood I stared defiantly, triumphantly, over my shoulder, into those unregarding cold blue eyes. I marched past him, my rifle correctly at the slope, my right arm swinging to shoulder level, my feet under control and rejoicing in my heart. My war within a war was over. I had won it.

We formed three sides of a square around the parade ground. The general advanced into the middle and stood alone under the expectant gaze of over a thousand boys. He addressed us in the kind of voice used for public oratory, a shout with a lift at the end of each sentence, and long gaps between the words.

"I should like to say——" he shouted, tapping his palm with his

cane, "I should like to say—how pleased I am—with the very—er—
efficient turn-out—you have shown me to-day. I feel—er—I feel—we
need have no fear—about the keenness and—and bearing—of our future
officers—so long as you fellahs from the school corps—ah—can put up
damned good shows like this."

I wonder what he would have said if I had fallen down in front of
him. He paused and cleared his throat. He tapped his leg with his cane
and examined the ground for a moment or two.

"Now—ah," he went on. "Now—many of you—will soon be
going—er—over the other side—to show the Boche—what you can do.
Envy you. Wish I had your chance again." (They all say that, I thought,
the superannuated ones, safe in their sixties, from the general to Old
Tails.) "But there's one thing I want to say. It's—ah—about wind up.
Now, you'll get the wind up, I dare say. Everyone does. Had the hell
of a wind up—many times—myself. Stick it, that's all. Got to stick it.
Don't let the troops see you've got it. If they see you've got it—they'll
get it too. They'll feel let down—panic. But if you don't show it—
they'll follow you to hell. That's all. Thank you."

In that instant the war loomed up real and terrible for me, over-
whelming. It was to me he was speaking. It was I who would get the
wind up and mustn't show it and well I knew what a wind up I should
get. There was no escape for me or any of the other goblins in Corporal
Thomas's section. The gaunt buildings seemed to close in upon us
charged with the menace of the future. All these dismal surroundings
spoke of it. I wanted to run away, to flee to some place where there
might be silence, where I could be alone, face to face with a future suddenly grown dreadful as a nightmare.

After the general's address, when we had cheered him and watched
his stout figure disappear into the main gate of the barracks, we marched
to a large bare piece of land on the crown of a hill. I liked it up there.
All the town lay mistily below us, wreathed in veils of smoke. Far off
beyond it the fields and trees whitened into the winter haze. The wide
calm prospect made the future seem less dreadful. This was the present
anyway.

All the top of this hill was laid out as a miniature battlefield, or as
nearly like one as possible. Trenches and sand-bagged parapets zig-
zagged across it. Guns looked out from behind a hedge. Away on the
other side, beyond the crest of the hill, other trenches represented enemy
positions. We lined up and sat down on the hard frozen ground. I was
uncertain what we were about to see and did not care much for I was only
thankful to be able to sit down after so much marching. My tired feet

throbbed inside their heavy casings. Lines of khaki tin-hatted soldiers took up positions in the trenches so that only their tin hats were visible. These were the troops the general had spoken about. To-morrow, next week or the week after they would go "over the other side" to the real thing, to "show the Boche what they could do."

"If they don't know you've got it," the general had said, "they'll follow you to hell."

I looked curiously at their tough, tanned, good-humoured faces under their tin hats, their eyes like those of animals, innocent of much emotion, expressing only patience. Irregular teeth, coarse lips that grinned and spat. Why should they follow me?

"That's the front-line trench there," said an officer with a tooth-brush moustache, pointing with his stick. "That's the support trench. Those are the enemy positions over there. Now the first thing we shall do is to put down a covering artillery barrage for our infantry, who will attack behind it. Ready there!" he shouted, and went striding away towards the hedge where the guns were.

There was a few minutes' silence, broken only by the murmur of voices from the trenches. Then uproar broke from the guns behind the hedge. Everything became wreathed in smoke from which stabbed tongues of flame. The senses were flattened and stunned by the noise. Fountains of earth sprang up from where the enemy were supposed to be, beyond the hill top, until you could see nothing but a black curtain of earth and smoke draped around the crest. Then one by one the lines of figures rose from the trenches near us, some carrying Lewis guns and others rifles. Through the smoke they ran forward, flung themselves down, rose and ran on into the smoke towards the top of the hill. As they approached the wall of flying earth the black fountains suddenly stopped playing. The guns became mercifully silent but smoke still lay heavily all around. The khaki figures, small now in the distance, ran shouting into the enemy positions. The sound of their hoarse shouts of mock triumph came faintly to us. The position had been stormed.

"You see the idea don't you?" said the young officer.

It was nothing like a real battle, of course. I knew that, but I saw the idea. I saw it clearly enough for a question mark to outline itself in my mind. Should I be able to do it?

"Of course, we can't really reproduce battle conditions here," continued the officer. "But it gives you a picture."

It gave me a picture of the future which I carried away from that battlefield and kept at the back of my mind from that day onward. Coupled with it the general's words rang like Old Tails' bell in my head. "You'll get the wind up. Of course you will. Everybody does."

My dread of war and horror of its approach, which was so real a quarter of a century later, dated from that day. With it came a hatred of soldiering which was born on that dreary parade ground. I forgot about it for days and weeks at a time, however, for when one is young one cannot worry about anything for long. But from time to time things happened to stir up anew the fear that lodged somewhere at the back of my mind. It would not sleep.

Every holiday, when I returned home, the ugly evidences of war spread farther and wider over the green spaces around the house in the park. For several centuries it had looked out upon scenes of immemorial peace. Now, from the warlike clamour that increased around it, it seemed to shrink back among its trees. Stretches of grass where once we walked were now railed off. Rows of huts sprang up and the inevitable cookhouses and latrines accompanied them. Guns pushed up their snouts among the trees. Army lorries, disregarding the sacred rules enforced upon us for years by stately old gentlemen in top hats with gold braid round them, careered across the green levels and scarred them with their wheels. In the plantations they stood in rows like prehistoric monsters asleep. Captive balloons hung above, obese shapes in our familiar sky. Columns of soldiers marched and drilled, attracting from the purlieus down the hill troops of raffish vivandières, who wandered about in groups and made sly giggling invitations. The sound of rifle fire and bursting grenades echoed among the copses.

One day something happened that awoke the latent dread I lived with. Returning from one of my solitary walks which had become a habit with me, I saw a great disturbance among a crowd of people near the house. The crowd seemed to be running all in one direction across the grass towards me. As it drew near I saw that one of the crowd was running ahead of the rest. There seemed to be a desperate urgency in the way he ran, as though he were fleeing from something in wild panic. Still he came on towards me with the crowd shouting at his heels. The noise it made was confused and cruel like the baying of hounds on a scent.

He came straight for me and passed by without appearing to see me, running with mad abandon. He was a young soldier. His head was uncovered and his hair disordered. His uniform was torn open in front. White to the lips, eyes staring, breathing stertorously and looking neither to right nor left, he dashed past me and vanished over the brow of the hill. In those few seconds I looked into his face and saw fear.

It was a madness like that of a hunted animal. "You'll get the wind up. Of course you will. Everybody does."

The crowd raced after him crying "Stop him! Stop him!" and was soon all around me.

"Why didn't you stop him, you fool?" shouted someone.

"That's a deserter," said another, a fat red-faced man, stopping and puffing to get his breath back. "Why the hell didn't you do something? Broke from his escort just ten minutes ago. And all you do is just stand there."

For that was all I had done. I had just stood there. It was all I had been capable of doing. I had seen fear for the first time face to face.

I said nothing about this when I got home. In truth I was a little ashamed. Why, whenever a crisis occurs demanding swift action, do I just stand still, completely immobilized, and do nothing? But even if I had wanted to, which, on reflection I found I didn't, I doubted whether I could have stopped him. I was glad presently that I had done nothing. I still hope he got away.

That evening my grandmother looked at me across the dinner-table, "Well, dear boy, I suppose, soon——"

XVI

MY sixteenth year was a milestone in my life. It marked the end of one chapter and the beginning of another. I was no longer a child and my dreams were fading. Those that were left I began to grow a little ashamed of, to disown, as though they were garments I had grown too big for. Whenever I found myself in their familiar toils I reminded myself that I was a man, or almost, and blushed at my own thoughts as I had never done before. They faded very slowly and I hardly knew just when they left me. Perhaps they never did leave me altogether, for sometimes they return to trick me even now. Now, however, I am too old to blush for them and welcome them like old friends, dear and foolish ghosts of the past, beckoning in vain with faint fingers. But at sixteen their place was taken by the painful stirrings and fevers of adolescence. I was at the spotty age of unnameable desires. For all the wealth in the world I do not think I would be sixteen again. I was moody and irritable for reasons that I could not define. A restlessness used to drive me out alone and send me home again discontented. I ached, without knowing what I ached for, and longed for something I dared not admit even to myself. I quarrelled suddenly and violently about nothing, usually with Mary, who was now living an intriguing life of her own at school. She dominated me completely now and her exciting adventures with her school friends, which she recited with herself as the central figure, filled me with envy. How wonderful, I thought, to be so witty, so popular, so sure of oneself. She never seemed to be in doubt about her next step or to worry where life was carrying her. No one is so sublimely assured and serene as a schoolgirl of fourteen after two terms at school. She had found a new world for herself. Mary faced life undaunted in a gymn costume and two plaits.

But I was assailed by doubts and questionings. I tried to cover them by being over-assertive. I lost my temper over trifling arguments and stuck obstinately to foolish statements which I knew were wrong, but which I thought it would be a sign of weakness to unsay. When worsted in a battle of words over something utterly unimportant, or more often when my arguments were drowned in laughter, I would leap to my feet and shout and bang on the table.

"It is!" I would shout, having nothing to back up my argument with but the loudness of my voice, now beginning to let me down by cracking disconcertingly at the critical moment. "It is! I know it is!"

And ended by choking back unmanly tears of impotent rage while laughter followed me from the room.

"Really! That boy is becoming quite unmanageable!" my parents would say when I had gone. It was true, for the boy was unable to manage himself. Poor sixteen! He was his own worst enemy.

"You know, darling boy," my mother said, in one of those moments of reconciliation which always followed these scenes and which made me feel so bitterly ashamed. "You really must learn self-control." She stroked my head as it sank slowly into her lap. "You're growing into a man now and it will go terribly hard with you in the years to come if you can't learn to control yourself. You mustn't lose your temper like this. I sometimes wonder if you aren't a little unbalanced."

I was unbalanced. Who is not at that age of darkness and nightmares? I always think that those who talk of early adolescence as the best and happiest time of life are talking nonsense. They have forgotten their own youth. And how strange it is that grown people never remember their own difficult years when confronted with the moody, feverish, petulant young. Or were the youthful fires that burnt then so chill or so remorselessly damped down that no flame appeared? Or did they smoulder beneath the surface? Was youth so cold and unemotional in those days that it presented no similar trials and problems? However that may be I became a problem once again, the subject of frequent anxious debates. These sometimes took place in my presence and eyes looked gravely at me across the dining-table. But more usually they took place in my absence when I had gone for a long solitary walk or bicycle ride across the park. From these I would come back very late with my nameless discontent and restlessness deadened by healthy fatigue. Often I missed supper and received a scolding for being so late. Then I retired to my little room with the round window, where I fell asleep reading Keats or Shelley or Rupert Brooke. They seemed to burn with kindred fires.

At sixteen I left school without very much glory. No one mourned my departure, I think, and it is safe to say that two terms after I had left only a few remembered me. I did not leave a name engraved in gilt letters in the dining-hall. No silver cup gleamed in my honour above the high table. The Headmaster's final comment was: "He could do well if he tried harder, but he is a charming boy and I shall be sorry to lose him." I was touched by that, for I had felt that since I had so grievously fallen from grace the Headmaster had not found much charm in the grubby lanky youth who always seemed to be mooning about. Perhaps at the last moment he relented and remembered how he used to take me on his knee. For myself, I was delighted to leave school, believing, as the young do, that any change must necessarily be for the better. On the day I left I turned back at the top of the hill and took a last look at the school buildings and the octagonal tower lying in the valley among the distant elms. They remained stamped on my memory as I saw them then, bathed in the morning sunlight with the black specks of rooks circling about them. In the months and years afterwards I remembered only the fields and lanes where I went with Ronald, the evening shadows on the playing field, the moon among the cedar-trees and Bobbie's melancholy gentle smile. Perhaps this is the best tribute that memory pays to one's schooldays, that these tender images remain. The pain is forgotten, the sweetness lingers.

Bobbie had left the term before I did. I had seen the taxi that took him and his wife to the station surrounded by boys clamouring to bid him a last farewell. "Good-bye! God bless you, sir!" I felt that school was not the same place after that good and upright man had gone. For that alone I was glad to go too.

My departure from school was the solution to the problem I presented. I was doing no good there. I must be taught something useful. To feel the warmth of friendship, to learn to take one's place in a miniature rough society—these things were not useful. These are not often, for some reason, held to the credit of schools.

"All this Latin and Greek," my father said. "Never did me any good!"

"Have the boy taught something that will be of use to him in after life, my dear," said my grandmother. "Have him taught a trade."

"What the boy wants is to learn to rub shoulders," said my father.

In the world fit for heroes to live in that was threatened after the war, my parents rightly argued, shoulder-rubbing would be indispensable. So my father began to make all sorts of inquiries about trades and about shoulder-rubbing occupations. He interviewed, on my behalf, politely bored people behind desks and brought home quantities of booklets. He wrote tentative letters. "I should be glad to know what prospects such a career would be likely to offer to a boy with intelligence but without exceptional gifts."

The first question to be answered, obviously, was "What particular bent does the boy show?" Nearly all the bored people behind desks wanted to know this. They became even more bored when no very definite answer was forthcoming. They wrote as much in their letters. For to this crucial question there seemed to be no satisfactory reply. The truth was that I showed no bent at all. I was distressingly mediocre. I was not particularly good at anything, though remarkably bad at several things. I gave no sign of wanting to do anything much. I really wanted to be left alone and not bothered.

During all the discussions about my future that went on around me and over me I maintained an inert passivity, like a calf in a market stall. I showed no interest or enthusiasm for anything. I had given no indication of having any brains and my school reports had been successively lukewarm. They said, with wearisome reiteration, "Could do better if he tried," "Does not concentrate," "Inattentive." I had no hobbies. My only amusements, now that I was too grown-up to play under the beech-tree and now that Mary was almost a young woman and had left me behind, were those long lonely walks or bicycle rides or gardening, which I did in fits and starts, beginning enormous undertakings but seldom finishing them. I was no use with my hands and had tried carpentry at school but had split so much wood and bent so many nails trying to make some bookshelves that the instructor had given me up in disgust. And I had given up carpentry and nails defeat me still. So it is not surprising, perhaps, that my parents found me a knotty problem. The debates about my future were long and often fruitless and only resulted in the melancholy conclusion that my parents were faced with a son who was not much obvious use for anything. However, a certain amount of laughter arose out of these discussions. My brother was merciless and christened me "the Rotten." "Now let's talk about what to do with the Rotten," he would say when conversation flagged.

And yet, in spite of all this, I did have a bent. I had a heart's desire which I kept as dark as I could. For fear of the laughter which would follow I dared not confess it. I wanted to write. I did, in fact, write incessantly, although to no purpose. I seldom finished anything I wrote and hid my efforts or tore them up. However, I could not keep the secret hidden for long and one day my brother found something I had written and read it aloud to the family with cruel mockery. I wanted to sink into the earth but the cat was out of the bag. Yes, I confessed, I wanted to be an author. It was, and still is, my only ambition, the only thing I have ever really wanted to do. It is an urge that will not be denied, no matter how busy I may be with other occupations or how fully my time may be taken up. I still write, often late at night after the day's work is done. For a writer, indeed, the most important thing in life is that he should write. Wars and battles and sudden death cannot stop him. I once thought they could but I find they cannot. They take second place. And this gives the writer a curious aloofness and detachment from life and from death, especially in these days. He is armoured against fate.

"A writer?" said my parents, when at last I confessed to my only ambition. "But, my dear boy, there's no money in that."

It seemed to them a curious trait, a kink, but no more. Quite rightly they regarded writing as highly unlikely to provide me with a living, especially since everything I wrote was very immature. Even to me my efforts, however much they may have entranced me at the time, sounded somehow wrong when read out loud so that I felt ashamed of them and despaired of ever being an author. And my parents, thinking only of my good, wanted me to be a success. They wanted to make something of my life—that is, they wanted me to make money. Nowadays, perhaps —though who knows?—we might take a slightly different view and regard success as happiness, fulfilment, the attainment of the heart's desire. Yet happiness and fulfilment, and very often the attainment of the heart's desire, as my parents rightly said, are very much easier to achieve if this world's goods go with them, but bitterly hard in the face of that sordid struggle to live which is all that so many know of life. And it seemed that I should never be that kind of success as an author. I saw their point. I saw it better still later on when the editors' rejection slips came flooding in with all the disappointment and hope deferred that they brought. Money, I thought, was extremely desirable. The lack of it cramped the spirit and must be avoided at all costs. So, regretfully and with resignation, I put writing aside as a career, though I still wrote and filled the bottom drawer in my bedroom with sheets of foolscap. I turned with a faint heart to the selection of prospects that was opening up before me.

My father's inquiries and interviews had resulted in a mound of correspondence. It now filled the bureau in the downstairs bedroom, where I used to sleep when I was a child, and which my father still used as a dressing-room. That bureau had stood in the same place beneath the window for years and I could remember it from the time when I used to awake frightened in the night and see its friendly outline against the pale glimmer of the window. It was made of a dark, almost black, oak and was carved into a medley of whorls and convolutions of which the oft reduplicated centre-piece was an embossed lion's head in front view. A lion's head formed the centre of the flap which let down in front. Carved foliage radiated from it. Each drawer had a replica of the same lion's head for a handle. On one side there was a cupboard whose door had a lion's head in the middle. My father treasured this cumbrous piece of furniture for it was something that was indisputably his in a house which, he had always been deeply conscious, was not his house but very much the house of the indomitable old lady who had ruled in it for so many years. But here, within these oaken walls, was his narrow kingdom. It was monstrously hideous and took up a great deal of room but it was his own. It was so heavy that two men could hardly lift it empty. "My desk," as its owner always referred to it, was a secret and forbidden region, filled with a miscellaneous but glorious collection of "things." My father was always a great lover of "things" and would never throw anything away, however inconsequent and apparently valueless. After being kept for some months everything became part of the immortal company of his "things" and must not be touched. "Never know. Might come in useful some day." "That? Dear old thing that. Very fond of that."

Inside "my desk" was a number of pigeon-holes marked "Bills," "Receipts," "Securities" and "Letters." They were stuffed full of pieces of paper tied up in bundles. These were very dull, except perhaps for the letters which, I often thought, ought to be exciting if one had time to read them. For whenever I was alone in the house and free from interruption, I amused myself illicitly by rummaging among my father's "things." I was careful always to put everything back exactly as I found it because my father would have been very angry if he had discovered that prying eyes had been at work there. There was a pleasurable guilt in this illicit foraging. I always felt that I might find out something, though I had no idea what. And curiously enough I never did find out anything. The impression I got was of the guileless innocence of grown men and that my father was still a boy after all. In the drawers, among a tangle of wire, a disorder of nails and screws and rose labels, were his medals from the war and uniform buttons and a badge or two. Even the letters all seemed to be from aunts and uncles about the prospects and accomplishments of various cousins I hardly knew. There were occasional faded photographs of ladies I had never met, smiling alluringly out of a motor-car my father had once owned early in the war. There was a snapshot of officers sitting in rows and one of other officers, evidently in France, eating an *al fresco* meal with someone holding up a beer bottle. There were Ordnance Survey maps with parts painted in red and green—relics of his manœuvres with the "costumers." There were old copies of *La Vie Parisienne*. There was a coloured reproduction of a lady in back view with very little on showing a behind like two rosy apples side by side. There was another showing a lady, wearing only a camisole and a pair of stockings. These developed a fascination for me and, when I knew that no one was about, I used to pull them out and gaze at those two rosy apples and that long expanse of pink thigh, and then presently put them back feeling disturbed and unhappy and somehow hungry. Sometimes I trembled a little. And there was a baffling tin box that was always securely locked. These were my father's "things," which he dearly treasured. They had more value for him than all the money in the Bank of England. They testified to the innocence of his pleasures.

But now "my desk" was filled to overflowing with letters, brochures and pamphlets in wild disarray, for my father was a very untidy man. And they all had directly to do with me. No one, just at that time, illicitly rummaging in this Holy of Holies, could have doubted what my father's main preoccupation was at that moment. But out of all this mass of acquired knowledge about possible futures for a boy with intelligence but without especial gifts only three alternatives seem to emerge in the end.

Firstly, there was the Eastern Telegraph Company. How would it be if I went to their training school in Cornwall and then to a station in the East Indies or Singapore? "No," had said the man my father interviewed. "No. I don't know that any particular gifts are required. Of course," he added, as though stating something already taken for granted, "of course, we like our lads to be keen on sport. If your boy is good at games, for instance—especially cricket——" And here I was up against that English obsession for playing with a ball which closed so many avenues to me, for I was no good at games at all, especially cricket. And, at sixteen, the East Indies and Singapore seemed remote and savage places, full of Chinamen who stole and lied and cheated and tuans who played cricket all day long in the hot sun. The thought of endless cricket appalled me. And somehow I thought it was intended that I should become a telegram boy with "Via Eastern" written on his cap.

The second solution of my problem was proposed by my grandmother. Because it was proposed by her it looked at one time dangerously like winning the day, for she had a way with her where her decisions were concerned. It seemed that I had an uncle by marriage, whom I had never met in my life but who ran a fruit farm, rather precariously evidently, in British Columbia. This was not the uncle who had given me the silver mug but another. I understood that no silver mug was likely to be forthcoming from this one. I had to consult an atlas to find out where British Columbia was.

"It'll be the making of the boy," my grandmother said. "It'll make a man of him."

She agreed to pay for my passage out and my uncle wrote, on a page torn out of a twopenny exercise book, that he would be delighted to have me.

"I must say I think it's extraordinarily good of dear Cyril—or whatever his name is," said my grandmother, clinching the matter. "Really, my dear, I think it's too good a chance to be missed."

What a kind man my Uncle Cyril must be, I thought, to write so eagerly and to be so pleased to have an unknown boy, of undefined talents, planted on him. Nevertheless, I viewed the prospect of visiting him with loathing. But apples were not a very paying proposition, apparently, and, when I learnt that my grandmother had also agreed to pay handsomely for my keep, I began to suspect that it was not altogether kindness of heart that had made my uncle write, "Send the boy over to us as soon as you like. He will be sure of a good home and a healthy life." I began to dislike my uncle himself. However, it was agreed that I should go to Nelson at the foot of the Rockies ("lovely scenery, darling," said my mother) and learn how to make large, red, juicy, tasteless Canadian apples pay, under the tutelage of my kind uncle, whose past was unknown and whose future was doubtful. To me, I may say, this seemed like a living death, but I was saved from it in the nick of time by my uncle himself. He suddenly went bankrupt, sold the fruit farm for a song and vanished. Not very long afterwards we heard that he had died and apples had ceased to worry him. Grandmother was not very pleased when my distant uncle intervened thus on my behalf by dying and so frustrated her scheme for the solution of my problem.

"How tiresome and inconvenient of dear Cyril," she said.

There remained, however, yet a third avenue to explore—that of a business career.

I showed no more enthusiasm for this than for any of the courses proposed for me. I had no aptitude for business whatever and if sent down the village on a shopping errand always came back with short change. To be successful in business you must be quick and extremely shrewd—in other words, continually suspicious of the motives of your fellow men. I was very slow and took a long time to grasp things and was utterly guileless. I am not being a prig when I say that I could not swindle a village idiot and I am an exceedingly bad liar. However, I supposed I must do something so only the thought of endless cricket in the outposts of Empire stirred me into any opposition at all. Everybody at my age, it seemed, began to think about doing or being something and, now that I realized that my dreams of becoming either an engine driver or an author were unlikely to come true, I did not much mind what I did. So when an office stool and pin-striped trousers were proposed for me I accepted the prospect passively, with the same indifference I had displayed towards all the other futures my elders planned. It was better than the others since it would at least mean staying at home.

So it was finally decided to send me to a business training college on the outskirts of London for a year to learn shorthand, typewriting and book-keeping by double entry. And to rub shoulders. I left school and began to go daily, with an attaché case containing books and sandwiches, to a commercial college in a nearby suburb. Here I learnt, after a year, to write shorthand at a hundred and ten words a minute but not necessarily to read it back again, and failed to achieve the requisite hundred and fifty. I learnt to type rapidly but inaccurately and to keep books by double entry, very untidily because I always added up the totals wrong. I learnt to write inspiring business letters "We are in receipt of yours of the 10th inst. and in reply beg to state ... soliciting the favour of your esteemed commands, we remain ..." This was gall and wormwood to me. I thought how dreary must be the minds of those who work in offices that they should become capable of writing such stuff. I decided that I could never be a business man and mentally wrote off that future for myself also, but did nothing about it.

I worked harder during that year than I had ever worked before. It would not be the fault of the college if I were not efficient when I left. I was not, but one accomplishment I did learn there, though not without some difficulty at first. I learnt to rub shoulders and to mingle with people from a walk of life different from my own. I disliked this to begin with, for I was a stranger in their midst and they made me feel it in many ways. But in the end I succeeded and was not unhappy in the bare classrooms, crammed with working-class boys and girls, which had once housed a prosperous Victorian family. I found a rough kindness there.

At the end of the year I wrote, as I had been taught, but without the least enthusiasm, a letter of application for a post as junior clerk in an East India merchants' office.

"Dear Sir," I wrote, in a large artificial hand full of pot-hooks and hangers that I had been forced to acquire. "I beg to apply for the post of junior clerk advertised by you in to-day's *Times*. I am seventeen years of age and unmarried. I enclose two references and a copy of a testimonial from a commercial college. Hoping to be favoured with an interview, I am, Yours faithfully...." My hopes were rewarded. I was so favoured and as a result got a job in a dark city office. Its window looked out into a brick well and you could only see the sky by pressing your cheek against the glass and looking vertically upwards

Black dust lay inches deep over everything. I kept the job for three months.

When I was sixteen the war suddenly came to an end. I was busily engaged in increasing my wage-earning value and in rubbing shoulders in order to prepare myself for just this. Now, unexpectedly, it had come—the world fit for heroes to live in that was to prove such a cruel mockery before long. I saw that great and rather dreadful jubilation which took place on the night of November 11th, 1918. It was the expression of a great sigh of relief. At last the long agony, the outpouring of blood and treasure, the mourning and the partings were over. Soon the sons and lovers would return. It was the dawn. My mother and father and I stood in Piccadilly Circus that night on the pavement edge, watching the crowd go mad with joy. But we were spectators only, for somehow we did not feel that way. My father stood there stock still, gripping hard the handle of his walking stick, his lips trembling slightly. He was saying good-bye to the happiest time of his life. The war had brought him freedom from care, a return to youth, friendship. Eighteen months before the war ended he had been invalided home. Now, though still in uniform, he worked in an office again—the War Office, but still, an office. For him so much was over for ever, the jokes, the laughter, the happy times. Even the exhilaration of danger. Many years later, on September 3rd, 1939, when the wheel came full circle again and he was an old man, my father lifted his glass and said, "Ah, well. Here's to the memory of it all." And he looked at me and at my young brother in the R.A.F. with envy, believing that our war would bring to us what his brought to him. How very wrong he was.

But my mother took hold of my hand on the pavement edge in Piccadilly twenty-five years ago and pressed it. "Darling boy," she said. "Not you, thank God."

No, not me. I was glad when my father said, "Ah, well. Better be getting home," and led us into quiet streets back to Waterloo to catch the train home. In those streets the noise of rejoicing came distantly and London seemed to be brooding over the trials and sufferings of her people, which they, in their innocence, thought were over. "Not yet," the tall dark buildings seemed to say. "There is so much more to do and suffer." Only slowly and not on that wild night of rejoicing did I realize that it was not after all for me, that terrible ordeal. The choosers of the slain had passed me by. Many of my schoolfellows had been touched by their wands but I, and those of my age, had been left. Now the future stretched unbroken before us like a long empty road, calm and tranquil, if perhaps a little unexciting. Through the sacrifice of others we should see the spring and summer and autumn follow one another. The earth and the fullness thereof were ours—or so we thought. I wish I could say that I felt a moment of high purpose and dedication. I wish I could say that I resolved to be worthy of those who had died that I might go on living, increasing my wage-earning capacity, filling up sheets of foolscap and throwing them away. Did I pray that the life thus spared to me might be worth sparing, or that at the end of it I might leave the world richer than I found it? I did not. But I was not alone in that. For a quarter of a century I stood for two minutes once a year in silence in memory of the dead. And so in the end it came again inevitably to my generation and to me. Yes, to me.

But the end of the war left me in mid-air, with a question unanswered. How would I have stood that test if it had come to me as it had come to so many of my schoolfellows only a year or so older than I? I felt that there was a part of myself I did not know and now, it seemed, would never know. Thousands of young men of my age were asking themselves that question, for, after a relaxed and flaccid interval, a spate of novels and plays painting the war in realistic colours descended upon us. Those who had stayed at home were told what the war was really like for the first time. For during the war the Press had made it out to be all really rather jolly, as it does to-day. *Punch* had a cartoon of a laughing Tommy with a German helmet on his head binding up his hand. This, I think, appeared after a particularly bloody battle in which hundreds of thousands of Tommies had been killed. And behind the lines, we were assured, it was all sing-songs and Mademoiselle from Armentières. I think all our knowledge of that remote place called the "front" came to us after the war. Those who went there either never came back or, if they did return, never spoke of it. And those who talked constantly about "when I was in France" were usually safe behind the lines. I was curious, with a kind of anxious curiosity, to find out what it had really been like and so I read all those grim realistic books about it, saw the plays and the films. They were a great success, for thousands of young men besides myself were reading them and seeing them too. We read *Way of Revelation, Undertones of War, All Quiet on the Western Front, Sergeant Grischa, Under Fire.* We saw *Journey's End* and *What Price Glory?* Could we have endured and suffered like this too? Apparently we decided we could not, for after we had read them, a wave of pacifism and hatred of war swept over the country and undid all that those others had died for. Perhaps it was not our fault. Our thumbs were down. It was our verdict against ourselves.

As for me, I know that wishful thinking persuaded me that it could

The House in the Park

never happen again, not to us with our refrigerators and radiograms, cheap cars and Odeon cinemas. How could such a thing be possible in this pleasant world in which one booked a sleeper to the South of France in the Blue Train? Impossible with all those lights in Piccadilly! The monstrous darkness of 1914–18 was drowned in a flood of neon lights. And still, once a year, we stood to remember that foolish nightmare, like a small boy remembering faintly at high noon how he had awoken trembling with fear in the night.

But in the 'thirties, when Germany went back to her old gods, the shadow returned to my life, like a ghost revived after fifteen years. It gave a quality of unreality to the commonplace happenings of every day. People passing in the street seemed like figures in a dream. The conversation of my friends rang false. So soon they would all be swept away. And again there was that unanswerable question. When, after the emotional stress of 1938, the second war came at last, I met it, as did all my countrymen, with a sense of relief. Now at last I should know, and soon.

But at sixteen that was all very far ahead and nothing seemed to mar the calmness of the future. Except that my grandmother, that beloved, tyrannical, capricious old lady, began to fail in health. And the great elm-tree, which for many years had stood proudly by the front garden gate, fell with a soft swishing sound one windy night. It lay in the morning prone upon the lawn among a tangle of shattered branches and its naked roots had torn up the crocuses which had blossomed round its feet for so many springs. Its fall, too, meant the end of a chapter, but its delicate leaves took quite a long time to die.

180

XVII

NOW she was dead. In the drawing-room, surrounded by the satinwood furniture and the yellow wall-paper, she lay in a coffin beneath a mound of flowers, which filled the room with their heavy scent. It seemed to be the odour of death and spoke of the decay of mortal flesh and the vanity of human hopes. Only the white marble boy seemed to be imperishable, a trophy brought back many years ago from Italy. He kept guard over her remains from the corner where he had stood for so long, gazing upward at his raised forefinger. The wreaths and crosses that lay piled upon her, so that you wondered if she could feel the weight of them, each carried a little card; "In affectionate memory," "Deeply mourned," "R.I.P." The house was full of people as it had not been since the days when my aunts were married or when my father's soldiers had gathered there after their parades in the park. But the people who were here now were dressed in sombre black, moved quietly about almost on tiptoe as though afraid of awakening her who slept in the shuttered drawing-room. They spoke in solemn whispers about mundane subjects as though avoiding the dreadful issue, the grim fact of death, which had brought them all here, as though not to speak doggedly about the world were to remind themselves of their own inevitable end. Studiedly they talked about Lloyd George, about reparations, about what a lovely summer it had been and how nice the garden looked. Whenever, unavoidably, she entered briefly into their conversation they referred to her as "poor dear Emily," as though death were some terrible mistake which she had made, as though she had inadvertently died and caused all this pother and worry.

"I am particularly fond of this view over the park," said one. "You might be a hundred miles from London."

How could he, I reflected, who had never seen its infinity of changing moods and lights, its pearly magic in the early morning or its slumbrous evening quiet, be particularly fond of it? I wanted to tell him to stop talking about our view—my view.

"I see they're going to electrify the railway," said another.

"Of course that will ruin the place."

This was a family gathering such as collected together only at funerals and weddings, uncles and aunts and cousins whom one hardly ever saw and only heard spoken of occasionally. I looked at them as though they were museum specimens. Why should they have thought it necessary to come, I wondered, for in her life they had hardly known her. I sat in a corner, wearing a new black suit, feeling uncomfortable and resentful and somehow out of it all—out of something that touched me more nearly than all these people.

A long procession of carriages arrived at the gate and four men, in top hats and frock coats, bore her out through the french windows and laid her in a glass hearse with all her flowers around her. Then we drove to the cemetery with the blinds down. People took off their hats as we passed. We stood around her grave while the vicar, his surplice flapping round him, read the burial service in his loud healthy voice. "Let the dead bury their dead," his voice seemed to imply. As the first spadeful of earth fell on her her only remaining son, an elderly grey-haired man, stepped from the circle of mourners and threw into her grave a bunch of roses from her own garden. It seemed a more loving tribute than all those flowers, more fitting than the lilies turning brown, sweeter than the roses opening to show their hearts, kindlier than the carnations that hung their heavy heads. "I am the Resurrection and the Life saith the Lord." The earth covered her and one of the most beloved figures of my life was gone for ever. But not from my heart and for many years I used to think that, if I tried hard enough, I could feel again the touch of her hand on my head and hear her voice. "It's all right, darling, I'm not afraid." It is less easy now. And a few years ago I went back to that cemetery but, alas, I could not find where she lay.

We drove back to the house at a trot. The blinds of the carriages were up. When we arrived the men in frock coats took off their top hats and trooped into the kitchen where there was beer waiting for them. In the dining-room a large meal was waiting for the mourners. After all, life must go on. Body and soul must be kept together. Veils, which had hidden decorous sorrow, were raised to admit cold chicken and burgundy. Voices were less subdued now. There was no fear of waking her where she lay.

"Well, perhaps, another glass, my dear. It does one good on these occasions."

"So trying for you, poor dear," said someone to my mother. "But never mind. You have your children and flowers. They help so, don't you think?"

"I dare say we'll have a fine September."

"You mark my words. We won the war, but Germany will win the peace."

"A remarkably good burgundy of poor dear Emily's."

One of the frock-coated men appeared at the french window and

bowed to my mother through it. It was the undertaker. He was indicating that he had undertaken and was about to depart. A procession
of black figures followed him, wiping their moustaches. Presently there
was a movement upstairs to the library to hear the will read by a tall
grey-haired lawyer and I was left alone with the half-finished dishes, the
empty plates and glasses, thinking of the dead.

So my grandmother joined that shy and fitful company of ghosts that
haunted the house in the park. Severe and disapproving though some
of them undoubtedly were, I had grown so used to them that they were
friends, familiars who greeted me ever and again as, perhaps, a sudden
feeling in the library that I was not alone, some faint, half-suggested
noise, a fleeting inexplicable sense, maybe, that I was doing or saying
something that had been done or said before by someone else, or a sense
of being in circumstances not quite new. Or I would encounter them
as one of a hundred well-remembered smells, the mustiness of the
library, the fresh linen smell of the workroom, the oilcloth smell of the
pantry, the smell of warm stone on the veranda and, in the garden, the
smell of box hedges in the sun, of pine needles, of lavender, of earth.
It is these things, their faint scents, the tiny sounds they make in the
night, the way they look on still evenings, which give to old houses the
feeling they breathe that they are haunted by the sad spirits of those
who have lived in them and now cannot tear themselves away.

My grandmother had lived in the house in the park for thirty years.
Before her time it had been presented to my great-grandfather, Richard
Owen, for his lifetime by the Crown in the middle of Victoria's reign.
It was a gift in recognition of his services to science, a reward for lecturing
to rows of young royalties about natural (but not too natural) history,
and for coming down heavily on the side of the angels against the odious
Mr. Darwin. When his wife died, the Professor's sister came to live
with him and look after him. She was a severe old lady in rustling black,
with a chatelaine at her waist, who ruled her brother sternly and stood
no nonsense. But she was already an old lady when she came to live in
the house in the park and, after some years of her rigid and economical
regime, she died and the old man was left alone again.

Hers was a shade I hardly knew, for she died long before I was born,
but to my mother and my aunts she was real enough and would be
encountered occasionally sitting in the drawing-room before the lamps
were lit. A chair, known as Aunt Maria's chair, had stood in the drawing-
room for many years, becoming shabbier and shabbier. Eventually my
grandmother, who had no time for ghosts, ruthlessly had it re-covered.
But even the stiff flowered chintz in which it reappeared could not

exorcize the ghost of Aunt Maria. She still sat there in the twilight in her black dress and white ringlets, more severe than ever, disapproving of this unwelcome change.

The Professor had one son who was a civil servant, a quiet, mild, cultured man, who read a great deal, was fond of music, was an excellent artist and loved good conversation. On the death of his aunt he came to live in his father's house, bringing with him his attractive, energetic little wife, with her pretty brown hair and sharp, darting brown eyes. And he brought a large unruly family of four boys and three girls. He was an unhappy man, dominated by his determined little wife, and quite unequal to the burden of being a father to his uproarious children. And he was constantly at odds with his own distinguished and formidable father, who had no sympathy at all for his son's bookish inclinations and disliked being vied with in conversation. But all that this gentle soul wanted was to be left alone to read and make pen-and-ink drawings, to discourse learnedly with his friends and to play the violin.

His was a melancholy ghost. It was not easily evoked. But his violin, in a case lined with blue velvet and with one string broken, remained to call him back to earth. This, and his sketch-book, full of pen-and-ink drawings of soldiers on the march and people riding horses, drawn with a virility, strength of line and power of movement that seemed surprising in one so gentle and passive. Only these things, in which he had been happy, had the power to induce that poor shade to return fleetingly to the earth it had been so glad to leave for the silence and peace of the grave.

After her husband died, my grandmother was left alone to look after the aged Professor and her large family. She was undismayed and set about the task of placing her sons and marrying off her daughters, and, in the course of years, accomplished it. Her husband had never been of much help to her and latterly had left all decisions to her.

The Professor lingered for many years, a severe and terrifying presence in the library upstairs, whither he shuffled daily from his bedroom adjoining. This was that same bedroom in which, many years later, I bade my grandmother good-bye. One of its windows looked over the green expanse of the park where the pond lay like a bright plate of silver, or brooded dark and sullen like ebony. The other window looked over the garden which the old man had designed and planted himself and loved dearly. His library too had windows commanding the same beloved prospects. When the weather was fine, or when he grew tired of sitting in the library making marginal notes in all his books in his spidery hand, he would come unsteadily down the stairs and stand for a little while in the sun upon the lawn. There, leaning upon his stick, he would contemplate the beauty that was his and which he had made, as though bidding it farewell. Perhaps he was reluctant to leave so fair and sweet a world, unable to believe that the next one would bring him so many roses and snapdragons and yellow violas. Then presently he would turn and climb slowly and with difficulty up the winding stairs to the library. How melancholy old age must be for those of us who cannot conceive of any paradise half so lovely as the earthly one we are about to leave.

But mostly the old man sat in his library annotating his books, imperiously ringing his bell and calling for meals he had already consumed but swiftly forgotten, dozing or holding a book in front of him without reading it. Often the book he held was upside down. But sometimes, in the evening, his grandchildren in the dining-room below would stop in the middle of their chatter with their heads on one side, listening, in the grip of a sudden foreboding. Yes, sure enough, they would hear the tap of his stick on the stairs and the shuffle of his slippered feet.

"It's grandfather," they would whisper fearfully. "He's coming down."

This was always apt to happen if they had young friends in for supper, for the old man would hear the sound of young voices in the room below. Perhaps some ache for lost youth came over him. Perhaps he grew suddenly hungry for the company of young people, as the old often do. It may be that the sound of these voices reminded him that he was tired of the company of one old man, and that old man himself. Or he may have felt that there was something going on and he wished to be in it. So the dining-room door would open and he would slowly enter and sit sternly for the rest of the evening in a chair by the fire, grasping the handle of his ebony stick with his long knotted fingers. But the old, however sad it may be, are no company for the young. "Crabbed age and youth cannot live together." His grandchildren were convinced that he came down simply to spoil their fun, for the presence of the lantern-jawed old man, with his domed skull under a skull cap, from which the white hair descended to his neck, and his large smouldering eyes, acted as an immediate damper on the spirits of the young people.

"Oblige me," he would say, pointing with a trembling finger to the oil lamp in the centre of the table, "oblige me by extinguishing that brilliant illumination. I find it deleterious to the eyesight."

And they would obediently turn the light down and sit for the rest of the evening making conversation, now become stilted and difficult, almost in the dark. Soon his grandchildren's guests would regret that they really must be going.

Occasionally the old man, during these uncomfortable visitations, would demand imperiously to be entertained, like a caliph calling for dancing girls.

"I should be glad to hear the young lady sing something," he would say, turning his burning eyes upon some unfortunate and shy young woman, paralysing her like a snake hypnotizing a bird. "Perhaps," addressing my mother, "you would be good enough to accompany her on the pianoforte."

Those were the days, thank goodness now departed for ever, when all young ladies had an accomplishment. Usually they sang. Sometimes eagerly and sometimes reluctantly they did so whenever two or three were gathered together. Obediently, then, as she had been expensively trained to do, the young woman would rise and warble at the piano. When she had finished, with a sigh and a half-expectant smile, the Professor would solemnly clap his long gnarled hands once or twice.

"A very pleasing performance, my dear young lady." Then, after a pause in which everyone waited for words of praise, "When you have learnt to sing in tune the enjoyment of your audience will doubtless be greatly enhanced. I bid you good night."

And he would rise and, leaning heavily upon his stick, shuffle slowly from the room.

But these visitations became fewer and fewer until there came a time when he stood for the last time in the garden and said farewell to it for ever. The old man became bedridden and could only see the tops of the trees through the window on one side and the silver streak of the pond on the other. Distinguished callers came to see him on Sundays. In the hall they said, "How is the dear Professor to-day?" They were taken up to his bedroom where they stayed for a little while without taking off their overcoats. "Well, how are we to-day?" they said. "What a lovely view you have from here, Professor. You might be a hundred miles from London." Then they went downstairs, took off their overcoats and stayed to lunch. When they left they said they hoped the dear Professor would soon be up and about again, knowing that he would not and would never be about again any more. But they came less and less frequently, for soon the old man was unable to recognize them. "Your face is familiar but your name escapes me," he told a lifelong friend who had visited him regularly for many months. The friend gave up his visits from that moment. But he was glad when they ceased to come for he had finished with them and with life. He had grown very deaf, could not remember who they all were and shouting trivialities from his pillow wore him out. Those who lingered he got rid of by means of a formula which was never known to fail and which ensured that they never came again. He would peer at his enormous silver watch that lay on a table by his bed and, leaning back against the pillows, close his eyes and say:

"There is an excellent service of trains to and from the Metropolis. I think, my dear friend, if you were to leave about now——"

And his guest, hastening down to the station two miles away, would find that he had an hour or so to wait on a dingy and inhospitable platform.

Then my grandmother, unable to cope any longer with the double task of looking after a bedridden old man and a large family, imported into the house what, in those days, was a horrifying innovation, something regarded as slightly improper, a female nurse. The old man only consented to this monstrous proposal after several weeks of gentle but unceasing persuasion. The idea of a strange female hovering about in his bedroom while he was not only in the room but in that most compromising of all situations, in bed, seemed a scandalous impropriety. But, at last, having neither the strength nor the will to resist, he gave way. It was announced to him that the nurse was already in the house.

"In that case," he said, adjusting his skull-cap and smoothing the sheets, "you may tell the young woman she may approach my bedside. I shall attempt no liberties."

The last bastion, his personal privacy, had fallen.

And presently he died and was gathered to his fathers.

But it seemed that his soul could not rest in Heaven. It had loved its gracious and pleasant world too much. It came back to haunt the little house in the park and the garden into which it had instilled so much of itself. It clung lovingly to the library and was there instantly whenever you took down and opened one of the hundreds of dusty volumes that lined the walls. Blow the dust off the top and open it at any page. There, under some passage, was a thin unsteady line and, in the margin, "Nonsense!!!" And you must turn your head to be sure that he was not beside you. He was constantly in the drawing-room where the marble boy, which he had brought back from Italy years ago, proclaimed his presence with one finger upraised. But most of all he was in the garden where grew the monkey-puzzle tree that he had planted and the statue of Pomona, goddess of fruits and flowers, still standing where he had placed her in a niche of holly, brooding over a geranium bed, with moss growing on her breasts and ferns in the crook of her elbow. I knew his severe and unsmiling shade. I met him in the potting-shed or in the evening in the West Walk where the Michaelmas daisies shone like constellations of purple stars. I often thought I discerned him in the dark library, sitting all alone before an unlighted fire, poor homesick exile!

Now she, who in her lifetime had no time for ghosts at all and was impatient with us who felt their presence, had herself joined that silent company. Now she was gone her elusive presence lingered still, like a faint perfume, around those parts of the house and garden to which she had devoted so much energy and care for so many years. She had always been concerned with the essentials of life. Abstractions, such as her husband had dealt in, had no part in her existence. The Professor's activities had been something outside the domestic sphere she inhabited and therefore outside her interest. It was the practical side of life that occupied her, the running of a house, the bringing up of a large family. Now it was only natural that she could not rest in ignorance of the number of eggs laid down daily or the amount of tea "They" were consuming in the kitchen. Or without knowing whether the lamps had been trimmed that morning or how much coal was being burned in "that great range." For so many years she had put the eggs away in pickle, carefully marking each one with the date, although, lately—her memory failing her—she had forgotten the date. "Yesterday's egg," she would write in compromise, or "To-day's egg." It seemed impossible that she should suddenly cease to do this or that she should no longer dole out little packets of tea, currants or sugar for "Them." Every morning for many years, wearing a black apron covered with a pattern of little flowers, she had gone busily about the house which was as much part of her as her flesh and bones. Indeed we poor humans are so much bound to the earth which is our only home that it seems incredible and cruel that the world we loved so much should mourn so little when we are gone and remorselessly revolve without us. The poor spirits hover around the familiar precincts. How enviously they must behold the living going to and fro in them! Jealously they must watch other hands busy with the tasks they loved to do. How can death be anything but extinction when we are cut off from the world which is so much a part of us? And yet it seemed that the house did mourn for her. All those intimate and friendly regions, the pantry, the store-cupboard, the linen-cupboard, the workroom—with its lay figure, Angelina, round whose wire skirt and red female-shaped torso so many dressmakers had crawled on all fours with their mouths stuffed full of pins—the cool, dim, food-smelling larder; all these seemed to hold her presence and would not let her go.

We left the house in the park which returned to the Crown who owned it. So there came a day not very long after my grandmother's

death when I wandered round the garden and said farewell to it myself.
It looked as it did when the Professor took his leave of it twenty years
before me. There was more moss on Pomona's breasts, more ferns in
the crook of her elbow. She had sunk deeper into her niche of holly.
The monkey-puzzle tree was dying in its lower branches. I bade good-
bye to the rockery I had made, to the trees I had climbed, and noted that
in the dark corner where the ferns grew their fronds came only up to
my waist. I could remember when they arched over my head like a
green tunnel. It was autumn. The canopy that covered the great tent
of the beech-tree was beginning to grow thin and the pale September sky
showed through. On the mossy floor, where the roots ran like veins
upon a hand, the leaves lay red and gold and brown. They rustled
under my feet. To that temple of my youth, as to my youth itself, I
said farewell for ever. I should never play there again except in my
memory, in which I constantly return to it.

Indoors, while I mooned about brooding over the snows of yester-
year, my uncles and aunts and cousins were busy dividing the familiar
furniture and all Grandmother's household gods among themselves.
I did not want to be there to watch that. I had secured all I wanted—a
little leather-bound volume of Keats, annotated in the Professor's
quavering hand. The ink of his writing had turned yellow and faded
but the nightingale sang as sweetly as ever, imperishable.

So now, years afterwards, when I go to see my relations in their
Wimbledon villas and Kensington flats, old friends still welcome me in
strange surroundings, the marble boy in a narrow suburban hall, the
satinwood piano in the front room of a seaside bungalow, Aunt Maria's
chair in a self-contained flat, stoutly refusing to bear any resemblance to
a modern convenience.

And now the house in the park has central heating, so I am told, and
electric light and two bathrooms. There is even a garage I believe.
Some of the rooms have been thrown into one another—such an improve-
ment. The little dressing-room where I used to waken in the night has
become part of my parents' downstairs bedroom and together they make
a fine billiard room. They were never very nice rooms anyhow, were
they? And so damp. The great Scots fir that stood in the middle of the
lawn has been cut down to make room for a tennis court. In order that
people who knew not Joseph may hit a ball across a net a hundred years
of patient growth, a miracle of grace and beauty, a benediction of lovely
scents and solemn melodies has been laid low. From rows of little
lavatory windows people look down upon the West Walk where the
Michaelmas daisies shine in the dusk like purple stars. You pay twopence

for a ride in a paddle-boat, or did before the war, upon the silver pond which the Professor gazed upon from his deathbed. It has a concrete rim. The people from down the hill have come into their own. They play football in front of the house in the park and make love beneath the trees. Yet in my memory it is the same as when I knew it and never changes, a place of immemorial peace, hallowed by the ghosts that walk there. Every piece of furniture, every tree and every flower is there. They bloom for all eternity. Perhaps I myself have become one of those shades already for I am so often there in my imagination. I shall go back there when I die.